Jewish Heritage Travel

Also by Ruth Ellen Gruber

Upon the Doorposts of Thy House: Jewish Life in East-Central Europe, Yesterday and Today (Wiley)

JEWISH HERITAGE TRAVEL

A GUIDE TO EAST-CENTRAL EUROPE

Updated and Revised Edition

Ruth Ellen Gruber

John Wiley & Sons, Inc.
New York • Chichester • Brisbane • Toronto • Singapore

The quotations on the following pages are used with the generous permission of the copyright owners: Page 3, from *Time of Stones* by Monika Krajewska. From the introduction written by Anna Kamienska (Warsaw, Poland: Interpress, 1983). Page 5, from *Prince of the Ghetto* by Maurice Samuel (Philadelphia: The Jewish Publication Society, 1948, 1959). Page 19, from *The Golden Tradition* edited by Lucy S. Dawidowicz. From "I Enlighten a Shtetl" by S. Ansky (New York: Schocken Books, 1967). Page 21-22, from *Remnants, the Last Jews of Poland* by Malgorzata Niezabitowska and Tomasz Tomaszewski. From "No Fear in Me" by Szymon Datner (New York: Friendly Press, 1986). Page 27-28, from *The Family Moskat* by Isaac Bashevis Singer (New York: Farrar Straus and Giroux, 1950). Page 38, from *If This Is a Man* by Primo Levi (London: Abacus Books, 1987). Page 41, from *A Treasury of Yiddish Stories* edited by Irving Howe and Eliezer Greenberg. From "Tales of Chelm" (New York: Schocken Books, 1953). Page 46, from *The Golden Tradition* edited by Lucy S. Dawidowicz. From "When Hasidim of Ger Became Newsmen" by Moshe Prager (New York: Schocken Books, 1967). Page 50, from *Souls on Fire* and *Somewhere a Master* by Elie Wiesel, translated by Marion Wiesel (New York: Penguin Books, 1984). "Souls on Fire" copyright Elie Wiesel, 1972; "Somewhere a Master" copyright Elirion Associates, Inc., 1982. Page 193, from *The Jew in the Medieval World* edited by Jacob R. Marcus (Philadelphia: The Jewish Publication Society, 1938). Page 254-255, from *Black Lamb and Gray Falcon* by Rebecca West (London: Macmillan, 1941).

This book is printed on acid-free paper.

The photographs are by Ruth Ellen Gruber.

Copyright © 1992, 1994 by John Wiley & Sons, Inc.
All rights reserved. Published simultaneously in Canada.

Library of Congress Cataloging-in-Publication Data

Gruber, Ruth Ellen
    Jewish heritage travel : a guide to east-central Europe / Ruth
Ellen Gruber. — Updated and rev. ed.
      p.   cm.
    Includes bibliographical references and index.
    ISBN 0-471-04251-X
    1. Jews—Europe, Eastern—History.   2. Holocaust survivors—
Europe, Eastern—History.   3. Europe, Eastern—Ethnic relations.
4. Jews—Travel—Europe, Eastern—Guidebooks.   5. Europe, Eastern—
Guidebooks. I. Title.
DS135.E83G68   1994
947'.0004924—dc20   94-9890

Printed in the United States of America

10 9 8 7 6 5 4 3 2 1

To the memory of Flora, Joe, Becky, and Frank

Preface

Before World War II, nearly five million Jews lived in Poland, Czechoslovakia (today, the Czech Republic and Slovakia), Hungary, Romania, Bulgaria, and Yugoslavia (today Slovenia, Croatia, Bosnia-Herzegovina, and Yugoslavia). Most of them perished in the Nazi Holocaust, and most of those who survived the Holocaust emigrated, mainly to Israel and the United States, leaving fewer than 150,000 Jews in these countries today.

Despite World War II and despite more than four decades of communist rule, much still stands to bear witness to the rich Jewish culture that once flourished in the region. This book is a guide to these many remaining traces of Jewish culture and civilization. It is designed both as a practical guide for travelers to the various countries and as a sourcebook for armchair travelers interested in learning about a vital part of European and Jewish history—past and present.

The book is divided into chapters, one chapter for each country-area. Each chapter includes a brief historical survey of Jewish life in the country-area, plus addresses of the main Jewish communities and Jewish facilities, such as kosher restaurants. Where possible, I have listed locally available English-language guidebooks and other publications, which can provide more detailed information on Jewish heritage. **Boldfaced** terms are defined in the glossary at the back of the book. Asterisks (*) mark some of the sites I found personally most interesting, a selection that is purely subjective.

Readers desiring further information on specific sites may want to contact the United States Commission for America's Heritage Abroad in Washington, D.C., a body set up by Congress in 1985, or The Jewish Heritage Council of the World Monuments Fund, 174 East 80th Street, New York, NY 10021. Both organizations are involved in the ongoing process of documenting and preserving Jewish monuments, and in 1993 they completed a full-scale survey of Jewish sites in Poland, the Czech Republic, and Slovakia. This information has been loaded into a computer database.

The world is changing more rapidly than the changes can be recorded. Each visit to the countries discussed brings more information. I invite you to share in the thrill of these discoveries—and I thank those of you who have written to me to inform me of what you have discovered.

Ruth Ellen Gruber

ACKNOWLEDGMENTS

Many, many people have selflessly given me their time, advice, expertise, and encouragement in the preparation of this book. Without their generosity, I could not have written it.

Samuel D. Gruber, director of the Jewish Heritage Council of the World Monuments Fund, was in from the very beginning in more ways than one; our parents inspired us with a sense of family and family history that has expanded to encompass Jewish history as a whole. Edward Serotta has been a stalwart friend, phone-pal, and sounding board; I only hope I have been as helpful to him in his own research. Geoffrey Wigoder's encouragement from afar meant a great deal. Barbara Walsh Angelillo's eye was always constructively critical.

In Poland, friends became guides, and guides became friends. Monika and Stanislaw Krajewski, Maria and Kazimierz Piechotka, Jan Jagielski, and Tomasz Wisniewski are pioneers in the rediscovery and preservation of Jewish heritage. In the Czech Republic and Slovakia, Arno Parik of the Jewish Museum in Prague and Jiri Fiedler literally told me where to go—and I went. Ludovit Dojc shared his knowledge of Slovak Jewish heritage, as did local Jewish community leaders. Peter Wirth, in Budapest, went out of his way over and over again to make sure I was on the right track in Hungary, and Jewish community members in various towns welcomed me with warmth. In what was Yugoslavia, Milica Mihajlovic, of the Jewish Museum in Belgrade, Mladen Svarc in Ljubljana, Srdjan Matic in Zagreb, and Eugen Werber and Sasa Lebl in Belgrade, were my guides. Deep thanks go to Romania's chief rabbi, Moses Rosen, the Federation of Jewish Communities in Romania, and the individual leaders of Jewish communities all around Romania, for their hospitality and friendship. Likewise, many thanks to Eddie Schwartz and Izador Ajzner of the Shalom Organization in Bulgaria.

In addition, I'd like to thank Zvi Feine of the American Jewish Joint Distribution Committee for providing information on Romania. I'd like to offer particular thanks to my colleagues at the Jewish Telegraphic Agency (paying special tribute to the late Edwin Eytan) for enticing me into writing on Jewish affairs.

Many friends and colleagues not involved in Jewish research aided me with moral support, spare beds, translation, and enthusiastic willingness to act as guinea pigs on trips. I'd particularly like to thank the entire Zapotocky/Rexa family, Sonja Javorska, Paul Markovits and his parents, Gail Bensinger, Pablo Conrad and Diana Horowitz, Bill Rutkowski, Maja Razovic, Mirjana Tomic, the Stanic family, Rysia Zachariasz, George Jahn, Teddie Weyr, and S-patrol charter member Judy Meighan. The Associated Press bureaus in Vienna, Warsaw, and Bucharest were especially helpful; Drusilla Menaker's nonaspirins came in very handy in more than one country. Thanks, too, to Steve Ross, Nancy Marcus Land, Upton Brady, and to the various strangers who sent me pictures and information after reading that I was preparing this book. Special thanks to Charles J. Morris.

I have used oral and unpublished material by several of the above-named people, as well as the books listed in the bibliography, as source material for historical background. Some of my experiences recounted in this book were recounted in a different form in articles I wrote for the Jewish Telegraphic Agency, the *New York Times,* and the *Independent on Sunday.*

REG

CONTENTS

Jewish Heritage Travel

A TRIBE OF STONES

Beginnings

The seeds for this guidebook were sown in the bitter cold of December 1978, when my brother Sam and I accompanied Romania's chief rabbi, Moses Rosen, on the *Hanukiada,* his annual Hanukkah pilgrimage to Jewish communities scattered around Romania.

For years, during the eight days of the holiday, Rabbi Rosen traveled from synagogue to community hall to synagogue, visiting a good proportion of Romania's Jews, who in 1994 numbered about 14,000. He prayed with them, talked to them, had a festive meal with them. People huddled in their heavy overcoats; youth choirs sang, puffs of steam coming from their mouths; candles flickered in the cold.

Over the six days we traveled with Rabbi Rosen, we visited nineteen Jewish communities. We saw big, fancy synagogues and tiny prayer rooms; **shuls** painted with beautiful zodiac scenes and shabby meeting halls with no decoration. We experienced "big city" Jewish life and marveled at small towns reminiscent of the prewar **shtetls** we knew only from literature. We saw the mass graves of Holocaust victims and danced the *hora* with young Jewish students on New Year's Eve. We were warned about how to behave in a state tightly ruled by the communist dictator, Nicolae Ceausescu: Whisper, someone told us; they listen to everything.

One of the little towns we visited was Radauti, scarcely more than a village in the very north of Romania, a few miles from the then Soviet border—the village our paternal grandparents came from.

One old grizzled man, wearing the astrakhan hat that seems de rigueur in the Romanian winter, recalled members of our family even though our grandparents had both immigrated to America before World War I. One great-uncle, he told us, probably Uncle Kush, was the first man in Radauti to drive a car.

We picked our way through the Jewish cemetery and there found the grave of our great-grandmother, who survived the Holocaust and died in 1947. I was given my middle name, Ellen, in her honor.

Later, in a dimly lit apartment in Bucharest, I visited the only member of our family still living in Romania, the brother of our grandfather, Uncle Pinkas. He was then in his nineties, "the oldest man I ever saw," I told a friend at the time. Uncle Pinkas could scarcely remember his long-gone brother Frank, who had died in Ohio fifty years before.

That trip in 1978 was not primarily a search for family roots; I was a journalist writing news stories; the stop in the ancestral village and visit with Uncle Pinkas were a bonus.

Still, a chord was touched that has continued to resonate over the years. It is a chord that I am convinced resonates deep within any Jew whose ancestry lies in East-Central Europe—and also a chord whose harmonies cannot fail to touch the non-Jewish world as well.

A Jewish guide to East-Central Europe cannot help but take a visitor into a ghostly, multidimensional shadowland of *Then, Now,* and *What Might Have Been.* It is a journey particularly important now, as for the first time in half a century the recent political changes in the area have made it possible for Jews to worship freely and carry on a Jewish life. At the same time, the new freedoms have also unleashed worrisome new waves of anti-Semitism along with ancient nationalistic sentiments long held in a sort of suspended animation under the communist regimes.

Then, in the Jewish context, means before the Holocaust; the time when the region was the world's Jewish heartland, home to millions of Jews—most living in abject poverty, many solidly prosperous in their near-total assimilation, some exerting the most important cultural and intellectual influence of the time.

Then also means the horror; the story that must be told and retold: Auschwitz, Treblinka, Terezin, Warsaw, Lodz, Iasi, Jasenovac, on and on and on. The story of the Holocaust can be told here on the spot; visitors can walk the streets where martyrs defended doomed ghettos, make pilgrimages to the camps where millions were slaughtered, pause for prayer or reflection at monuments and memorials, and above all, see, feel, and experience the places where Jews lived for so many centuries and now live no longer.

Now is the current state of affairs. Countries whose prewar Jewish population made up a considerable part of their inhabitants now have only a handful of Jews remaining. In some places, like Prague in particular, there are well-kept synagogues, cemeteries, and museums presenting the rich history of Jewish society—as well as an enthusiastic, if minuscule, contemporary Jewish community. Even in some provincial towns, like Presov in Slovakia or Szeged in Hungary, where Jewish communities may number only a few dozen or a few hundred souls, there are some marvelous historic synagogues still in use.

All over the region, thousands of old Jewish cemeteries lie abandoned and untended; hundreds of former synagogues languish in disrepair or have been transformed for secular purposes, some still, however, marked by rusting Stars of David or Hebrew inscriptions. A number of them have been restored to their original appearance for use as museums or other cultural purposes. (Romania is an exception to the pattern: its 17,000 Jews are organized in more than sixty communities and, while the vast majority of prewar synagogues have been destroyed, the nearly eighty synagogues that remain still function as houses of worship and are maintained in excellent condition. The more than 700 Jewish cemeteries in Romania also are well cared for by the local Jewish communities, and at least half are enclosed by fences.)

Each cemetery, or ruined cemetery, and each synagogue, or ruined synagogue, is a monument to the **Shoah**—the Holocaust—just as much as or more than sculptures or museums or other constructed memorials.

What Might Have Been is a musing on past and present alike—and, indeed, on what is to come.

Many of our collective memories and intangible links as Jews were spawned over bowls of Bubby's East-Central European borscht and blintzes, pastrami on rye, smoked carp, and bialys. Many of us who have little idea of our own forebears before their emigration somehow identify with the ancestral legends and portrayals embodied in the stories of Isaac Bashevis Singer, I. L. Peretz, Sholom Aleichem, Sholom Asch; the paintings of Marc Chagall; even the stage-set Yiddish world of *Fiddler on the Roof.*

The fact that the names on the countless overgrown graves in the countless overgrown cemeteries in East-Central Europe read like the membership list of any American temple is an especially poignant reminder of how close we all are both to what was destroyed and to what has been left. So, too, are the endless lists of names on Holocaust memorials and at Holocaust monuments, such as Auschwitz.

In preparing this book, I traveled thousands of miles to seek out the physical remains of a vanished civilization. Often I felt like an archeologist, digging and delving into the ruins of a past: *my* past, *our* past.

I tried to detach myself; to investigate, to inquire, to write up descriptions of synagogue buildings and ghettos and graveyards and ignore the ghosts who clustered around the doorways or shimmered in the shadowy depths of young forests grown up around the weathered tombs.

Most of the time I was successful, more or less. After all, my father is an archeologist, and artifacts were a part of my childhood. I have lived for years in Italy, where the ruins of the ancients are a part of the landscape altogether taken for granted. Buildings are buildings after all; stones are stones . . . right?

Wrong. Stones are not just pieces of rock.

"To every thing there is a season and a time to every purpose under heaven," we read in Ecclesiastes. "A time to mourn and a time to dance; a time to cast away stones and a time to gather stones together."

In 1983, my friend Monika Krajewska in Warsaw published a book entitled *Czas Kamieni* (*Time of Stones*). It is a photograph album of Poland's Jewish cemeteries. Her brilliant pictures interspersed with quotations from the Scriptures, poets, and the graves themselves make it one of the most powerful evocations of our lost world I have seen.

In her introduction to the book, Polish writer Anna Kamienska described the weathered tombs as monuments to an exterminated people:

> a tribe of stones, a people of stones, an obstinate tribe which is
> ever marching and ever shouting and calling voicelessly. Against
> the background of native grasses, trees, nettles and blackberries,
> exotic Hebrew letters are still talking about those who lived here
> and passed away. About righteous men, just and charitable,
> about God-fearing and loving women who toiled for others.

No, stones are not stones, and Jews and non-Jews alike who visit the places described in this book should be prepared to deal with a maelstrom of emotions springing from this fact.

Holocaust survivors will have special emotions. But those of us whose links with these places are more distant also will feel their power.

As I traveled to research this book, I tried to be objective and detached, but the voiceless cries described by Anna Kamienska would penetrate when I least expected. The dignity and melancholy power of some of the standing synagogues or ruins brought goose bumps to my skin. The loneliness of a building or a tombstone, or of a small handful of people swaying in prayer in a dilapidated shul, brought tears to my eyes. It happened in Abony, in Hungary; it happened in Rymanow, in Poland; it happened when I attended a community Passover seder in Radauti, the town of my grandparents, in Romania.

In Satoraljaujhely, a town on the Hungarian border with Slovakia, Holocaust survivor Rozsika Roth, one of less than a dozen Jews left in the town, keeps the keys to a big mausoleum for a famous local Hasidic tzaddik. Pictures of bearded Holy Men line the dresser in her bedroom, and all the doorposts in her ramshackle home bear a **mezuzah**. She kisses the one on her front door over and over each time she leaves the house. In all the apartments I've occupied in the past two decades, I never (until some time after writing this book) followed the commandment to put up a mezuzah—a small case containing handwritten verses from Deuteronomy on a parchment scroll, which should be affixed to the right-hand doorpost of Jewish homes. But in certain villages in southern Poland, the sight of still visible scars where mezuzahs had been wrenched away fifty years ago hurt like raw wounds in my consciousness.

I felt pride, too, and some sort of elation at what I saw. It was uplifting to discover relics of our people stretching back centuries; to witness the unique beauty of what we created. Buildings very different from those constructed by Christians; glorious frescoes of Jerusalem and Old Testament stories; lions and stags, **menorahs**, and the mythical leviathan. Tombstones whose beautiful Hebrew inscriptions and delicate carving of our unique symbols—the hands of the Cohanim, the vessels of the Levites, the broken candles of death—reached out with mystical significance across the centuries.

I became mesmerized and at times a little obsessed. I wanted to visit, touch, see, feel as many places as I could. I almost felt it as a duty. As I entered broken gates or climbed over broken walls into cemeteries where a Jew may not have set foot in years, I wanted to spread my arms and embrace them all, embrace all the gravestones, all the people buried there; all the memories. I'm here, I told them mentally; SOMEONE is here.

Maybe the strength of my reaction lies partly in the fact that I grew up as a typical, nonobservant American Jew whose connection with the "Old Country" and **Yiddishkeit** came more from reading than from practice or direct knowledge. Among the twenty-one grandchildren of my grandparents from that faraway Romanian village of Radauti, only one of us has married another Jew.

In the introductory first chapter of his wonderful book on Yiddish writer I. L. Peretz, *Prince of the Ghetto*, Maurice Samuel discussed, somewhat apologetically, his own rediscovery of the Jewish world after a lifetime of assimilation:

> I had for years been indifferent to the destiny of the Jews and willingly ignorant of their peculiar creations. When, for reasons that are not relevant here, I felt again the irresistible tug of the relationship, the recall was incomplete. I was of the Western world and would never wholly relinquish it; English was my language, and so remains in a sense that will never be true of Yiddish and Hebrew. Moreover, I was already uncentered, with a certain cosmopolitanism which has its charm and uses, but which excludes me from the tacit inmost circle of Jewishness.
>
> I long ago recognized the defect and decided to exploit the opportunity. If it is impossible for me to be a genuine insider because I have known what it is to be an outsider, I will at least put my reborn interest and affection at the service of permanent outsiders. If I cannot be a creator of Jewish values, I will try to be the interpreter of some of them.

Samuel's words in a way became my own credo in preparing this book.

The fact is, that when thinking about places of Jewish interest in East-Central Europe, or of the Holocaust, people tend to think more about the places of horror where Jews died by the millions than those places where they lived in even greater millions.

Jews made up ten percent of the population of Poland; over fifty percent of the population of many towns and villages. Their presence in East-Central Europe dates back originally to Roman times, and continuously for the past millennium.

Most mainstream guidebooks scarcely touch the subject aside from major centers like Prague or Budapest. Ruined castles and churches are pointed out aplenty: Former synagogues, ruined or not, are mentioned hardly at all.

I have tried to fill that gap, not just for Jews—but for everyone.

Practical Information

Within the limited scope of a guidebook, it would be impossible to include all Jewish relics and sites of Jewish interest remaining still in East-Central Europe: After all, this is a guide, not an encyclopedia or a genealogical handbook.

In the countries I have included—Poland, Hungary, the Czech Republic, Slovakia, Romania, Bulgaria, and the former Yugoslavia, all within today's post–World War II borders—hundreds of synagogue buildings

still stand, in one form or another; thousands of Jewish cemeteries still
exist, most in very poor condition and difficult to find.

I have tried to describe in some detail a representative selection of
these sites from each country, marking some of the places I personally
found most interesting with an asterisk. In addition, I have added basic
lists of some of the other sites visitors can also explore, though even these
do not encompass all Jewish relics.

Some practical hints, based on my own experience, on how to visit
Jewish heritage sites in East-Central Europe should prove helpful.

What You Will See

Jewish cemeteries, known in Hebrew as **Bet Hayyim** (houses of the living), are the most common remaining physical relic of Jewish civilization
in East-Central Europe. Several thousand of them still exist, most of them
abandoned to the elements.

Aside from a few tomb inscriptions dating from Roman times and
other archeological finds, the oldest Jewish cemeteries still in existence
date back to the late Middle Ages; others have tombstones dating to the
sixteenth and seventeenth centuries. These are found primarily in the
Czech Republic, with a few in Poland and Romania. Most remaining Jewish cemeteries were founded in the eighteenth and nineteenth centuries.

The physical appearance of gravestones, called **mazzevahs**, varies
somewhat from country to country depending on local cultural influences
and, starting in the nineteenth century, on the degree of Orthodoxy or assimilation of the local Jewish community.

Orthodox Jews—with some regional variation, particularly in
Balkan areas where Sephardic Jews predominated—tended to retain the
traditional stelelike form and design of mazzevahs, with symbolic carvings and inscriptions in Hebrew.

Often, particularly in Poland, Romania, and parts of the Czech Republic and Hungary, these carvings are very intricate. The designs in many
cases refer to the name, tribe, or profession of the person commemorated.

Among the more common carved symbols you will find are two
hands in the spread-fingered gesture of priestly blessing on the gravestone of a Cohen (priest), that is, a descendant of the High Priest Aaron,
the brother of Moses. Another common symbol is a pitcher (ewer) or
pitcher and bowl, marking tombs of Levites, or descendants of the tribe of
Levi, priestly assistants who traditionally washed the hands of the priests.

Lions, symbolizing both the tribe of Judah and personal names such
as Lev or Leib, meaning lion, also are common. Books mark the graves
of particularly learned people; hands placing coins into charity boxes de-
note those who were particularly generous or philanthropic. Candlesticks
often mark the graves of women, since in Jewish ritual women light the

candles on the Sabbath. Numerous tombstones bear symbols referring to death, for example, broken candles or broken trees. In addition, there is often a wealth of purely decorative carving—flowers, plants, birds, vines, and various folk designs derived from both Jewish and local folklore.

Much care, too, was devoted to elaborating the Hebrew inscriptions, and a wide variety of carving styles can be seen. Often there is no other carving on the tombstone than the epitaph, and the decorative script serves as ornamentation in itself. In Poland and Romania especially, gravestones were often painted in bright colors. Many stones bear traces of this decoration.

Famous rabbis, scholars, or other particularly revered people were sometimes buried in more elaborate tombs or mausoleums. These are often, even today, places of pilgrimage. Visitors place pebbles or candles on the tomb and often leave messages or prayers written on paper, known as **kvittleh**. Around the tombs of some of the great rabbis, particularly great Hasidic **rebbes** or **tzaddikim** (revered, holy men), present-day followers have erected little buildings or other protective shelters. These are known as **ohels** from the Hebrew word meaning tent or tabernacle.

Non-Orthodox Jews—comparable to present-day Conservative or Reform communities—wrote tomb inscriptions in local languages and eventually erected elaborate grave markers virtually identical to those erected by the contemporary non-Jewish community. Even they, however, often retained the traditional convention of writing the Hebrew letters *P N* or *P T*—an abbreviation for the words meaning "Here Lies"—above the epitaph.

Some Jewish cemeteries have a ceremonial hall near the entrance or on the grounds where bodies were prepared for burial and funerals took place.

Hundreds of synagogue buildings still remain in the region, though most—including Poland's unique wooden synagogues—were destroyed during or after World War II. The Nazis carried out a systematic program of defiling or destroying thousands of synagogues, beginning on the infamous *Kristallnacht* (Crystal Night), November 9–10, 1938, when scores of synagogues in Germany and German-occupied territory were ravaged. During the war years, local Jews were forced to help in the destruction; in some cases, as in the Polish city of Bialystok, Jews were herded into a synagogue before it was put to the torch.

The synagogues that remain date from the thirteenth-century Old-New Synagogue in Prague to several big structures erected in the 1930s. Their conditions vary widely, from devastated shells or those used as warehouses or workshops, to those that have been totally rebuilt so that nothing remains to identify them as former synagogues, to those still in use as synagogues, to some that have been beautifully restored and are used as museums or for other cultural purposes.

The architectural style of synagogues also spans a broad spectrum. The one constant is that synagogues were almost always built in such a way as to never resemble or be mistaken for a Christian church—indeed, under many Christian rulers, they were forbidden to do so. Sometimes synagogues were also forbidden to be taller than nearby churches, so some were built with foundations below ground level.

Elements to look for in synagogues are:

- The **Aron ha Kodesh**, or Holy Ark. This is the place where the Torah scrolls were kept, built against or set into the east wall of the synagogue sanctuary. It was often highly decorative, and even in ruined buildings it is usually possible to see where this was.

- The **bimah**, or pulpit. In Conservative and Reform Jewish synagogues, this tends to be in front, a platform beneath the Ark. In Orthodox Jewish synagogues, the bimah is characteristically in the center of the sanctuary; in East-Central Europe it was often surrounded by an iron grille. A typical Polish architectural style was to construct the synagogue around a central bimah whose four massive pillars rose to the roof and supported the vaulting. These four pillars are all that remain of the Old Synagogue in Tarnow, Poland.

- The women's gallery. In Orthodox Jewish practice, women are separated from men in the synagogue. Synagogues often had an upper gallery reserved for women.

- Fresco decorations. Many old synagogues had beautiful wall and ceiling paintings that survive to some extent. Often these designs had biblical themes or encompassed texts of the Scriptures. Jewish tradition forbids the portrayal of the human figure, but elaborate plant and animal motifs are common. Among the most striking frescoes are the numerous representations of the animals mentioned in a Talmudic exhortation to "be as strong as a leopard, light as an eagle, fleet as a stag, and brave as a lion to perform the will of thy father who is in heaven." Imaginary scenes of the Holy Land and Jerusalem also were a fairly common motif. Many Romanian synagogues are decorated with brilliant and very well-maintained frescoes vividly incorporating this imagery.

In many towns and villages, numerous buildings still remain in the old Jewish quarters or ghettos. These include not only buildings used by the Jewish community, such as schools, community offices, the rabbi's house, or the **mikvah** (ritual bath), but also homes and shops of ordinary people. Some of these old neighborhoods, such as in Trebic or Golcuv Jenikov in the Czech Republic, give an eerie evocation of the vanished Jewish world. In Poland in particular, large sections of a number of entire villages, such as Bobowa or Checiny, look pretty much the way they did when they were Jewish shtetls. On some houses, you can even still see the places where mezuzahs once were affixed.

There are hundreds of monuments and memorials to the Holocaust all over East-Central Europe. In addition to museums or memorials at the

sites of major Nazi death camps, there are many local monuments commemorating victims. These range from large sculptural memorials to
plaques commemorating mass graves or individual martyrs. In addition,
there are several Jewish museums or other exhibitions of valuable Jewish
artistic and ritual objects.

Things are changing rapidly in East-Central Europe. A cemetery
that was overgrown and desolate this year may be cleared up and restored
by next year. Likewise, it only takes one wet spring for nettles and grasses
to make a once-cleared cemetery look totally abandoned.

Many of the abandoned, empty synagogues have been able to remain
ghostly wrecks in the middle of towns simply because of the inefficient
communist economy, which was not oriented toward profit making or
town beautification. This, too, may change with the introduction of a private, market-oriented economy in these countries.

Try, however, not to blame today's local people for the state of disrepair in which you find Jewish monuments. Unfortunately, if you look
around, you will find many non-Jewish historic buildings in terrible condition, too, thanks to war damage and more than forty years of neglect by
communist authorities.

There are many plans—or at least hopes—on the part of local officials and remaining Jewish communities to restore synagogues and
ghetto areas. Lack of money and complications involving ownership ham-
per these initiatives. I hope that by the time you visit them, some of the
places I describe here as sadly abandoned will have been restored. Some of
them, I fear, may have been torn down.

BEFORE YOU GO

It is a good idea, particularly if you have not been to East-Central Europe
before, to do some pretrip reading both on Jewish history and on local
history in the region. It can be pretty depressing reading, but having
some background on the tumultuous events over the centuries may help
deal with the shock of seeing what remains today and the emotions that
come with this shock: sadness, grief, pain, anger, and other less easily de-
finable feelings.

Oddly enough, among these complex emotions, the Jewish traveler
to these areas should additionally be prepared to feel an inexplicable, vis-
ceral identification or familiarity with the art and architecture: This, in
turn, can lead to a broader sense of tranquility or communion.

Since the end of World War II, there has been much Jewish theological debate over whether the Holocaust was unique—or whether it was but
the latest, and most terrible, of a series of disasters afflicting the Jews.

The "ghettoization" and mass expulsions from the Middle Ages on,
the devastation and atrocities carried out from 1648 to 1649 during the

Cossack uprising led by Bogdan Chmielnicki in eastern Poland and the Ukraine, the Russian pogroms of the late nineteenth/early twentieth centuries recall all too well the Nazi Holocaust, without the modern methods of mass extermination used in death camps.

There are many books available about Jewish history in the region. There is also, of course, a vast and growing literature specifically on the Holocaust and the World War II period. At the end of this book, the bibliography lists a number of reference, historical, and fictional works that should help you prepare for your trip. The list only skims the surface of the literature available, but it should get you started.

One invaluable preparatory tool, if you have access to it at a library, is the *Encyclopaedia Judaica*. It is worth spending a few hours browsing through these information-packed volumes, which include short histories of many individual Jewish communities.

GETTING AROUND

Many visitors trying to trace their family origins may be concerned that the town or village from which their relatives or ancestors came might not exist anymore. This is rarely, if ever, the case. The villages are still there, as they have been for centuries, even though they may look completely different and even though many or most Jewish traces may have vanished.

Some old Jewish centers, such as Humenne in eastern Slovakia or Mateszalka in northeastern Hungary, appear to have been almost totally leveled during or after the war and rebuilt by the communist authorities as ugly collections of raw concrete boxes. The most shocking examples of this can be found in Romania, where massive urban renewal projects in the late 1980s destroyed almost all traces of the historic centers and Jewish quarters in dozens of towns and cities like Focsani, Falticeni, Dorohoi, and Tirgu Neamt.

Major cities and towns can be reached by plane, train, or bus, but in the countryside a car is the best means of transportation. Cemeteries, for example, are often a mile or so outside the town or village, sometimes down rutted dirt roads, in the middle of fields, or on the top of a hill. Cars, with or without drivers, can be rented in capital cities and some provincial cities.

Infrequent train and bus connections may make it impractical to visit more than one site a day; however, with a car one can see several related places in the space of a few hours, for example, the cluster of very interesting villages in northeast Hungary near Tokaj, or the historic little towns in southeast Poland near Lublin or Tarnow.

Roads are generally good, though in remote country areas or within villages there could be stretches of dirt road (which can be very muddy in wet weather).

Make sure you have a good map, drawn to the largest scale possible. Often maps published within the countries themselves are more detailed.

You can increasingly find booklike road atlases, which are often the most detailed of all and also have indexes of place names. Compared to North America and most of western Europe, gas stations in some countries of East-Central Europe are still few and far between, so keep your tank topped up!

FINDING THE SITES

Ask, ask, and ask again after you get lost trying to follow the first person's directions. In this book, we use English spellings but also include local spellings in parentheses for each entry.

In the few towns where there is a Jewish community, the local Jews—most of them elderly—will be happy to have you visit. Members of these communities have gone out of their way to show me places of Jewish interest or even offer me a bed for the night! Many older Jews speak Yiddish or German; the relatively few younger people may speak English.

If you do not contact the Jewish communities or if there is no Jewish community, ask people on the street who appear to be over sixty years of age and thus would remember both the war and the time when Jews lived in their town. Young people, unfortunately, may have no idea at all what you are talking about.

Many older people speak German; some will offer to accompany you to where you want to go, and many will be eager to share their memories—particularly memories of the war. Don't forget that these wartime memories are often painful for local non-Jews as well as for Jews.

I have found that simply saying—in an interrogatory tone—the words "synagogue?" or "Jewish cemetery?" in either German or the local language often works. I also strongly suggest you carry a notebook or drawing pad on which local people can draw maps for you.

The word for *synagogue* is pronounced more or less "seen-ah-goh-ga" all over the region.

Jewish cemetery translates as the following:

- Polish: Cmentarz Żydowski (Smen-tazh Zhih-dov-sky)
- Czech: Židovský Hřbitov (Zhidovskee Zhbee-tov)
- Slovak: Židovsky Cintorin (Zhidovskee Sin-tor-een)
- Hungarian: Zsidó Temető (Zheedo Tem'-eh-too)
- Serbo-Croatian: Jevrejsko Groblje (Yev-ray-sko Gro-blee-yeh)
- Romanian: Cimitir Evreiesc (Chim-iteer Yev-ray-esk)
- Bulgarian: Evraysko Grobishte (Yev-ray-sko Groh-bish-te)
- German: Jüdischer Friedhof (Yoo-dish-er Freed-hawf)

In many cases, I have included names of the streets where the synagogue or cemetery can be found; where I have not, it is because, frankly, knowing the street name or specific address would not be much help—either there are no street signs or it is easier (and often more effective) simply to ask for the synagogue or Jewish cemetery than to ask for a particular street.

Many former synagogues and cemeteries are kept locked. In places where there is a Jewish community, the community office generally has the keys. Sometimes there will be a note on the locked gate of a cemetery telling where the key can be found. Sometimes it is possible to enter through a break in the fence or climb over the wall.

People in houses near synagogues or cemeteries also often either have a key or know where one is kept. In many towns and villages, depending on the country, keys to empty synagogues can be obtained from the local town hall or municipal museum.

Synagogues used as art galleries and cultural centers generally have opening hours posted on the door. Workers at synagogues converted into warehouses, workshops, schools, and so on usually have no objection to visitors taking a look.

In the wake of the ouster of communist regimes, many street names with communist associations are being changed back to earlier names or to new, noncommunist ones. Be prepared to be confused. Older maps are of little use when it comes to names.

If an elderly, obviously poor person, particularly in a village, has gone out of his or her way to help you, you may want to give him or her a tip. Use your judgment, though. It is not necessary, and some people will be offended if you offer them money.

Also, beware the hangers-on (Jewish or otherwise) at some major sites of Jewish interest who latch on to you, make a show of guiding you around, then insist on a big handout. I had some unpleasant experiences with such people at the cemeteries in Cracow and Lublin in Poland. In the latter case, the elderly man demanding money made a terrible shouting scene inside the cemetery itself, demanding more money than what we had given him.

WHAT TO BRING

Bring with you medicines, batteries, personal supplies (like tampons), and anything else you cannot do without.

The economic situation is different from country to country in the region, but all are going through the torturous process of changing from a communist to a market economy. Many items taken for granted in the West are simply not available in some of these countries—or they are not available all the time, or if they are available in capital cities they are not available in the provinces. Always carry your own soap, because many hotels and restrooms do not provide it. Also, carry toilet paper—many toilets do not provide it.

Be sure you bring enough reading matter! In capital cities and, in some countries, other major cities you can generally find English-language newspapers, magazines, and books—but it can be difficult in the provinces. I also always carry a small shortwave radio with me, to listen to the BBC (British Broadcasting Corporation) or Voice of America news and entertainment programs.

Keep your clothes casual. Most cemeteries are totally overgrown or have sections that are totally overgrown with weeds, shrubs, and trees; to reach many cemeteries requires walking through fields or down country roads. You may have to clamber through weeds, and so on, to reach synagogue buildings, too. Mud is a constant factor at the slightest hint of rain. Therefore, wear athletic or other sturdy, comfortable shoes—not sandals. When out in the country, women should wear trousers, or risk having their stockings shredded.

Also, wear a money belt and bring at least some cash dollars. Credit cards are not accepted everywhere (particularly in remote areas), and travelers checks are also sometimes hard to change.

FINALLY, A WORD ABOUT ANTI-SEMITISM

Anti-Semitism has existed in this part of the world as long as Jews have lived here, and it still exists even today, when only a handful of Jews remain.

Under the communist regimes, anti-Semitism (also masquerading as anti-Zionism) was from time to time official policy: in Czechoslovakia in the 1950s, in Poland in 1968, for example. At the same time, strict control of the population kept open expressions of popular anti-Semitism to a minimum.

Now, after the political changes, newfound freedoms of speech, thought, and deed mean that anyone can say whatever he or she wants. And everyone does. Anti-Semitism—like other ethnic prejudices and hatreds—has come out of the closet in some places. In most of the countries, it is almost an abstract phenomenon, though, as local people—Poles, for example—scarcely know anymore what a Jew might be.

Foreign tourists are unlikely to experience any open anti-Semitism directed against them, but be prepared to see occasional anti-Semitic slogans daubed on walls or on gravestones. And be prepared for occasional shocking remarks by people you might meet. (On the other hand, you may also be shocked by hatred expressed, for example, by a Serb against an Albanian or Croat, or a Slovak against a Hungarian or Czech, or Romanians and Hungarians about each other.)

Remember, too, that anti-Semitism is not simply an East-Central European phenomenon. A survey by the Anti-Defamation League of B'nai Brith counted more than 1,600 anti-Semitic incidents in 1990—in the United States.

POLAND

Population: 38 million
Jewish Population before World War II: 3.3 million (within prewar borders)
Jewish Population in 1994: 6,000 to 15,000

A LITTLE HISTORY

Rabbi Moses ben Israel Isserles, the great sixteenth-century sage known as *Remuh*, once wrote that it was preferable to live on dry bread and in peace in Poland than to enjoy better material conditions amid the greater danger and insecurity found in other countries. Remuh, who lived and is buried in Cracow, is also reported to have noted that the Hebrew word for Poland—*Polin*—could be formed from two other Hebrew words, *Poh lin,* meaning "here he shall rest."

Over the past thousand years, Poland has been both a harbor of refuge and a scene of horror for Jews. Here, Jewish culture rose to some of its greatest glories; here, Jewish society suffered some of its most devastating defeats. Long a haven for Jews fleeing persecution elsewhere, Poland eventually became home to 3.3 million Jews—a vibrant, varied population embracing rich and poor, religious and secular, artists and fools, businessmen and jobless *luftmenschen* (literally, people who lived on air, without visible means of support). Poland was the heartland of the Jewish Diaspora, the largest Jewish community in Europe; and as such it became Nazi Germany's main killing grounds.

Jews were living in Poland as early as the tenth century—there is even a legend about a Jewish merchant, Abraham Prochownik, who was reputed to have been offered the Polish crown in the ninth century.

The first Jews came as merchants and peddlers fleeing persecution in the German Empire, particularly during the Crusades, and the earliest Jewish settlements were established in Silesia, in what is now southwest Poland.

Poland's nascent Jewish communities were devastated in the thirteenth century, when Tartar invaders laid waste to Christian and Jewish settlements alike. Following this, immigrants were welcomed by local rulers anxious to repopulate their towns. In 1264, Prince Boleslaw the Pious of Kalisz issued a body of laws known as the Calisian Privilege, which guaranteed Jews the right to live in the town. In the fourteenth century, King Casimir the Great, who was sympathetic to Jews (legend even credits him with a Jewish lover named Esther, or Esterka) and who favored the creation of a Jewish urban population, extended the Calisian Privilege to encompass the right of Jews to live all over his kingdom.

From the thirteenth to the fifteenth centuries, waves of Jews from Germany, Bohemia, Moravia, Spain, Italy, and elsewhere eagerly flocked to Poland, fleeing massacres, persecutions, and expulsions at home. It is estimated that by the end of the fifteenth century, between 20,000 and 30,000 Jews lived in at least sixty Jewish communities in towns scattered over Poland and Lithuania (with which Poland had united in 1358). Living

in tight communities under the protection of the king and usually established near the marketplace or town fortifications, Jews were craftsmen,
peddlers, moneylenders, and merchants dealing in livestock, exotic spices,
wine, textiles, dyes, and many other goods.

The burgeoning Jewish population did not go unopposed by the
Catholic church or by local non-Jewish merchants (many of them German)
fearing competition. Anti-Jewish violence erupted in the wake of the
Black Death plague in the thirteenth century; the first blood libel—the accusation that Jews kill Christians to use their blood for ritual purposes,
particularly to make Passover matzo—was reported in 1347.

Church leaders repeatedly tried to force Jews to wear a special badge
and called for other tight restrictions. A Polish church council meeting in
Wroclaw in 1267 declared Jews to engage in "superstitions and evil habits"
that could contaminate Christians. Various towns were granted the privilege *de non tolerandis Judaeis*—laws that barred Jews from living there.

In the mid-fifteenth century, as part of a pressure campaign to force
King Casimir IV Jagiello to revoke Jewish privileges, bitterly anti-Jewish
Cardinal Zbigniew Olesnicki invited to Poland John of Capistrano, a Fran-
ciscan monk whose persecutions in Germany had already earned him the
nickname "Scourge of the Jews." In Wroclaw, thanks to Capistrano's
preaching, almost the entire Jewish community was burned at the stake
or expelled from the city because of their alleged blasphemy. Anti-Jewish
riots linked to his preaching also broke out in Cracow and Warsaw.

In 1454, the king bowed to pressure and declared the repeal of all
Jewish charters. This decision was relatively short-lived, however. New
privileges ushering in a Golden Age for Polish Jewry were granted to
Jews, particularly during the reign of Sigismund I (1506–1548).

In 1551, King Sigismund II Augustus, who was sympathetic to the
Jews and tried to combat the increasingly frequent accusations of blood
libel, granted the leaders of Jewish communities wide-ranging judicial
and administrative powers over Jewish life. Each Jewish community was
to elect a council of elders called a *Kahal*, which was to oversee tax collection and the administration of Jewish courts, schools, and other institutions—even the rabbis.

This laid the groundwork for the foundation, around 1580, of the
Council of the Four Lands, a supreme governing body that for nearly 200
years ruled over virtually every aspect of secular and religious Jewish life
in Poland and, as such, served practically as a state within a state.

The Council, which lasted until 1764, was based in Lublin and joined
representatives from the regions of Great Poland, Little Poland, Volhynia,
and Red Russia (East Galicia and Podolia). Lithuania originally was part
of the Council but from 1623 had its own central organization.

Even greater waves of Jewish immigrants surged into Poland after
1500. Most came from western and central Europe, but some Italian and
Sephardic Jews also made their way to the Polish haven. One of these was

the doctor Isaac Hispanus, who served as court physician in the late fifteenth and early sixteenth centuries.

Between 1500 and 1648, the Jewish population of Poland and Lithuania swelled from 30,000 to as many as 500,000, making it the largest concentration of Jews in the world. An extremely high level of scholarship and cultural and religious life developed in centers like Lublin, Warsaw, Poznan, and Cracow.

By the beginning of the sixteenth century, Poland boasted famous yeshivas where scholars like Moses Isserles Remuh, Solomon Luria, and Shalom Shachna flourished. Hebrew printing houses turned out splendid, sometimes illuminated, books, and magnificent synagogues, some still standing today, were built.

Then, in 1648–1649, a bloody uprising headed by Cossack chieftain Bogdan Chmielnicki ushered in three decades of war, destruction, and chaos still referred to in Polish history as "The Deluge." Chmielnicki led hordes of fellow Cossacks, Ukrainian peasants, and Tartars in an orgy of plundering, pillaging, and massacre. The uprising of the Greek Orthodox Cossacks and peasants was aimed against both the Roman Catholic Polish landlords who oppressed them and against the Jews—many of whom served as tax collectors and stewards on the Polish estates. Tens of thousands were slaughtered amid scenes of unbelievable carnage: One image that has been repeated both by historians and in literature is that of Jewish women slit open and then live cats sewn into their bellies.

The Chmielnicki uprising was followed by yet another Cossack rebellion and by invasions by Sweden and Russia, which kept the country in a constant state of turmoil and warfare for years. As many as 700 Jewish communities were destroyed during these decades; estimates of Jews killed range from 100,000 to 500,000. The destruction forced thousands to migrate to the west and south and in many cases pushed Jews into mysticism, superstition, self-isolation, and expectations of the imminent coming of the Messiah.

Numerous false Messiahs claimed followers. The most influential was the remarkable Shabbatai Zevi, born in Smyrna in 1626, who proclaimed himself Messiah in 1665 after attracting a huge following of believers during widespread travels. Belief in Shabbatai Zevi swept Poland, as it swept tens of thousands of Jews all over Europe and the Middle East from England to Jerusalem, and pockets of his sect remained even after Zevi himself converted to Islam to save his life and died in exile in Albania in 1676. (See Ulcinj, Yugoslavia.) Another popular false Messiah was Jacob Frank (1726–1791), who came from Podolia, then part of Poland. He was influenced by the lingering Shabbatai Zevi sects he had come into contact with while traveling in the Ottoman Empire. Frank returned to Poland, where he claimed he was the reincarnation of Shabbatai Zevi and gathered around him many followers into a sect whose beliefs mingled elements of Judaism, Catholicism, and Islam. They were widely believed to indulge in sexual orgies as part of their rituals. Polish rabbis excommunicated the Frankists in 1756, and Frank and several thousand followers converted to Catholicism in 1759.

Another important spiritual movement began at the same time as the Frankists: **Hasidism**. Hasidism, still widespread among Jews today, grew up as a revival movement that was actually a revolution against the increasingly dogmatic and circumscribed Judaism as preached and practiced by the rabbis, who had become all-powerful in most Jewish communities in Eastern Europe. In many communities, esoteric Talmudic dispute had replaced spirituality.

Israel ben Eliezer, known to his followers as the Ba'al Shem Tov (Master of the Good Name), or the *Besht,* was born around 1700, probably in the village of Okop in Podolia—the same part of the Polish Ukraine that produced Jacob Frank. He wandered throughout the region (see Piatra Neamt, Romania), preaching joyous communion with God through faith and love—rather than through book learning or scholarship. Little is known specifically about the Ba'al Shem Tov's life; he left no writings, and the stories passed down by his disciples are the stuff of legends. At the time of the Ba'al Shem Tov's death in 1760, however, he had gathered around him as many as 100,000 followers.

The Ba'al Shem Tov's disciples carried on his work, bringing the Hasidic gospel of joy and love to all corners of Eastern Europe. Eventually, Hasidism evolved a system under which individual communities of Hasids were led by a tzaddik or rebbe, a charismatic, saintly leader who was revered as a worker of miracles and a direct mediator between man and God. In 1772, the Mitnagdim, or opponents of Hasidism, grouped around the powerful and strictly Orthodox Rabbi Elijah ben Soloman Zalman (1720–1797), known as the Gaon (Eminence or Spiritual Leader) of Vilna, Lithuania, and excommunicated Hasidism as a "new sect." This did not stop the movement from spreading and becoming the most powerful Jewish force in Eastern Europe in the nineteenth century.

The Jewish enlightenment, or **Haskalah**, grew at much the same time as did Hasidism. The Haskalah movement began in Germany in the late eighteenth century, particularly through the reforming work of Jewish philosopher Moses Mendelsohn. The Haskalah penetrated slowly and with difficulty into the East, introducing modern ideas and western European cultural influence. The movement was bitterly opposed by both traditional rabbinical Orthodoxy and by Hasidism. In the nineteenth century, as the movement made some inroads, families were split apart over adhesion to modernism or tradition. Young people particularly turned to the Haskalah as a way to pull themselves out of the backward, isolated world of the shtetl.

The Yiddish writer S. Ansky (1863–1920) wrote how he, a convinced **maskil**, or follower of the Haskalah, had to hide his beliefs when he went to work as a teacher in a shtetl:

To avoid provoking malicious acts against me from the start, I put on a mask of piety and showed that my only purpose was to earn my keep. I played my role well, I obtained lessons, and soon I was in touch with several boys. Despite the isolation from the great world, the town nevertheless had a few "infected" young people, who reached out for light and knowledge and thirsted for a word of haskalah. They understood immediately I was not as pious as I made out, and wordlessly, but with expressive glances, they hinted they wanted to establish contact with me. They soon succeeded. Once, late at night, I heard a cautious quiet tap on my window. Opening it, I saw before me two boys who, quietly but joyously and spiritedly, told me they came to discuss an important, a most important matter. Not waiting for an invitation, they entered my room through the window.

A conversation began which lasted till dawn. It would be hard to define what we talked about. The conversation consisted almost entirely of passionate exclamations (whispered, of course, so the landlady would not overhear) extolling the radiant and sacred haskalah. I do not remember what I told my new comrade-pupils, but the substance was not in my words but in the exalted mood of the listeners, who saw some sort of prophecy in my words. They left, joyous, as if newborn, with a firm decision to throw off their yoke, run away from home, and begin a new life, bright and promising.

Between 1772 and 1795, Poland disappeared as an entity, partitioned among Russia, Prussia, and Austria. It did not reappear as an independent state until after World War I. Western Poland went to Prussia. Southern Poland and Galicia, including Cracow, went to Austria. The largest part of Poland, the eastern and central regions, went to Russia. In 1794, Polish patriot Tadeusz Kosciuszko led an abortive revolt against the Russian and Prussian armies. A Jewish regiment led by Berek Joselewicz (see Kock) fought with Kosciuszko.

The Russian czars created the so-called Pale of Settlement, a strip of land along Russia's western border, including the Polish territory gained by Russia in the partitions, where all Russian Jews were forced to live. Life was miserable here for the majority of the millions of Jews living in the Pale. They suffered brutal persecution and often violence. In 1882, the so-called "May Laws" expelled Jews from all villages in the Pale and sharply restricted the right of Jews to travel and carry out trade. The late nineteenth and early twentieth centuries saw pogrom after pogrom directed against the Jews.

All of this sparked the mass emigration of Jews to the west: Between 1880 and 1914 it is estimated that 1.5 million Jews left the Pale of Settlement—the vast majority went to America.

The terrible conditions and constant persecution also contributed to Jewish political activism, particularly among labor unions and left-wing parties like the Jewish Labor Bund, a militant socialist party founded in Vilna in 1897, Zionists, and conservative parties like the Orthodox Agudas Israel founded in 1912.

Conditions were not quite so dire in Galicia, which became part of the Austro-Hungarian Empire. Jews here were granted some measure of freedom in the 1780s through the Edicts of Tolerance issued by Josef II and gained further rights over the years. Nonetheless, poverty and anti-Semitism eventually prompted mass waves of emigration. As many as 300,000 Galician Jews immigrated to the United States between 1891 and 1913.

When Poland was re-formed as an independent state after World War I, its eastern border stretched far into what is now Lithuania, Belarus, and Ukraine, and much of what today is western Poland belonged to Germany. Its new leaders formally promised to guarantee the rights of minorities—of which the Jews were one, making up about ten percent of the population. These guarantees were never fully honored, however, and were revoked in 1934.

Anti-Semitism was a constant throughout the interwar period. Right-wing extremists agitated for forced Jewish emigration; pogroms against Jews were not uncommon; the number of Jews allowed into universities was strictly limited; and economic restrictions on Jews led to widespread poverty and unemployment. Following the rise of Hitler in Germany and after the death of Poland's military dictator Marshal Jozef Pilsudski in 1935, things got worse as anti-Semitism became an active part of government policy.

Nonetheless, Poland's 3.3 million Jews did form a world for themselves that was full of spirituality, learning, culture, political activity, and all other components of a rich Jewish life. In the mid-1980s, Jewish historian Szymon Datner recalled those days of his youth:

> The world of the Polish Jews was extraordinarily varied, rich, and colorful. And above all it was big and it was what I would call present: very visible. Jews made up 10 percent of the population of the country, but since they lived predominantly in the towns, their numbers there were proportionately much greater. In large cities, from 30 to 50 percent. In smaller towns, particularly in the eastern lands, the number of Jews ran as high as 80 or 90 percent. Those were the famous Jewish shtetls. And a splendid, exuberant, and creative Jewish life flourished everywhere in those towns and villages. There was complete freedom of observance and autonomy in religious matters, exceptionally well developed education of all types, at all levels, and in all special-

izations, as well as an enormous number of publications in all three languages: Yiddish, Hebrew, and Polish. Thirty Jewish newspapers and a hundred and thirty of the most varied magazines were being published just before the war. Literary giants, reformers, thinkers, scholars, and politicians grew up and worked in Poland. Dozens of political parties of all colorations were active. They had their delegates and senators in the Polish parliament. There were charitable and cultural organizations, unions of writers and journalists and workers.

World War II began on September 1, 1939, when Germany invaded Poland. One sentence can sum up the horror of the Holocaust in Poland: Out of the 3.3 million Jews living in the country at the outbreak of war, only 300,000 survived. Along with 3 million people, almost the entire infrastructure of a civilization was erased: Thousands of synagogues, prayer houses, and other Jewish buildings were razed to the ground; tens of thousands of books and ritual objects were destroyed. Tombstones were uprooted from ancient cemeteries to be used to pave roads and build pigsties.

After the horrors, tens of thousands of survivors emigrated—particularly after the pogrom in Kielce in 1946 (see Kielce) reminded them that anti-Semitism had not been killed along with Poland's Jews. Mass emigrations left about 30,000 Jews living in Poland by the beginning of the 1960s. A final mass emigration took place in the wake of a sweeping anti-Semitic campaign by Poland's communist regime in 1968–1969. This ostensibly had been touched off by student demonstrations in 1968 and by the Six-Day War in 1967, after which Poland, like other communist states, broke off relations with Israel. After 1968, all but a few thousand Jews left Poland, and Jewish culture and life in Poland virtually came to a standstill.

The situation began to change in the late 1970s and particularly after the rise of the Solidarity movement in 1980. At about this time, a number of young Polish Jews discovered their roots and began trying to pick up threads that had been cut decades before. Young Jews and non-Jews alike, many affiliated with the anticommunist political opposition, also began caring for Jewish cemeteries and other Jewish monuments. Numerous books on Judaism and Jewish topics were published. These trends have flourished since the ouster of the communists.

For the Traveler

Where

Poland is in northern East-Central Europe, bordering the Baltic Sea, Lithuania, Russia, Belarus, Ukraine, Germany, the Czech Republic, and

Slovakia. Except for the hilly and mountainous southern fringes of the country, the overwhelming majority of Polish territory is a flat or slightly rolling landscape, much of it dense forests or agricultural land.

When

With its chill northern climate, Poland is no treat in the late fall or winter. It is at its best in the late spring (May can be beautiful), summer, and early fall—the famous "Golden Septembers."

How

The Polish airline LOT, as well as many international carriers, fly to Warsaw and Cracow. There are also international train connections from Berlin, Prague, Vienna, and Moscow, as well as ferry connections with Scandinavia.

Roads in Poland are generally good, though there are only a few four-lane highways. Driving can be a strain, though, particularly at night in rural areas, due to poor lighting and numerous horse-drawn farm vehicles.

Visas

Americans do not need visas for Poland.

Languages

Polish is the native language. Many people, particularly in western Poland, speak German, however. As everywhere, English is becoming more and more widespread as a second language, particularly among young people.

Helpful Phrases

English	Polish (Pronunciation)
Synagogue	Synagoga/Bóżnica (Seenagoga/ Boozh'-nit-sa)
Jewish cemetery	Żidowski cmentarz (Zhee-dov'-ski smen'-tazh)
Yes	Tak (Tahk)
No	Nie (Nye)
Hello/Good day	Dzień dobry (Dzhin doh'-bree)
Good-bye	Do widzenia (Do vee-dzen'-ya)
I don't speak Polish	Ja nie mówię po polsku (Ya nye moo'-vye po pohl'-skoo)

English	Polish (Pronunciation)
Please	Proszę (Proh'-sheh)
Where is . . . ?	Gdzie jest . . . ? (Gje yest)
Thank you	Dziękuję (Dzhin-koo'-yeh)
Entrance	Wejście (Vaysh'-cheh)
Exit	Wyjście (Veesh'-cheh)
Toilet	Toaleta (Toh-a-let'-a)
Men	Panowie (Pahn'-oh-vyeh)
Women	Panie (Pah'-nyeh)
Is there a room free?	Czy jest wolny pokój? (Chee yest volny pokooy)
How much does this cost?	Ile to kosztuje? (Eelay taw kawsh-too'-yeh)
One	Jeden (Yed'-den)
Two	Dwa (Dvah)
Three	Trzy (Chi)
Four	Cztery (Chteh'-ry)
Five	Pięć (Pyench)
Six	Sześć (Sheshch)
Seven	Siedem (Shed'-dem)
Eight	Osiem (Osh'-em)
Nine	Dziewięć (Dzheh'-vinch)
Ten	Dziesięć (Dzhesh'-inch)

Money

Poland's monetary unit is the zloty. In mid-1994 the exchange rate was about 22,000 zloties per U.S. dollar.

Kosher Cuisine

A kosher restaurant, Menora, opened in Warsaw in 1991, the first kosher restaurant in Poland in thirty years. Contact individual Jewish community offices or the Our Roots Jewish travel office in Warsaw for information on obtaining kosher meals elsewhere. Some packaged kosher food may be available in specialty shops.

If You Only Have a Few Days

Warsaw and Cracow are the main points of interest, and numerous easy side trips can be made from each. Auschwitz is about an hour from Cracow, so is Tarnow. If you drive from Warsaw to Cracow, you can make a zigzag route and see a number of interesting sites, including Karczew, Przysucha, Szydlowiec, Checiny, Kielce, Pinczow, Wodzislaw, and Dzialoszyce. Most Polish Jewish relics are in the eastern and southern parts of the country. The areas around Lublin, Zamosc, and Bialystok are particularly rich in Jewish history. The Jewish museums in the old synagogues at Tykocin and Lancut are well worth seeing.

Helpful Addresses

(The direct dialing code to Poland is 48.)

Our Roots Jewish travel agency. Edits local guidebooks, has information on specific sites, can provide guides, and is generally very helpful.
ul. Twarda 6
Warsaw 00-104
Tel. and fax (22) 200-556

Federation of Jewish Communities
ul. Twarda 6
Warsaw
Tel. (22) 204-324

Ronald S. Lauder Foundation. Active in promoting Jewish youth groups, education, and Jewish revival.
ul. Twarda 6
00-104 Warsaw
Tel. (22) 200-793

Jewish Historical Institute
ul. Tlomackie 3/5
Warsaw 00-090

Research Center on Jewish History and Culture in Poland
Jagiellonian University
ul. Batorego 12
Cracow 31-135
Tel. (12) 337-058; fax (12) 344-593

Jewish Research Institute, Rzeszow
ul. Boznicza 4
35-959 Rzeszow
Tel. (17) 32670; (17) 32689

Tomasz Wisniewski is an English-speaking, independent researcher on local Judaica who also sells postcards made from old pictures of Jewish monuments in the Bialystok region.
ul. Bema 95/99, Box 351
15-001 Bialystok
Tel. 21246

Jano-Tour
Specializes in Jewish tourism
Sw. Filipa 5/5
Cracow 31-150
Tel. (12) 336146

Ariel Cafe is a Jewish-oriented coffeehouse, art gallery, restaurant, and bookstore in the heart of Cracow's old Jewish section.
ul. Szeroka 17
Cracow
Tel. (12) 21-38-70

Orbis Polish Travel Bureau
ul. Bracka 16
Warsaw 00-028
Tel. (22) 26-02-71

"Routes to Roots" provides genealogical tours, traces family roots and ancestry, and offers research packets on ancestral towns.
c/o Miriam Weiner
136 Sandpiper Key
Secaucus, NJ 07094
Tel. (201) 866-4075; fax (201) 864-9222

U.S. Embassy
Al. Ujazdowskie 29/31
Warsaw
Tel. (22) 28-30-41

Main Active Jewish Communities

The communities listed below have regular Friday night and holiday services, usually in prayer rooms attached to the community center. Most communities are very small, and most are located in the southwestern Silesia region. Check with communities for time and location of services and for the possibility of obtaining kosher food.

Warsaw	Nozyk Synagogue, ul. Twarda 6
Bielsko Biala	Mickiewicza 26
Bytom	Smolenska 4
Chrzanow	Chojnowska 16
Cracow	Skawinska 2
	Remuh Synagogue, ul. Szeroka 49
Dzierzoniow	Krasickiego 28
Gliwice	Dolne Waly 9
Katowice	Mlynska 13

Legnica	Chojnowska 17
Lodz	Zachodnia 78
Lublin	Lubartowska 10
Szczecin	Niemcewicza 2
Swidnica	Boh. Getta 22
Walbrzych	Mickiewicza 18
Wroclaw	Wlodkowica 9
Zary K. Zagania	Armii Czerwonej 3a

Local Jewish Interest Guidebooks

Our Roots publishes very useful detailed guidebooks to Warsaw, Cracow, and other areas. They are on sale at some tourist bookstores, hotels, the Our Roots office, and at the Jewish Historical Institute.

- *The Guide to Lublin Area* by Andrzej Trzcinski is packed with information. You can find it in Warsaw at the Jewish Historical Institute.
- A guide to the Lodz Cemetery is available in some bookstores as well as at the Jewish Historical Institute.
- *A Tribe of Stones* by Monika Krajewska. A large-format photographic essay with extremely valuable text on Jewish cemeteries in Poland, this is an expanded and updated version of Krajewska's earlier book, *Time of Stones,* which is out of print.
- *Poland's Jewish Heritage* by Joram Kagan. Hippocrene, New York, 1992.
- If you read Polish, there are an increasing number of local Jewish guides to specific cities, such as Tarnow and Cracow, or regions, such as the area surrounding Bialystok. A guide to Jewish sites all over Poland, by Przemyslaw Burchard, is also available, as is a very helpful map of Poland locating many Jewish sites.

JEWISH HERITAGE IN POLAND

Thousands of synagogues, including numerous unique wooden synagogues built between the seventeenth and twentieth centuries, stood in Poland before World War II. Today, there are about 245 known synagogue buildings still in existence. All of the wooden synagogues were destroyed.

Thanks to the work of dedicated individuals like Jan Jagielski, Maria and Kazimierz Piechotka, Eleonora Bergman, and Monika and Stanislaw Krajewski, as well as the renewed interest in Judaism in Poland and the new political climate, all remaining synagogue buildings and their current functions are listed at the Jewish Historical Institute in Warsaw. They range from synagogues used for religious services (as in Warsaw and Cracow) to synagogues used as museums. Most, however, are in secular use as warehouses, cinemas, factories, or even fire stations. Many are empty or simply in ruins.

In 1981, a group called the Citizens' Committee for the Protection of Jewish Cemeteries and Cultural Monuments in Poland was founded. Volunteers in the Committee have spent endless hours studying and restoring devastated cemeteries and holding lectures or writing articles alerting both the public and official bodies to the plight of the monuments. Several cemeteries, too, have been cleaned up or restored by private people or groups, generally Polish Jews now living abroad.

Today, there are about 400 Jewish cemeteries in Poland that still have tombstones, but only 140 of these have more than 100 tombstones left. About 50 cemeteries have tombstones dating back to before 1795.

In addition to the cemeteries and synagogues, a number of Polish towns still have neighborhoods whose old buildings recall the old shtetl. There are many monuments and museums commemorating the Holocaust.

WARSAW

(Polish: Warszawa)

Jewish Community: ul. Twarda 6, Tel. (22) 204324

Kosher Restaurant: Menora, Plac Grzybowski 2

Before the Holocaust, Poland's capital was the most important Jewish center in Europe. The city's more than 350,000 Jews made up one-third of its population. More Jews lived in Warsaw than in all of Czechoslovakia; roughly the same number of Jews lived in all of France. Out of all the cities in the world, only New York had a greater Jewish population.

Here is how Nobel Prize-winning author Isaac Bashevis Singer described Plac Grzybowski—then as now a center of Jewish life in Warsaw—in his epic novel *The Family Moskat*:

> The sidewalks were crowded with gaberdined Jews wearing small cloth caps, and bewigged women with shawls over their heads. Even the smells were different now. There was a whiff of the marketplace in the air—spoiled fruits, lemons, and a mixture of something sweetish and tarry, which could not be given a name and which impinged on the senses only when one returned to the scene after a longish absence. The street was a bedlam of sound and activity. Street peddlers called out their wares in ear-piercing chants—potato cakes, hot chickpeas, apples, pears, Hungarian plums, black and white grapes, watermelon whole and in sections. Although the evening was warm,

the merchants wore outer coats, with large leather money pouches hanging from the belts. Women hucksters sat on boxes, benches and doorsills. The stalls were lighted with lanterns, some with flickering candles stuck on the edges of wooden crates. Customers lifted and pinched the fruits or took little exploratory nibbles, smacking their lips to savor the taste. The stall-keepers weighed purchases on tin scales. . . .

In the middle of the street, truckmen guided overloaded wagons. The heavy, low-slung horses stamped their iron-shod hoofs on the cobbles, sending out sparks. A porter wearing a hat with a brass badge carried an enormous basket of coal strapped to his shoulders with thick rope. A janitor in an oil-cloth cap and blue apron was sweeping a square of pavement with a long broom. Youngsters, their little lovelocks flapping under octagonal caps, were pouring out of the doors of the Hebrew schools, their patched pants peeping out from between the skirts of their long coats. A boy with a cap pulled low over his eyes was selling New Year calendars, shouting at the top of his voice. A ragged youth with a pair of frightened eyes and disheveled earlocks stood near a box of prayer shawls, phylacteries, prayer books, tin Hanukkah candlesticks, and amulets for pregnant women. A dwarf with an oversized head wandered about with a bundle of leather whips, fanning the straps back and forth, demonstrating how to whip stubborn children. On a stall lit by a carbide lamp lay piles of Yiddish newspapers, cheap novelettes, and books on palmistry and phrenology. Reb Meshulam glanced out of the window of the carriage and observed: "The land of Israel, eh?"

Today, Plac Grzybowski bears little resemblance to that colorful scene. Here, though, surrounded by modern but already shabby concrete and glass apartment blocks, are buildings housing the Yiddish Theater and offices of the Jewish newspaper, the Jewish travel bureau Our Roots, and other Jewish offices. Around the corner is the only remaining synagogue in the city, the Nozyk Synagogue on ul. Twarda.

In all of Warsaw, only a few hundred (or maybe a few thousand, as many Jews do not identify themselves with the community), mainly elderly Jews remain out of the city's more than 1.6 million people.

Jews settled in Warsaw in the late fourteenth and early fifteenth centuries, but not long afterward were expelled. Jews were officially banned from living in the city from 1527 until 1768, but during this period various Jewish settlements were established in privately owned towns called *jurydykas* on the estates of Polish nobles outside the city limits.

The Jewish population grew rapidly after the residency ban was lifted, and particularly after the partition of Poland among Russia, Prussia, and Austria in the late eighteenth century, when waves of immigrants flowed in. In the first years of the nineteenth century, Warsaw's 11,600 Jews made up over seventeen percent of the local population. By 1910, more than 300,000 Jews lived in the city, forming nearly forty percent of the population.

This extraordinary Jewish community encompassed all facets of Jewish life, all colors of the Jewish spectrum. Most Warsaw Jews remained Orthodox in their religious practice, and many were fervent Hasidim living highly traditional lives—mostly in poverty. But there was also a sizable Reformed community whose ranks included many prosperous and influential businessmen.

Educational, scholarly, cultural, and intellectual life was extremely vibrant. There were Jewish theaters, Jewish newspapers, Jewish bookshops, numerous religious schools and yeshivas, Jewish sports clubs, social clubs, and organizations. Politically, too, Warsaw was fertile ground for many Jewish parties and movements, particularly worker parties like the Bund and Orthodox ones like Agudas Israel.

A list of famous Jews who were born or lived and worked in Warsaw would take pages: writers such as Isaac Bashevis Singer, Sholom Asch, I. L. Peretz, David Frischmann, and Nachum Sokolow; theatrical and film personalities like Esther Rachel Kaminska and her daughter, Ida; historians such as Majer Balaban; scholars like Samuel Poznanski, Chaim Solowiejczyk, and Isaac Cylkow.

Most Warsaw Jews lived in a district southeast of the picturesque Old Town, and it was here that the Nazis set up the Warsaw Ghetto in November 1940, a year after they occupied the city and imposed vicious anti-Semitic restrictions. About 450,000 Jews were crowded into two sections known as the Small Ghetto and Large Ghetto. They were placed on starvation rations, and in little more than a year some 100,000 are estimated to have died from hunger or disease. Mass deportations began on June 22, 1942, and hundreds of thousands of people were herded into cattle cars at a siding near Umschlagplatz and shipped to their deaths at Treblinka.

On April 19, 1943, some 300 Jews in the ghetto staged an abortive uprising that, despite bloody fighting for three weeks, ended in defeat. Cornered in their bunker at ul. Mila 18, most of the uprising leaders committed suicide rather than allow themselves to be captured by the Nazis.

The ghetto was reduced to a pile of smoldering rubble.

Only about 300 Jews survived in the city when it was liberated on January 17, 1945.

Most of Warsaw, not just the ghetto, was leveled in the war—today's postcard-perfect Old Town actually was painstakingly rebuilt, based on photographs and old paintings. Aside from this restored part, most of the city now consists of rather ugly modern buildings and apartment blocks. Only a few isolated Jewish monuments remain—otherwise, there are merely plaques to mark what used to be.

Major Places of Jewish Interest in Warsaw

• Synagogue: ul. Twarda 6

The Nozyk Synagogue, the only surviving synagogue in Warsaw, was founded in 1900 by Zalman and Rywka Nozyk. It suffered serious damage during World War II, when the Nazis used it as a stable, and it was further damaged during and after the Warsaw Ghetto uprising. It was repaired to some extent in the immediate postwar period and later underwent a full six-year restoration completed in 1983.

Services are held here daily, and there is a kosher canteen for community members (tourists can also make arrangements to eat here). Services can, in fact, be a little unnerving. On one Sabbath not long ago, prayer books were unavailable (apparently they are kept hidden in order to prevent theft). Most of the congregation—a few dozen elderly men—didn't seem to be paying attention anyway. Acoustics were terrible. It was hard to hear either the leader of the service or the reader during the reading of the Torah. People stood around talking—and getting louder and louder to the point where the *shammas* had to pound on a railing for quiet! Rabbi Pinchas Menachem Joskowicz, a Hasidic Jew with a long white beard who returned from Israel to become Poland's only rabbi in 1988, gave a lengthy sermon in Yiddish, while members of the congregation gathered round the bimah.

Warsaw—The Nozyk Synagogue, the only synagogue in Warsaw. Looming through the fog in the background is the tower of the Stalinist-era Palace of Culture.

Afterward, a **kiddush** (ceremonial refreshments) was held in the community house next door—Israeli matzo, Israeli gefilte fish, and kosher Polish vodka produced by the Nissenbaum Foundation, an organization founded by a family of Polish Jewish Holocaust survivors.

• Old Cemetery: entrance at ul. Okopowa 49/51

Established in 1806, the cemetery contains the graves of about 250,000 people. Covering thirty-three hectares, it is the largest—and one of the few still functioning—Jewish cemeteries in Poland. Despite recent cleanup and restoration efforts by Jewish organizations and volunteer civic groups, much of the vast cemetery is choked by shrubs, weeds, and young trees that have grown up over the years among the tombstones.

The cemetery displays a panorama of Jewish history in Warsaw, and tombstones range from intricately decorated mazzevahs in the older section to massive sculptural monuments and family tombs erected in the late nineteenth and early twentieth centuries.

Numerous prominent Polish Jews from all walks of life are buried here. They include rabbis and revered Hasidic tzaddikim, as well as writers I. L. Peretz and S. Ansky, actress Esther Rachel Kaminska, historian Majer Balaban, and Lazarus Ludwik Zamenhof, the inventor of the artificial language Esperanto. (See Bialystok.) There is also a striking sculpted monument erected in 1982 to honor Janusz Korczak (Henryk Goldszmit), who ran the orphan's home in the Warsaw Ghetto and went to his death at Treblinka with the orphanage children.

The most impressive tomb in the older section of the cemetery is that of the wealthy merchant Ber Sonnenberg (1764–1826), an ancestor of French Nobel Prize–winning philosopher Henri Bergson. Designed by architect and artist David Friedlaender, it is a large, rectangular structure with two extremely elaborate sculptural relief panels of complex landscapes. One of the panels depicts the suburb of Praga, across the Vistula River from central Warsaw, including its Jewish cemetery. The other is a remarkable vision of biblical Babylon.

• Jewish Historical Institute and Museum: ul. Tlomackie 3/5 (open daily, 9 A.M.–1 P.M.)

The Institute complex, housed in the prewar building that once was the Judaic Library, includes the museum, a library, and Jewish archives. Just across the narrow street is a big, modern glass and steel skyscraper that stands on the site of the former imposing Great Synagogue, built in 1878 and destroyed in 1943.

The precious archives in the Institute include documentation dating back to the seventeenth century, memoirs from the Holocaust period, contemporary Jewish documentation, and a collection of over 30,000 photographs.

The library contains tens of thousands of books, manuscripts, prints, and periodicals, most of them salvaged from the yeshiva in Lublin, the library of the former theological seminary in Wroclaw, and the main Jewish library in Warsaw. The oldest items date back to the twelfth century.

The museum includes fascinating exhibits of artworks, Jewish ritual objects (the textiles are particularly valuable), and historical objects, many from the Holocaust period. There is a museum bookshop selling some English-language material, including local guidebooks.

• Jewish Theater: Plac Grzybowski 12/16

The modern concrete building housing Warsaw's Jewish Theater also houses the offices of a number of Jewish organizations and the Jewish newspaper *Dos Yiddishe Wort*. Today's theater gives regular performances of Yiddish classics as well as Polish works. You can buy striking posters advertising these plays at the theater office.

• Warsaw Ghetto Monuments

Much of what was the Warsaw Ghetto and, earlier, the main Jewish quarter of Warsaw was razed during the war and today is mainly the site of high-rise apartment blocks and empty lots.

A few old buildings do remain, however, as well as a few fragments of the former ghetto walls, in the courtyard of ul. Zlota 60, and the prison on ul. Pawia, now a museum. There are also a number of monuments and markers, including a Memory Lane—a lane of Jewish memory, martyrdom, and struggle—inaugurated on April 19, 1988, the forty-fifth anniversary of the Warsaw Ghetto uprising. This lane is a route through the former ghetto area marked by plaques, inscribed blocks of black marble, and other monuments to events, individuals, and the ghetto heroes in general. The route starts at the crossroads of ul. Anielewicza and ul. Zamenhofa, where there is a plaque noting that this was the site of the ghetto.

Among the sites it passes are:

- The impressive Monument to Ghetto Heroes, with a dramatic sculpture by Natan Rapaport, on ul. Zamenhofa.
- The site of the Jewish resistance bunker at ul. Mila 18.
- The buildings on ul. Stawki, which were the headquarters of the SS and the Jewish hospital.

The Memory Lane route ends further down ul. Stawki with the simple, stark monument marking Umschlagplatz, the staging area from which tens of thousands of Jews were deported from the ghetto to Treblinka.

At ul. Jaktorowska 8, there is a monument to Janusz Korczak (Henryk Goldszmit) at the site of his Jewish orphanage.

• Brodno Cemetery in Praga

Praga is a district of Warsaw across the Vistula River from the main part of town. Jews settled there in the eighteenth century. The Jewish cemetery in Praga is in the Brodno neighborhood, at the corner of ul. Odrowaza and ul. Wincentego. Founded in about 1780, it was devastated by the Nazis, who used some of the gravestones for paving.

Restoration work was begun in the mid-1980s to replace and repair the thousand or so gravestones that still remain.

CRACOW

(Polish: Kraków)

Jewish Community: ul. Skawinska 2. Tel. (12) 662-347; 661-756

Cracow, the ancient capital of Poland, is a splendidly beautiful city of 750,000 people whose fairy-tale castle, centuries-old university, and many other historic monuments and buildings spread out like a living museum around the vast and colorful Market Square.

Unlike Warsaw, Cracow was scarcely damaged during the war. Pollution and acid rain (including that from a huge steelworks built in the 1950s just outside town) may be taking their toll on ancient stone and brickwork, but—as residents are quick to point out—Cracow's historic buildings are real, not re-creations based on old records. Emphasizing historical links, every hour on the hour a trumpeter atop a church tower in the Market Square plays a fanfare that is cut off in midnote, in memory of a trumpeter slain by the Tartars with an arrow in the throat at just that point when he was playing the same fanfare centuries ago.

The old Jewish district, Kazimierz, and many former Jewish buildings have remained intact—albeit in poor repair—to this day, forming the country's richest and most important complex of Jewish relics.

Jews were living in Cracow by the early fourteenth century. At the end of the fifteenth century, they were expelled from the town proper and forced to move to the suburb of Kazimierz—today well within the city limits. The Jewish community in Kazimierz, bolstered by immigrants from Germany, Bohemia, Spain, and Portugal, became a semiautonomous Jewish Town, protected by the king. It flourished as a trading center and forged particularly close links with Prague, partly because many Jews emigrated from Prague and Bohemia to Cracow.

Jewish culture and scholarship in Cracow reached high peaks in the mid-sixteenth to mid-seventeenth centuries, when great sages like Rabbi Moses Isserles Remuh (c. 1525–1572) drew students and other scholars around them. Isserles is particularly known for his commentaries and amendments to the **Shulchan Aruch**, the codification of Jewish law prepared by the Sephardic Jewish scholar Joseph Caro and published in 1567. Isserles's commentaries expanded the Shulchan Aruch so it could be used as a guide to Ashkenazic as well as Sephardic Jewish practice.

Cracow came under the Austrian partition zone and, as elsewhere under the Hapsburgs, a concerted effort was made to get Jews to assimilate, though they were not granted full civil rights until the mid-nineteenth century.

In the twentieth century, the population grew quickly. Jews moved out to settle all over the city, though the core of Jewish life remained in Kazimierz—and here, too, the Orthodox, mainly Hasidic and poor, part of the population remained.

In 1938, more than 64,000 Jews lived in Cracow. The Germans occupied the city on September 6, 1939, less than a week after the beginning of the war. Two days later, all Jewish businesses were ordered to show a Star of David. Further stringent anti-Semitic measures followed in short order: All Jews over twelve had to wear a Star of David; Jews had to turn in cars and motorcycles; Jews were forbidden to move to a different house; Jews were forbidden to use public transportation; Jews were assigned to forced labor brigades. A ghetto was set up in March 1941 for Jews from Cracow and numerous surrounding towns and villages. Mass deportations began in June 1942.

Only about 2,000 Cracow Jews survived the Holocaust. Some 200 or so mostly elderly Jews live in Cracow today. There has, however, been a renewal of interest in Jewish history and culture in Cracow among Jews and non-Jews alike. A well-equipped Jewish research institute has been set up within the Jagiellonian University, with a Jewish Culture Center in Kazimierz itself. Every two years the picturesque district is also the scene of a rich festival of Jewish culture including music, dance, film, and theater.

Major Places of Jewish Interest in Cracow

• Kazimierz District

Walking through the old streets and markets and peering into apartment house courtyards, one somehow feels as though he or she is passing through a ghost town. Everything is dilapidated, but it is easy to imagine the bustle of the past. Most major surviving Jewish relics in the district are grouped around ul. Szeroka, an elongated square, which was the center of life in Kazimierz's Jewish Town.

• Old Synagogue: ul. Szeroka 24

Erected in the fifteenth and sixteenth centuries and remodeled many times since, the Old Synagogue is a massive, fortresslike building in the late Gothic-Renaissance style. The Nazis used it as a warehouse, and later it was ravaged and savagely looted. Following total restoration after the war, it became a Museum of Jewish History and Culture—a branch of the Cracow History Museum—in 1958.

The collections displayed are extensive and precious—liturgical items, ancient Torahs, textiles, dishes and utensils, shofars. There are also photographs, documents, and artwork detailing the history of the Cracow Jewish community before and during the Holocaust.

The primary exhibit, however, is the synagogue itself, with its two-aisle Gothic plan, elaborate wrought iron bimah, original masonry Ark, and other decorative and architectural elements.

In the broad plaza outside the synagogue is a monument to thirty Poles shot here by the Nazis.

• Remuh Synagogue and Old Cemetery: ul. Szeroka 40

Built in 1553 and remodeled several times, the synagogue is still used to-day and is the center of Jewish religious life in Cracow. It was founded by Israel Isserles, father of Rabbi Moses Isserles Remuh, for whom it is named. The Nazis looted it, but there was a full-scale restoration after the war. Right next to the synagogue is the Old Cemetery, which was used from 1551 through 1800.

Strictly speaking, this is a collection of cemetery art rather than the remains of a cemetery, as the cemetery, already in poor condition in the 1930s, was totally devastated by the Nazis. During archeological excavations in 1959, however, hundreds of ancient tombstones and fragments were found buried under the surface—some believe they were deliberately hidden before the Swedish invasion of 1704. About 700 tombstones, dating back to the sixteenth century, were reerected in the places they have today. Many nineteenth-century tombstones were brought from another cemetery and erected after the war. Fragments of tombstones were used to create a very moving mosaic wall (see cover of this book).

The tomb of Rabbi Moses Isserles Remuh and members of his family are in a fenced-off plot.

• Bociana, or Popper's, Synagogue: ul. Szeroka 16 (through yard)

Built in 1620 by the wealthy merchant Wolf Bocian, the synagogue today is a culture center. All the rich interior decoration has been destroyed.

• ul. Szeroka 6

This building was the site of the community bathhouse and mikvah from the sixteenth century.

• Tempel Synagogue (Also called Reformed Synagogue): ul. Miodowa 24

This synagogue was built from 1860 to 1862 for use by the Reformed Jewish community and was remodeled several times. The ornate interior includes colorful frescoes and stained glass windows. It is still consecrated as a synagogue but rarely used. A full-scale restoration of the building was expected to begin in 1994.

• Izaak's Synagogue: ul. Kupa 16

Built in 1638 with funds from the wealthy community elder Izaak Jakubowicz, this synagogue was remodeled several times but preserves its massive form. When the synagogue was under construction, a local priest complained that it was being positioned too close to a street where Christians lived. The Nazis looted its once rich interior decoration. It has been undergoing restoration.

• High (or Tall) Synagogue: ul. Jozefa 38

Built between 1556 and 1553, this synagogue was a prayer room on the second floor of the building, above ground-floor shops. Little of the original decoration is left, and today it houses a monuments restoration workshop.

• Kupa Synagogue: ul. Warszauera 8

Built in the first half of the seventeenth century, this synagogue was turned into a matzo factory after the war. Little is left of any original decoration, but there are some twentieth-century frescoes.

• New Cemetery: ul. Miodowa 55

The cemetery, in use today, was founded in 1800 (after the Old Cemetery was closed) and was devastated by the Nazis. It was restored in part after 1957 and has thousands of gravestones, some of them very beautifully decorated. The oldest date to the 1840s; it is interesting to note that some of the tombstones have inscriptions in Polish and German, an illustration of assimilation. There is also a Holocaust memorial.

• The Ghetto

The Cracow Ghetto was set up by the Nazis in March 1941 in the Podgorze district on the other side of the Vistula River from Kazimierz.

Just across the bridge is Bohaterow Ghetta (Ghetto Heroes) Square, the place from which Jews were deported to death camps, mainly Auschwitz-Birkenau and Belzec.

At No. 18 is a Museum of National Commemoration, set up in 1983 in what during the war was the "At the Sign of the Eagle" pharmacy, containing exhibits on the wartime ghetto and the Nazi occupation. Fragments of the ghetto walls are also visible.

• Plaszow

Southeast of the former ghetto is the site of the Plaszow concentration camp, which was built on top of a Jewish cemetery. It was here that German industrialist Oskar Schindler managed to save 1,100 Jews by having them work in his factory. There is a monument to the tens of thousands who did not survive. Not far away, on ul. Lipowa, is Schindler's factory, which now makes electronics parts. A new monument is in the factory's courtyard.

ELSEWHERE IN POLAND

Auschwitz-Birkenau (Oświęcim)

The biggest and most notorious complex of Nazi extermination camps is situated in and around the south-central Polish town of Oswiecim, about forty miles west of Cracow.

Before the war, Oswiecim was a typical shtetl, more than half of whose population was Jewish. In the town there is still a former synagogue, the former Jewish quarter, and the Jewish cemetery. The cemetery was totally demolished by the Nazis, but the tombstones were reerected in neat rows around 1980.

Auschwitz (the German name for Oswiecim) has become synonymous with the Holocaust. The most recent historical research shows that 1.5 to 2 million people, the overwhelming majority Jews from all over Europe, were murdered here.

The camps at Auschwitz and Birkenau were declared monuments and designated as museums/memorials in 1947. At Auschwitz, exhibits were set up in barracks and administrative buildings and, in addition, so-called national pavilions were created. These displayed exhibitions on how citizens of various countries suffered under the Nazis. Many of these exhibitions were pure communist propaganda.

Jews, who made up ninety percent of Auschwitz victims, were assigned a national pavilion . . . but so were the East Germans! Throughout the Auschwitz museum complex, the fact that ninety percent of the victims of Auschwitz were Jewish was scarcely mentioned.

Since the fall of the communist regime, an international committee has been at work to make much-needed changes at the museum—above all to stress at last the overwhelming Jewish character of the victims.

In contrast to Auschwitz, the Birkenau camp has been left much as it was: a vast, eerie, ghost-haunted expanse of ruined barracks, with a few brick and wooden structures left. From the entrance gate, where the old railway tracks still recall the tragic shipments of human cargo, a long, long central path stretches into the distance to a big monument to the victims. Nearby are the ruins of destroyed gas chambers. The long walk to the monument—it took me about half an hour—gives much time for thought and meditation; the sheer size of the camp as left is horrifying.

I was disappointed and frustrated by what I saw at Auschwitz. The meaning of the Holocaust, the painful, crucial meaning of what went on at Auschwitz, has been buried beneath the sterility of what the place has become and the crudity of the communist-era propaganda.

I was angered, rather than moved or horrified, by the piles of human hair, of shoes, of suitcases, of eyeglasses preserved behind glass, as if in some commercial Madame Tussaud–type chamber of horrors.

The brick barrack buildings, planted with trees and flower beds, made the place look like a college campus.

Later, reading Auschwitz survivor Primo Levi's moving account of his experiences, *If This Is a Man*, I found particularly apt what he said in the afterword:

> I returned to Auschwitz twice, in 1965 and 1982 . . . I didn't feel anything much when I visited the central Camp. The Polish government has transformed it into a kind of national monument. The huts have been cleaned and painted, trees have been planted and flowerbeds laid out. There is a museum in which pitiful relics are displayed: tons of human hair, hundreds of thousands of eyeglasses, combs, shaving brushes, dolls, baby shoes, but it remains just a museum—something static rearranged, contrived. To me, the entire camp seemed a museum . . . I did, however, experience a feeling of violent anguish when I entered Birkenau Camp, which I had never seen as a prisoner. Here nothing has changed. There was mud, and there is still mud, or suffocating summer dust. The blocks of huts (those that weren't burned when the Front reached and passed this area) have remained as they were, low, dirty, with draughty wooden sides and beaten earth floors. There are no bunks but bare planks, all the way to the ceiling. Here nothing has been prettied up.

Belzec (Bełżec)

In the woods near this village in eastern Poland south of Zamosc near the Ukrainian border is the site of one of the major extermination camps set up by the Nazis on Polish territory. The Nazis destroyed all traces of the camp in 1943, even plowing under the land and planting trees.

A monument commemorates the 600,000 people, including more than half a million Jews, who were murdered here.

*Bialystok (Białystok)

Before World War II, Bialystok's 40,000 Jews made up about half the population of what is now a drab industrial city of over 260,000 people northeast of Warsaw. Most shops and businesses were run by Jews, and Jews played a major part in the development of Bialystok's large textile industry in the nineteenth century.

Under the Polish partitions, Bialystok was under Russian occupation, within the Pale of Settlement. Due to the big textile and other industries, Bialystok became a focal point of Jewish labor union activities and the Bund party, as well as an intellectual center for the Haskalah (Jewish enlightenment).

Little is left of old Jewish Bialystok. Today, the big Jewish cemetery outside town on ul. Wschodnia is the only one of the six prewar Jewish cemeteries to have survived the war. At one time, there may have been 100,000 gravestones here—today there may still be as many as 10,000 that survived the Nazi devastation. The oldest date to the beginning of the nineteenth century.

The cemetery is very much overgrown by trees, bushes, grass, and weeds; you have to push your way through what used to be paths as if pushing your way through a jungle. In the late 1980s, however, a new wall and gate were built.

There are all types of gravestones, ranging from traditional mazzevahs to elaborate nineteenth-century sculptural monuments. There are even stones shaped like tree trunks—a particularly haunting sight amid the real saplings and undergrowth that choke the area.

One large black marble memorial, standing alone in a clearing, commemorates the terrible pogrom in 1905 in which seventy people were killed. "It's a miracle that it still exists," said Tomasz Wisniewski, a non-Jew who discovered his city's Jewish history while jailed for dissident activities during martial law in the early 1980s. He now devotes his time to recording what is left of Jewish culture and history in the Bialystok region. "This whole area," he said, throwing out his arm to go beyond the Jewish cemetery, beyond Bialystok, to include everything in this corner of Poland, "this whole area is one big cemetery. Its history is only wars, invasions, pogroms. There is nowhere else like it."

A big, ugly war memorial in the town center stands on the site of one of the other Jewish cemeteries. A large open market where Poles, Russians, Gypsies, and Romanians buy and sell everything imaginable, occupies the site of another Jewish cemetery.

Just off ul. Proletariacka, in the center of what was the wartime Bialystok Ghetto, established by the Nazis in August 1941, a small park marks the site of the ghetto cemetery. In the park, set in a rose garden, is a memorial tablet to 3,500 Jews killed there in August 1943.

Only three synagogues survive in one form or another out of the dozens that existed here before the war.

On ul. Warynskiego in the heart of what was the ghetto, a synagogue built just before the war in 1936–1937 still stands, cheek by jowl with modern apartment blocks and beautiful old wooden houses remaining from the historic old Jewish section. The synagogue today is used as an art restoration center. Around the corner, cobbled ul. Czysta, lined with sagging wooden houses, gives a good idea of the way Bialystok once used to look.

Another synagogue, built in the early twentieth century, stands at ul. Branickiego 3. It has been turned into a sports hall, and there is no indication it ever was a synagogue except for the projecting niche for the Aron ha Kodesh, which can still be seen from outside in the rear.

One other synagogue, today a burnt-out shell, stands on ul. Piekna near the old Jewish Market Square. It was built in the late nineteenth century, and there are plans to restore it and to place a memorial plaque.

This old Market Square, lined by a handful of old wooden houses, is one of the few neighborhoods still retaining some of the prewar atmosphere of the Jewish city—the effect is intensified by the contrast evoked by new high-rise blocks across the street.

At various points throughout Bialystok, plaques and street names recall the Jewish past. Near the courthouse downtown, a plaque marks the site of the Main Synagogue, burned down by the Nazis in 1941 with more than 1,000 Jews inside. In the same neighborhood, a plaque marks the former Jewish school attended by former Israeli Prime Minister Yitzhak Shamir. At ul. Warszawska 8, a plaque commemorates local son Lazarus Ludwik Zamenhof, the creator of Esperanto. An eye doctor born in 1859, Zamenhof published in 1887 his major opus, "An International Language," under the pen name Dr. Esperanto—"the Hoping One." He was convinced that the national and racial hatred he saw around him were only made more intense by linguistic barriers. His new language, he thought, could help bring peace.

Bobowa

This small village, set amid rolling farmland in southern Poland near Nowy Sacz, was once a Hasidic center and home to the court of the revered Bobower rebbe. Much of the town center retains its old Jewish character—and quite a few of the crooked wooden houses still bear scars on their doorposts where mezuzahs were torn away.

The picturesque former synagogue is an eighteenth-century masonry building with wooden-galleried front and steep sloping roof. It is in good condition—the Ark is intact—and is used as a weaving workshop.

The cemetery, high on a hill above town in the middle of cultivated fields, is fenced (watch out for nettles when you climb under) and much of it is well maintained, as pilgrims still come to pay respects at the ohel of the rebbe. There are about 100 mazzevahs, the oldest dating to the eighteenth century.

Checiny (Chęciny)

The impressive hilltop ruins of a large castle dominate this small town in central Poland just south of Kielce. Quaint little houses and shops cluster around the market square and the former synagogue, giving the authentic feel of an old shtetl. Some buildings still show places on the doorposts where mezuzahs were once affixed.

The stone synagogue, built in 1638, has a typical, two-tiered Polish mansard roof and retains other original architectural features. It has been converted into a cultural center including a cinema, reading room/library, and games hall. There is still a Hebrew inscription inside the Ping-Pong room, and the library retains the vaulted ceiling and massive door.

Above town there is an extremely overgrown but very picturesque hilltop cemetery, with about 200 carved gravestones. The oldest date from the early seventeenth century.

Chelm (Chełm)

In Jewish folklore, this town in southeastern Poland is famous as a town whose inhabitants are fools—or if not fools, then deceptively wise simpletons.

A Chelmite once went about on the outskirts of the town, searching for something on the ground.

"What are you looking for?" a passer-by asked him.

"I lost a ruble in the synagogue courtyard, so I'm hunting for it."

"You poor Chelmite," the stranger mocked him, "why are you hunting for it here when you lost it in the synagogue courtyard?"

"You're smart, you are!" the Chelmite retorted. "The synagogue courtyard is muddy, whereas here the ground is dry. Now where is it better to search?"

There was a wedding in Chelm. The guests noticed that the bride and groom were facing westward, though according to custom they should be facing eastward.

Checiny—The doorpost of this house in this former shtetl in central Poland clearly shows where the mezuzah once was placed.

So they began to turn the wedding canopy, but no matter how much they turned it, the bride and groom still faced westward instead of eastward.

"Imbeciles!" cried out a stranger. "Why do you turn the canopy? Turn the bride and groom."

And so they did, and saw that the stranger was right. And to this day they have never ceased to tell one another how much wisdom remains in the world.

In reality, the Jewish community in Chelm was one of the oldest in 'oland, dating back to the Middle Ages and possibly as far back as the welfth century.

One of its most famous personalities was the sixteenth-century mystic Elijah Ba'al Shem, about whom the same sort of legends concerning creation of the golem—an artificial man—grew up as were later told about his contemporary, Rabbi Loew in Prague. (See Prague.)

Much of the Jewish population was slaughtered during the Chmielnicki uprising in 1648. In the eighteenth century, Chelm became an important trading town, and from the early nineteenth century it became a Hasidic center.

Half of Chelm's prewar population of 31,000 was Jewish; few survived the Holocaust. The Nazis destroyed the centuries-old main synagogue and most other Jewish sites. Gravestones from the sixteenth century cemetery were torn up and used as paving blocks.

Today, one synagogue, built in the early twentieth century, still stands at the corner of ul. Kopernika and ul. Krzywa. It has been remodeled as offices. Much of the devastated cemetery has been made into a park, but a few dozen old gravestones remain.

Chmielnik

Before the war, Jews made up as much as seventy percent of the local population of this small, tree-shaded town in south-central Poland near Kielce.

The once splendid synagogue was originally built in the 1630s, then partially rebuilt in the eighteenth and again in the nineteenth centuries. The Nazis turned it into a warehouse, causing serious damage.

It is a massive stone building with barrel vaulting, in poor condition despite recent attempts at renovation that were halted due to lack of funds. Graffiti covers inside walls—and when I visited it in 1990, the word "Hitler" was scrawled on the exterior.

Stucco work dating from the eighteenth century remains on the ceiling, and there are still traces of polychrome decoration, including frescoes of primitive lions and neoclassical geometric forms, as well as fragments of zodiac signs that surrounded the now vanished Aron ha Kodesh.

There is an old Jewish cemetery in Chmielnik; it is abandoned.

Dabrowa Tarnowska (Dąbrowa Tarnowska)

In this small town in the rolling hills of southern Poland near Tarnow there is an unusual-looking synagogue dating from 1863 that has a striking multi-story arcaded facade between two towers. Inside the synagogue there are traces of various decorative elements, including fine, delicate polychrome frescoes of animals, plants, zodiac symbols, birds, texts, and curtains.

Across the street is a cemetery with a Holocaust memorial. It was here in June 1942, according to an eyewitness quoted by Martin Gilbert in his book *The Holocaust*, that the doomed local rabbi and a group of his followers went to their deaths in a remarkable display of bravery. Somehow they managed to bring a bottle of vodka with them when the Nazis herded them to the graveyard. In a gesture of both faith and defiance, they toasted each other with the traditional wish *l'chaim*—to life—then joined hands and began to dance. The Nazis shot them down as they were dancing.

*Dzialoszyce (Działoszyce)

This dusty village in south-central Poland between Cracow and Kielce was a center for the leather and fur trade, brickworks, and the clothing industry, and from the mid-eighteenth century the majority of its inhabitants were Jews.

The roofless wreck of the neoclassical synagogue, designed in 1845 by architect Felicjan Frankowski to replace an earlier wooden synagogue, is a particularly moving ruin, a stark monument to a vanished people dominating the village just off the main square. Only the outer walls remain, punctuated by tall, round-topped windows set amid sculpted outer ornamentation. Inside, a few patches of flaking blue paint are all that remain of decorated walls.

In 1939, 7,000 of the town's 10,000 inhabitants were Jewish. In 1941, 3,000 Jews from other localities in Poland were deported there. On September 2, 1942, the Nazis rounded up all the Jews in town. Amid horrific scenes described by the tiny handful of survivors, they slaughtered 2,000 of them and tossed them into mass graves near the Jewish cemetery outside town. The remaining 8,000 were deported to the death camp at Belzec.

On ul. Skalbmierska, at the site of the cemetery destroyed by the Nazis, there is today a monument to these victims, erected on September 1, 1989, the fiftieth anniversary of the outbreak of the war, by one of the handful of survivors.

Foreign visitors are rare in Dzialoszyce. Children are likely to cluster around, eager to know who you are and what you are doing. A group of children, rambunctious boys and giggling teenage girls, followed us into the synagogue, out to the cemetery monument, and back to the village square.

Dzialoszyce—Teenagers hang out by the video arcade and bumper cars in front of the ruin of the synagogue.

An old woman living across the square from the ruined synagogue spoke to us about the past. She recalled how she used to work for the local rabbi.

"I will never forget what he told me," she said. "He said that when the birds go away from here, the Jews will go away, too. One year there was a hard winter; there were no birds. And after that . . ."

Gora Kalwaria (Góra Kalwaria) (Yiddish: Ger)

Jews were allowed to settle in this small town twenty miles south of Warsaw in 1795, and in the nineteenth century, Gora Kalwaria became the seat of one of the most famous and powerful Hasidic dynasties in Poland, founded by the Tzaddik Isaac Meir Alter (1789–1866), who was a disciple of Menachem Mendel of Kock.

So renowned and revered was Rebbe Alter and his court that the town became known as *Nowy Jeruzalem*—New Jerusalem—and the *Ger dynasty* made Gora Kalwaria a focal point for the Hasidic community.

Isaac Meir Alter's grandson, Tzaddik Abraham Mordechai Alter (1866–1948), was a founder of the Agudas Israel party, which sought to defend Orthodox Jews from influences ranging from Reform Judaism to Zionism. He made his court a meeting place for Hasids and non-Hasidic Orthodox Jews to join forces for their common goal. He had a deep belief in the power of the press and was involved in the establishment of several Orthodox Jewish newspapers.

He appealed to old-fashioned values when writing to his followers for support for one of his papers, Dos Yidishe Vort, founded in 1916:

> Long have I wanted a newspaper true to the Jewish spirit, where free-thinking and indecency would have no place. How many of you have come to me weeping, seeing your sons and daughters turn from us and flee elsewhere because they read wicked books and newspapers which poison the body and soul? Now I appeal to you: Let this undertaking not appear trivial in your eyes, because with only a few pennies a day you can help this paper grow and benefit the community.

Rebbe Alter managed to flee to the Holy Land in 1939, and the dynastic seat carries on to this day from Jerusalem.

The brick Ger Synagogue is now used as a furniture warehouse. There is a ruined cemetery, with about fifty gravestones dating back to the nineteenth century, and also the former house of the tzaddik at ul. Pijarska 10.

Gorlice

Jews, many of them involved in the wine trade, settled in this pleasant town in southern Poland near Nowy Sacz in the nineteenth century—an era when the town was the center of a small petroleum industry. Some 4,500 to 5,000 Jews lived here before the war. None live here today.

The nineteenth-century former synagogue, now a bakery, is near the broad central square. None of its original decoration remains, but—a rarity in Poland—it bears a plaque commemorating the thousands of local Jews who were slaughtered by the Nazis.

The cemetery, a mile or so outside town on the road to Bobowa, has memorials to Holocaust victims as well as the ohel of a local Hasidic tzaddik (get the key from the farmer in the house next door). The cemetery is on two levels. Below, there is a pile of gravestones torn up and heaped together. The Nazis tore up many gravestones for use as paving material. There is also a Holocaust monument commemorating local Jews and Gypsies.

Beyond this, atop a steep hill, is the main cemetery, partially cleared of undergrowth. In the cleared part, one of the few Jewish survivors of the Holocaust years ago erected two monuments, reinterring, respectively, 90 and 160 victims of the mass slaughter into two grave areas covered with tombstones.

*Grybow (Grybów)

There is nothing really special about this pretty little town in southern Poland near Nowy Sacz, but there is something particularly moving about the abandoned state of its scallop-roofed nineteenth/twentieth-century synagogue, almost next door to the soaring red brick Catholic church, and the desolation of the small, overgrown cemetery, set high, high on a spectacularly beautiful hilltop amid waving wheat fields and rich pastures on a dirt road beyond the Catholic cemetery.

Jaroslaw (Jarosław)

Jaroslaw, a town of 30,000 or so on the San River in the southeast corner of Poland, looms large in Polish Jewish history. It was famous in the sixteenth/ seventeenth centuries for its big fairs, held three times a year, at which Jewish livestock traders and other merchants were major participants. Jews came from miles around, particularly at the Autumn Fair, to buy and sell.

So important were these gatherings that temporary synagogues were set up and the Council of the Four Lands—the Jewish governing body whose seat was in Lublin—held sessions there at fair time.

The first permanent synagogue was built in 1640. Today, an early nineteenth-century synagogue with characteristic four-pillar central bimah, still stands, now used as an art school, and there are several other former Jewish buildings.

There is also a small overgrown cemetery outside town near the hamlet of Pelkinie.

Jozefow Bilgorajski (Józefów Biłgorajski)

Jews settled in this town in southeast Poland near Zamosc after it was founded in 1725 as a private town owned by the Zamoyski family. Jozefow became a typical shtetl, where Jews lived in little wooden houses. By the end of the eighteenth century, Jews made up well over half the population, and by 1921 the village had 1,050 Jews out of a total population of 1,344—nearly eighty percent.

An important Hebrew publishing house was established here in the mid-nineteenth century, and in the latter part of the nineteenth century local Jews came under the strong influence of Hasidism.

The Nazis set up a ghetto here for local Jews and Jews from some other nearby villages: In 1942, about 2,000 Jews were shot dead outside town on Winiarczykowa Mountain. A memorial now marks the spot of the mass slaughter.

Today, a baroque-style, nineteenth-century synagogue remains. Used as a warehouse during the war, it fell into ruin afterward and now is being restored.

There is also a fascinating Jewish cemetery, whose oldest gravestones date from the 1760s. Some of the mazzevahs still bear traces of polychrome decoration.

*Karczew

In Isaac Bashevis Singer's novel *The Family Moskat*, the female protagonist, Hadassah, is killed by Nazi bombs in the first days of World War II and is buried in the Jewish cemetery of this small town on the Vistula River about fifteen miles southeast of Warsaw.

At that time, Karczew was known for its numerous little Jewish-run shops of all types. It was also in an area in which well-to-do Warsaw Jews kept summer houses.

Today, the cemetery at Karczew is an eerie, disconcerting wasteland—one of the most striking and moving of Poland's abandoned Jewish graveyards and a sight that is absolutely unforgettable.

Karczew—The moving cemetery near Warsaw where weathered gravestones are drifted over by the sand.

The cemetery is totally forsaken, the three dozen or so gravestones broken or eroded or tipped over and drifted over by pale river sand, which has sifted over the entire open expanse. The smooth surface of the sand is criss-crossed by the footprints of people and dogs; bones (animal? human?) litter the sand. A timeless hush hangs over the place, and even local noises—birdcalls, motors, children's voices—seem far, far away.

*Kazimierz Dolny (Yiddish: Kuzmir)

Picturesquely situated on the Vistula River between Radom and Lublin and dominated by the hilltop ruins of a sixteenth/seventeenth-century castle, Kazimierz Dolny is one of the loveliest towns in east-central Poland and has long been a favorite tourist spot and artists' retreat.

Jews settled here in the late fourteenth or early fifteenth century and by the sixteenth century were well established, with a synagogue and cemetery. One legend even has it that King Casimir the Great, who reigned in the fourteenth century and after whom the town was named, had a Jewish lover, Esterka, who lived here. Many resident Jews were merchants, using the river route of the Vistula to carry timber, grain, and other goods to the port of Gdansk.

By 1830, the town's 1,200 Jews made up nearly sixty percent of the population. During the nineteenth century, a Hasidic court was established.

Before World War II, some 3,000 Jews lived in Kazimierz, making up nearly two-thirds of the local population. Many Jewish (and non-Jewish) artists and writers, including Efraim Seidenbeutel, Menashe Seidenbeutel, and Natan Korzen, had summer homes in the town. Jewish names among graffiti scratched in prewar years by visitors to the ruined castle on a hill above town overlooking the river are a poignant reminder of the community.

The town is centered on a large, beautiful market square lined with centuries-old Renaissance buildings. The impressive former synagogue, dating to the second half of the eighteenth century, is just off this square. Devastated by the Nazis, it was rebuilt to its original outer appearance in the 1950s and turned into a cinema (soft porn was showing when I visited). A plaque commemorates its original function and memorializes the 3,000 or so local Jews murdered by the Nazis. (Jewish officials said the cinema was to be closed in 1994.)

The Goldsmith's Museum at ul. Senatorska 11 exhibits some Jewish silver ritual objects.

Both of Kazimierz Dolny's Jewish cemeteries—the old one dating to the sixteenth century and the new one established in 1851—were devastated by the Nazis, who used gravestones as paving material.

At the site of the New Cemetery, on ul. Czerniawy just outside town, stands one of the most original and moving monuments to Holocaust victims. Here, in the mid-1980s, hundreds of recovered gravestones and fragments found in the town and at the sites of the cemeteries were built into an immense mosaiclike wall, rising up on the hillside. The wall is split by a jagged vertical crack symbolizing the sudden extinction of the Jewish community.

Stepping through the crack behind the wall, you find yourself in a dense, peaceful forest, where the remnants of the New Cemetery stand isolated amid the trees that have grown up over the past half century.

The transition from sunlight to deep shadow makes you catch your breath—and is a very powerful evocation of the tragic past.

Kielce

This bustling, modern industrial city of 210,000 lies in central Poland, roughly halfway between Warsaw and Cracow. Jews were barred from settling here until the early nineteenth century; by 1939, there was a Jewish population of about 25,000.

Kielce is infamous as the site of the last pogrom in Poland, a massacre of forty-two Jews by a Polish mob on July 4, 1946. The bloody attack was sparked by rumors that Jews had kidnapped and murdered a Christian boy for ritual purposes. A monument in the town outside the house on ul. Planty 7-8, where the pogrom was centered, now commemorates the slaughter—which itself was a factor that spurred the mass emigration of thousands of Polish Jews who had survived the Holocaust.

A synagogue built between 1902 and 1904 still stands, but it has been totally rebuilt and is now used as the district archives. The cemetery has been under restoration and has a striking monument to Holocaust victims.

Kock

Somewhere in Central Europe, beyond the horizon, between Warsaw and Lublin, there was once upon a time a small village whose name made people dream and shiver: Kock.

The year is 1839.

It is winter. And snowing. Nestling close to one another, huts and cabins slowly vanish into the soundless night. The sky hangs low over deserted streets. The village is holding its breath; seen from the outside, it is a ghost village.

So Nobel Peace Prize–winner Elie Wiesel has described this remote little town, famous in Hasidic lore as having been the seat of the great nineteenth-century tzaddik, Menachem Mendel Morgenstern.

Jews settled in Kock from the early seventeenth century and by 1820 made up thirty percent of the population. On the eve of World War II, about fifty-five percent of the town's 4,500 inhabitants were Jewish.

After 1829, when Rebbe Menachem Mendel settled in the town, Kock became an important center of the Hasidic movement. The Morgenstern Hasidic dynasty lasted until 1939, when the then-reigning tzaddik was killed in an air raid.

Born in nearby Goraj in 1787 and trained as a pharmacist, Menachem Mendel drew around him a huge following of the faithful. A mysterious and still unexplained incident in 1839 prompted him to go into seclusion, spending the last twenty years of his life locked in his room, following prayer services through holes drilled in his door, and only rarely seeing outsiders. This bizarre behavior spawned numerous mystic tales and legends. Nothing was ever explained, however, and before his death Menachem Mendel ordered all his writings to be destroyed.

Yiddish writer Joseph Opatashu (1887–1954) wrote about mid-nineteenth-century Hasidic life in Kock in his historical novel *In Poilishe Velder* (*In Polish Woods*).

Today, a new monument replacing the former ohel of Menachem Mendel's tomb is at the center of the walled cemetery and draws pilgrims from all over the world. The other grave markers in the cemetery are unusual—irregular uncut stones with simple inscriptions rather than mazzevahs.

In the village itself, quaint wooden houses recall prewar times. One such house, with a small tower, was the dwelling of a twentieth-century tzaddik.

Outside town, on ul. Berek Joselewicz, there is a large, irregularly shaped inscribed stone on a mound marking the grave of Berek Joselewicz (1760–1809), a Jewish Polish army colonel and calvary chief who led the Jewish regiment that fought with Kosciuszko's forces against the Russian and Prussian armies in 1794 and who died near Kock in battle during the Napoleonic wars.

*Krynki

Thanks to its large Jewish population, Krynki was a thriving commercial and industrial town near the center of prewar Poland, but today, about thirty miles east of Bialystok, it is an isolated farming village only a mile or two from the Belarus border. Some of the thatched wooden farmsteads date back well over a century and are fine examples of Polish vernacular architecture.

Jews settled here in the seventeenth century. During the Polish partitions, Krynki belonged to Russia and was located in the Pale of Settlement. It grew to be a mainly Jewish town, the center of a thriving leather industry. A textile factory was opened in 1827, and around the turn of the century the town was a hotbed of Jewish political activity and the site of one of the first Jewish labor unions to be established in Russia.

Some 3,500 Jews lived in Krynki in 1939, the great majority of the local population.

Traces of three synagogues and the cemetery survive. One of the synagogues is now the town's cinema, the Krokus, a salmon pink building with low eaves and sloping roof. When I visited, a double feature was playing: *The Witches of Eastwick* and *Greystoke, the Legend of Tarzan*. On the wall next to the entrance someone had scrawled the English word "Slayer"—the name of a popular heavy metal rock group.

As we stood taking pictures, a villager, his face as brown and wrinkled as a walnut, came out of the rickety wooden house next door and beckoned to us. He held out a book. "Here," he said. "Take this. I don't understand anything about it." It was a Hebrew book, the Psalms, and bore the publication date 1845. Its leather binding was cracked and falling apart. The whole book was on the point of disintegration.

The old man came from the part of Poland that became Soviet territory after the war. He fled across the new border in 1948, settling as close as possible to where he had come from originally and taking over one of the houses left by Krynki's slaughtered Jews. He found the book of psalms stuffed into the attic.

Another synagogue today is a warehouse; the third, the former imposing Great Synagogue, built in 1754, is a huge pile of rubble in the center of town. Nothing is left of what was a striking neoclassical building but its foundations—you can still see the base of flat pilasters. The size of the ruins, however, indicates that it must have been the most imposing building in town.

The cemetery is spread out on a peaceful hilltop behind some beautiful thatched wooden farm buildings probably 200 years old. The hundreds of eroded gravestones are overgrown by vines and weeds. Intense pink wild roses bloom in the meadow amid the high grass. A horse grazes among the tombs; insects hum. Butterflies sparkle amid the wildflowers. Roosters crow in the distance.

Belying the peaceful scene, the foundations of a pigsty and a dairy the Nazis used beautifully inscribed gravestones to build still exist in a nearby potato field. "Look," said a local farmer. He pried away one of the weathered stones to reveal a once polished surface and Hebrew inscription.

A little later, in just about the only blatantly anti-Semitic episode I encountered while researching this book, we were hassled by five or six drunks propping up vodka bottles on the steps of the village's greasy-spoon restaurant. "Are these people Jews?" one of them said to the Polish man we were traveling with. "If they are Jews we are going to torch their car."

The car had Dutch license plates and a sticker reading "NL" for Netherlands. These men actually believed our friend when he pointed to the NL sticker and told them that the N meant that No, we were Not Jews, and that they should leave us alone.

*Lancut (Łańcut)

A pretty town of about 15,000 in southeastern Poland near Rzeszow, Lancut is mainly noted for its magnificent seventeenth-century palace, once owned by the Lubomirski and then the Potocki families. The palace, set in a lush park, is now a museum; it also has a hotel/restaurant in one wing. In the vestibule of the palace is a huge Hanukkah menorah, given by the Jewish community to the rulers.

Jews settled here in the sixteenth century and over the centuries made their living as merchants, shopkeepers, and innkeepers. In 1939, there were more than 2,700 Jews, perhaps fifty percent of the local population.

Just outside the palace gates is the outwardly simple, cream-colored former synagogue, built in 1761, that has been beautifully restored as a Jewish museum. Take note of how it appears and remember it when you view the ruins of other synagogues. It has numerous brilliant polychrome decorations, including wall prayers, stucco bas-reliefs, frescoes, and even false marble. The motifs include lions, unicorns, monkeys, grapes, birds, deer, and flowers in rich greens, blues, oranges, and yellows.

Particularly striking is the fresco of the leviathan devouring its tail, curled around the inner cupola of the central bimah—a motif symbolizing the time of the Messiah. On the outside of the bimah's cupola are frescoes depicting biblical tales—the sacrifice of Isaac, Adam and Eve, the Flood, a menorah. The figures, however, are shown only by their hands and feet, in accordance with the stricture against human imagery.

Hasidic influence became strong in Lancut in the nineteenth century; the old Jewish cemetery is a pilgrimage place to the tomb of a famous Hasidic tzaddik, Reb Hurwitz.

*Lesko (Yiddish: Lisk)

Jews settled in this small town in the southeastern corner of Poland in the sixteenth century and eventually made up the great majority of the local population. Local Jews developed a "wise fool" reputation similar to that of the Jews of Chelm.

The striking synagogue on ul. Moniuszki, dating probably to the seventeenth century, has been restored for use as the local museum. The impressive exterior includes a curving gable, bas-relief Hebrew inscriptions, the tablets of Moses, and a round tower that was added during restoration.

Nearby is the old cemetery with perhaps 2,000 richly carved, well-preserved tombstones dating back three centuries crowded together amid underbrush and saplings. Situated on a slope near a forest, it is one of the most picturesque Jewish cemeteries in Poland, with massive stones containing some elaborate carvings heavily influenced by folk motifs as well as Jewish symbolism.

Lezajsk (Leżajsk) (Yiddish: Lizhensk)

In the late eighteenth century, this small town in the far southeast corner of Poland became one of the most important centers of Hasidism, thanks to the fact that one of the greatest of the early Hasidic sages, Elimelekh, lived here from 1777 until his death eleven years later.

Elimelekh, born in 1717, was a mystic who became one of the chief developers of the concept of the Hasidic tzaddik as a peerless holy man and revered leader of his community whose followers believed he could work miracles and serve as a mediator between them and God. Elimelekh's ohel, a place of pilgrimage, is in the Jewish cemetery.

*Lodz (Łódź)

Jewish Community: ul. Zachodnia 78, Tel. (42) 335156

Today a recession-hit industrial city of more than 850,000 people, Lodz was home to Poland's second largest Jewish community before the war, a dynamic mix of wealthy capitalists, a comfortable middle class, and a proletariat underclass that often lived in squalor. More Jews lived in prewar Lodz than in all of Yugoslavia and Bulgaria put together.

Lodz was a small, insignificant town until the mid-nineteenth century, when, largely thanks to Jewish (and German) input, it began to develop into a major industrial center specializing particularly in textiles and clothing. In the late 1930s, more than seventy percent of all Polish textile workers were employed in the Lodz mills.

Today, Lodz is still a major center of light industry and textiles, but it is poor and run-down. Some of the factories still in use were built by Jewish industrialists in the nineteenth century. The city's former grandeur can still be glimpsed, however, in the elaborately decorated buildings along ul. Piotrkowska, the main thoroughfare, as well as in the Jewish cemetery.

Jews, who began settling here in the late eighteenth century, played a particularly important role in the city's development—as factory owners, bankers, merchants, and wealthy industrialists, as well as members of the proletariat.

By the twentieth century, there was an enormous gap between the elite Jewish upper class of wealthy capitalists and white-collar professionals, who lived in luxury and practiced Reform Judaism, and the poorer working class and artisan class in the Jewish quarter, who maintained traditional Orthodox and often Hasidic lifestyles—or else were secular socialists. Israel Joshua Singer wrote about this in his book *The Brothers Ashkenazi.*

Before World War II, there were more than 200,000 Jews in Lodz—over one-third of the city's total population. Pianist Artur Rubinstein was born here, as was famed poet Julian Tuwim, a Jew who wrote in Polish, not Yiddish or Hebrew as did most Jewish writers.

In the spring of 1940, the Nazis instituted one of the most notorious Jewish ghettos; fewer than 900 Lodz Jews remained in the Lodz Ghetto after the war. A few hundred Jews live in the city today.

Lodz's splendid main synagogues were all destroyed. A late nineteenth-century synagogue, at ul. Rewolucji 1905 28, is in use for services now.

The most fascinating site of Jewish interest in Lodz is the New Cemetery, founded in 1892 to replace an earlier cemetery, which no longer exists. It is one of the most important Jewish monuments in Poland.

Between its founding and the outbreak of the war, some 180,000 grave monuments—including traditional style mazzevahs, sarcophagi, and elaborate mausolea—were erected. Styles include inscriptions and carvings based on Judaic symbols and folk art, as well as examples of mainstream nineteenth- and twentieth-century tomb sculpture—much of it very elaborate and incorporating styles such as art nouveau and neoclassicism.

The most impressive mausoleum is that of the family of textile magnate I. K. Poznanski: a huge domed edifice as big as a house.

Poznanski was one of Lodz's leading citizens, sort of a Jewish Great Gatsby. He built a stupendous domed mansion at ul. Ogrodowa 15 (now the city's Historical Museum) right next door to his sprawling red brick textile factory, once one of the biggest in Europe and still in use, in the middle of town. A museum dedicated to pianist Artur Rubinstein was opened in a wing of the mansion in 1990.

Two other mansions owned by the Poznanski family also still stand. One, at ul. Gdanska 32, is the Musical Academy; one, at ul. Wieckowskiego 36, houses the Museum of Art, which has an acclaimed collection of modern art. Other turn-of-the-century buildings with Jewish heritage include another nineteenth-century textile factory, built by Jewish industrialist Markus Silberstein at ul. Piotrkowska 242/248; the former mansion and bank of Maksymilian Goldfeder at ul. Piotrkowska 77; the beautifully ornamented former bank of Wilhelm Landau at ul. Piotrkowska 29; and the former Jewish hospital at ul. Senatorska 13.

*Lublin

Jewish Community: ul. Lubartowska 10

This shabby but beautiful city of 340,000 in eastern Poland was one of the most important historical centers of Jewish life, commerce, culture, and scholarship in Europe.

Jews may have settled here as early as the fourteenth century. They lived in a district near the castle that by the mid-sixteenth century was virtually an independent Jewish city existing side by side with the Christian main town. In 1568, the Jewish town was granted the privilege of barring Christians from living there. The privilege—*de non tolerandis christianis*—

was similar to the legislation many Christian towns had preventing Jews from living there.

Lublin's famous yeshiva was established in 1515, and a Hebrew printing house was established in 1547. Great scholars, both in Talmudic teaching and cabalistic mysticism, earned the city the reputation of being the "Jewish Oxford." Among them were Moses Isserles Remuh (1520–1572), who studied at the yeshiva and eventually gained fame in Cracow, and Jakov ben Itzhak, who published a Yiddish treatise on the Bible aimed at Jewish women in 1662.

For about two centuries in the late Renaissance and afterward, the city was the site of the Council of Four Lands, the ruling political body of Jews in Poland and Lithuania, which was established around 1580 and joined together rabbis and laymen representing the regions of Great Poland, Little Poland, Volhynia, and Red Russia (made up of East Galicia and Podolia). The Council, which lasted until 1764, had control over the whole range of Jewish secular and spiritual life. Among its duties were to collect taxes, regulate religious observances, sit as a court, and represent Polish Jewry to Polish officials. Typical laws it promulgated dealt with punishment of Jewish tradesmen who violated the Sabbath, the regulation of whether non-Jewish employees of Jews had to observe the Jewish Sabbath, how bankruptcy procedures should be carried out, and how charity should be extended to the needy.

An interesting view of Jews in Lublin dating from this period can be seen in a large painting just inside the entrance of the Dominican Church in the Old Town that shows the Jewish town in flames during the Great Fire of Lublin in the seventeenth century.

The city became one of Poland's most influential Hasidic centers in the late eighteenth century with the arrival of Tzaddik Jacob Isaac ha Hozeh (1745–1815), a charismatic figure known as the Seer of Lublin, whose practically blind eyes were said to be able to see into men's souls. He and two fellow tzaddikim, Menachem Mendel of Rymanow and the Maggid of Kozienice, became convinced that the wars raging in the early nineteenth century between the forces of Napoleon and those of the Russian czar heralded the end of the world. The Messiah would come and redeem the Jews, they believed, if Napoleon conquered the world and turned it over to the Redeemer. All three prayed fervently for such a victory; all three died in 1815, the year of Napoleon's final defeat at Waterloo. The Seer of Lublin's death followed a mysterious fall from his window.

By the mid-nineteenth century, Lublin's more than 8,700 Jews made up over half the local population. Before World War II, the Jewish community had grown to 40,000, or nearly forty percent of the local population. The Jewish quarter was a bustling labyrinth of streets, squares, and alleys with numerous synagogues and study houses, and four Jewish cemeteries.

Few traces, however, of this rich Jewish past remain. Only a handful of elderly Jews still live in the city. Only plaques and monuments help recall what was destroyed.

The Nazis razed most of the Jewish quarter as well as both great synagogues near the castle. They established two ghettos and either deported the Jewish population to death camps at Majdanek and Belzec or shot them in nearby forests. A monument to Holocaust victims stands in the square between ul. Rady Delegatow and ul. Hanki Sawickiej. The only remaining synagogue is a shabby prayer room situated on an upper floor at ul. Lubartowska 8/10. There is a small commemorative display here of ritual and historical materials relating to the Lublin Jewish community.

A plaque below the castle commemorates the magnificent MaHaR-SHal Synagogue, originally built in the sixteenth century and believed to have been the first synagogue to use the typical Polish central bimah plan.

A plaque at the base of the castle steps commemorates the old Jewish town that once spread out around this spot, and another plaque inside the city walls at ul. Grodzka 11 marks the former Jewish orphanage and memorializes Jewish children murdered here by the Nazis on March 24, 1942. The current Medical Academy building, at ul. Lubartowska 85, was the former Yeshiva.

The Old Cemetery, with entrances on ul. Kalinowszczyzna and ul. Sienna, is the most important Jewish relic left in Lublin. Founded in the first half of the sixteenth century, it is the oldest Jewish cemetery still existing in Poland. On a hill enclosed by a wall, it was ravaged time and again during centuries of war and violence. The Nazis tore it up and used its stones for paving. Still, some gravestones remain.

The oldest tomb—the oldest Polish gravestone in situ—is that of scholar Jakob Kopelman ha Levi, who died in 1541. The austere tomb of Talmudic scholar Shalom Shachna, who died in 1558, is impressive in its simplicity: a rectangular slab whose face is totally covered by Hebrew inscription. Another historically important tomb is that of the Tzaddik Jacob Isaac ha Hozeh (1745–1815), the Seer of Lublin. It is a place of pilgrimage for his followers even today.

The New Cemetery, on ul. Walecznych, was seriously ravaged during the war, but it is still used by the tiny Jewish community and there are Holocaust memorials. Restoration work has recently taken place; the cemetery has been enclosed by a fence made of symbolic mazzevahs, and a modern little synagogue has been erected here.

On the outskirts of Lublin is **Majdanek**, site of the Nazi death camp where over 350,000 people, including 100,000 Jews, were murdered. A monument incorporating a huge mound of human ashes commemorates the victims, and there is also a museum.

Mszczonow (Mszczonów)

This village is about thirty miles south of Warsaw on the main Warsaw-Katowice highway and has an easily visited and quite interesting Jewish cemetery dating back to the eighteenth century that is situated right on the edge of the road. Most of the cemetery is overgrown, but there are several mazzevahs with exceptionally vigorous and detailed carving, as well as the ohel of a local Hasidic rebbe.

The keys are kept by an elderly woman in an adjacent farmhouse. Before the war, she worked for the Jewish community, cleaning the synagogue and caring for the rabbi's house, and she has vivid recollections of life in what was a lively town before the Holocaust.

"Dear lady," she says, "I liked them, they were good people. When I was sick, they took good care of me, they gave me everything. In those days, dear lady, the shops were filled. What did the Jews do? Business! Trade! There was everything. It was better than it is today. But it was a long time ago. It was before the war!"

A sad look crosses her face as she mentions the names of Jews who lived in the town, as she conjures up the past world of bustling streets, busy shops, crowded synagogues, and study houses that gleamed on Shabbat. The memories show in her eyes as she talks.

She is alone. Her husband and son are dead—before her son died, he used to keep the grass cut in the cemetery. Today, she receives a little money from foreign Jews to keep the keys and try to clear the area around the ohel.

Inside the ohel, a hand-lettered paper sign in Hebrew and English asks visitors to give a tip to the caretaker.

Olesnica (Oleśnica)

The first sizable Jewish settlements in Poland were established in the early Middle Ages in Silesia, in the southwest, and synagogue buildings remain in two small Silesian towns, Olesnica and Strzegom.

The red brick building on ul. Luzycka near Olesnica's shabby market square has a steep peaked roof over the sanctuary, one squat tower topped by a pagodalike roof, and traces of tall Gothic windows. It was built in the fifteenth century, but already in the sixteenth century it was transformed into a church. Today it is an Evangelical church, set in a small plot of land surrounded on all sides by modern housing blocks.

Orla

Before World War II, Jews made up seventy-seven percent of the population of this village in northeast Poland near Bialystok—more than 1,160

Jews out of a little over 1,500 people in all. Today, there are no Jews. The local population is mainly comprised of Byelorussians, who practice the Russian Orthodox faith.

Nonetheless, despite funding problems, the town is restoring the old synagogue. The building was devastated during the war, when the Nazis used it as a field hospital and later turned it into a warehouse for chemical fertilizer. In 1990, the entire facade was covered by rickety scaffolding and more scaffolding filled the sanctuary inside. The mayor and other town officials seemed almost obsessed by the project, eagerly showing visitors around the building. They hope to make it a town cultural center, preserving the sanctuary in its original synagogue form.

The synagogue probably dates back originally to the first half of the seventeenth century, but it was rebuilt in the second half of the eighteenth century and again in the nineteenth century. The sanctuary has a vaulted ceiling and central four-pillar bimah. Traces of polychrome decoration, including floral wall motifs, remain. Old photographs show that the building once had marvelous frescoed lions above the outer entrance.

Remnants of the devastated nineteenth-century cemetery still stand: a score or so of lonely, very weathered gravestones in a field at the edge of town. The shape of many of the stones can no longer be distinguished, although it is still possible to make out some of the carving.

*Pinczow (Pińczów)

This charming little historic town in southern Poland between Kielce and Cracow was founded in the fifteenth century and became an important stoneworking and market center. Jews lived here as early as the sixteenth century—in 1673 some 496 of the town's 1,273 people were Jews. Before the war, about 3,500 Jews lived here.

The massive, cube-shaped synagogue, empty and damaged when the Nazis used it as a warehouse during the war but structurally unaltered, dates back to the late seventeenth century.

Restoration is under way (slowly, due to lack of funds) to convert the synagogue into a museum. Inside, there are traces of precious polychrome decoration, including wall texts, brilliant blue ceiling paintings, and some badly damaged floral and vegetal motifs dating from the eighteenth century and attributed to the Jewish painter Jehuda Leib. The elaborate bimah—known from photographs—has been destroyed, but the Renaissance carved stone Aron ha Kodesh has been preserved almost intact and is being restored.

A plaque outside the synagogue commemorates the local Jewish community. A mosaic wall nearby has been built from broken fragments of Jewish gravestones.

A corner of the local Town Museum is devoted to an excellent little exhibit on local Jewish history and culture.

Piotrkow Trybunalski (Piotrków Trybunalski)

This run-down county seat of over 60,000 in central Poland is on the main Warsaw-Katowice highway and easily visited.

Before the partitions of Poland in the late eighteenth century, the town was an important administrative center. Jews settled here in the sixteenth century. Some 15,000 Jews lived in Piotrkow before World War II, and the town, occupied by the Germans four days after they invaded Poland in September 1939, was one of the first in Poland to suffer from the Nazis' "Blitzpogrom" of death, destruction, and humiliation. Jewish homes and stores were ravaged; synagogues, homes, and shops were put to the torch; people were herded into forced labor and concentration camps or shot dead in the streets. By October, the Nazis had set up one of their first ghettos.

Today, the 1,000 or so fine tombstones in the large cemetery on ul. Spacerowa, near the Catholic cemetery, recall the richness of Jewish life in a town where there are no more Jews. The oldest tombstones date from the late eighteenth century and contain some extraordinary detailed carvings incorporating ritual symbolism and imaginary beasts.

A woman who lives alone at the edge of the grounds cares for the cemetery and is very helpful to visitors, offering to help find particular graves of particular families. She attempts to maintain the cemetery—trees are being cut down, brush is being cut—but it is a vast area, and saplings, brush, and tall grass encroach everywhere. At one point, I was startled by a pheasant breaking cover a few yards away.

Much of the area is empty where gravestones were torn up, and one part of the newer section is now dedicated to the mass graves of Holocaust victims and memorials to those killed during the war.

The nineteenth-century Great Synagogue on ul. Wojska Polskiego has been turned into the town library—the outer shell remains in good condition, but the only exterior indication of the building's former function are ironwork Stars of David incorporated into lamp holders. The small synagogue, from 1781, is a children's library.

*Przysucha (Yiddish: Pshiskhe)

A sleepy little town in central Poland, about twenty-five miles west of Radom, Przysucha was a famous Hasidic center, and the former synagogue, today empty, is one of the largest of Poland's remaining synagogue buildings. Local authorities have been trying for years to effect repairs but have been prevented by lack of funds.

The village was founded in 1710 as a settlement of German ironworkers. Jews were here from the beginning, and the synagogue was built in 1750. By 1921, the town was a typical shtetl, and two-thirds of the local population of 3,200 was Jewish.

Though heavily damaged during the war, when the Germans used it as a warehouse, traces of considerable structural and decorative detail remain inside the barnlike stone building, including the central bimah, the women's gallery, a few faded prayer frescoes on the wall, and much of the Aron ha Kodesh, with stucco work above it.

Also still existing is a rare example of a pillory, or *kune*, attached to the outer wall. Here Jews sentenced for various offenses by the Jewish community court would be locked in punishment.

Przysucha is one of the few former synagogues or cemeteries where I encountered another visitor. A Polish woman from Warsaw had brought some of her friends there to show them the tragedy of the abandoned building.

"Just look what they have done!" she said angrily. "Look what these communists allowed to happen!"

Jewish philosopher Martin Buber, who wrote extensively about the Hasidim and collected Hasidic stories, mentioned seven tzaddiks from Przysucha. The Hasidic dynasty founded by Jacob Isaac ben Asher Przysucha (1766–1814), known simply as "The Jew," became influential all over Poland. The Jew had been the favorite disciple of the influential Hasidic master, the Seer of Lublin.

Nearby the synagogue is the fairly well-maintained, fenced-in Jewish cemetery, which is still a center of Hasidic pilgrimages to the tombs of The Jew and other famous sages.

*Radomsko

In this nondescript industrial town of more than 30,000 in central Poland just off the main Warsaw-Katowice highway is a very fine, large Jewish cemetery behind a tall red brick wall, prominently marked outside as a war memorial site.

I pushed open the green metal door and really found myself in a different world.

Dogs from a farmhouse where the caretaker lives at the edge of the cemetery started barking furiously; chickens scattered among the gravestones straggling up the hill. A startled jackrabbit took off through the long grass up a slope and into the distance.

All around me were 1,000 or so tombstones carved with fantastic renditions of lions, deer, birds, and mythical beasts, like winged griffins and the leviathan. Some of the grave markers were made of iron, not stone.

In the center, standing alone, was a monument to the 8,000 Jews from Radomsko deported to their deaths during the war.

*Rymanow (Rymanów)

If one ruined synagogue could stand as a memorial to the barbarity of the Holocaust, it could be the tragic ruin in this nondescript village in the southeast corner of Poland where Jews settled in the fifteenth century.

Perched on a low hilltop at the edge of town, the synagogue, probably dating back to the eighteenth century, is a hulking and highly evocative mass of brick and stone that looks as if it fought hard against its destruction—and lost. Fragments of beautiful frescoes—including a lion, a tiger, and a scene of the Wailing Wall in Jerusalem—remain on its inner walls despite exposure to the elements through shattered windows and a nearly collapsed roof.

Rymanow was once a bustling commercial town whose Jewish population at one time specialized in the import of Hungarian wine into Poland. It was also one of the most influential Hasidic centers in Poland, seat of the court of the Tzaddik Menachem Mendel (1745–1815), a Talmudic scholar and disciple of Elimelekh of Lizhensk (see Lezajsk). Like his friends, the Seer of Lublin (see Lublin) and the Maggid of Kozhenits (Kozienice), Menachem Mendel believed that the Napoleonic wars foretold the coming of the Messiah, and, together with the other two tzaddikim, he prayed for a Napoleonic victory to ensure the coming of the Redeemer. One story told that during battles in which he was victorious, Napoleon always saw the vision of a red-haired Jew praying for him. As he went into his last great battle at Waterloo, he no longer saw the vision of the red-haired Jew. Waterloo, in 1815, spelled the crushing defeat of Napoleon. The red-headed Menachem Mendel and his two friends all died that year.

Pilgrims still come to pray at his tomb and the tombs of other tzaddikim in the ruined Jewish cemetery, which spreads out on a low hilltop amid lushly cultivated fields outside town.

Rzeszow (Rzeszów)

This historic county seat of 150,000 in the southeast corner of Poland at the foot of the Carpathian Mountains has a long Jewish history. Rzeszow was a privately owned town, and Jews settled here in the sixteenth century under the authorization of King Stefan Batory. The Jewish population grew large and prosperous. In the eighteenth century, local Jewish tailors and goldsmiths were particularly famous.

On the eve of World War II, some 14,000 Jews lived here, and the Nazis established a ghetto. At one point during the war, over 1,000 Jews were taken to the cemetery and shot; a monument stands on the spot today.

Two austere, heavy-walled synagogues with central four-pillared bimahs dating to the seventeenth century remain in the center of the town off Plac Zwyciestwa. Both have been well restored for cultural use and are marked with memorial plaques commemorating the vanished Jewish community.

One, the so-called New Town Synagogue built after 1686, is an art and culture center. The other, the Old Town, or Small, Synagogue built after 1617, is around the corner on ul. Boznicza (Synagogue Street) and is part of the local Archives. Today, it houses a Jewish Research Center, founded in 1989 to study, collect, and publish materials on the history of Jews in southeast Poland. In it is a small exhibit of local Judaica, including documents, books, photographs, drawings, maps, and diagrams.

Rzeszow's Jewish cemetery, on ul. Rejtana, dates to the nineteenth century and has about fifty gravestones.

Strzegom

This small town in southwest Poland near Wroclaw has one of the two medieval synagogues remaining in Silesia. Like the other one, in Olesnica, the medieval synagogue in Strzegom was already converted for use as a church in the Middle Ages.

The tiny, red brick building on ul. Dabrowskiego has slit windows and two squat towers with pointed steeples. It was built in the fourteenth century but was transformed into a church in the fifteenth century.

Szczebrzeszyn

Jews settled in this town in southeast Poland near Zamosc in the early sixteenth century. By the latter part of the sixteenth century, the Jewish population numbered about 100: They were merchants, trading up and down the country; some of them were involved in the trading of exotic spices.

Like most Jewish towns in the southeast, the local community suffered heavily during the Cossack uprising led by Bogdan Chmielnicki in 1648. A survivor from the town, Meir ben Shmuel, published an eyewitness account of the horrifying massacres in 1650. In the nineteenth century, the community became strongly influenced by Hasidism and seat of the Tzaddik Elimelekh Hurvic.

In 1939, there were about 3,200 Jews, about half the local population. They were deported to the Belzec death camp in October 1942.

The early seventeenth-century synagogue on ul. Sadowa was devastated by the Nazis but was well restored and is now used as a local cultural center. Much of the external and interior decoration has been maintained, including the vaulted ceiling, stuccos, Hebrew inscriptions, and the late Renaissance Aron ha Kodesh. The roof, with the double mansard characteristic of many Polish synagogues, preserves the original form.

Strzegom—This tiny red brick building in this Silesian town was erected in the fourteenth century as a synagogue but was transformed into a church in the fifteenth century. It and a similar medieval synagogue in nearby Olesnica are the oldest remaining former synagogue buildings in Poland and bear witness to the early medieval Jewish settlement of Silesia.

The Jewish cemetery was founded in the late sixteenth century, but its earliest gravestones date from the early eighteenth century. The graveyard, which was destroyed by the Nazis, is still in overgrown, ruinous condition but contains numerous richly carved mazzevahs incorporating Jewish ritual symbolism. A few have lingering traces of polychrome decoration.

*Szydlow (Szydłow)

Szydlow is a tiny but exceptionally interesting walled village in south-central Poland between Kielce and Tarnow. Set amid beautiful rolling farmland, it is considered the best example of a Gothic urban architectural complex in central Poland.

Its three main buildings are the castle, the synagogue, and a Gothic church: all massive masonry structures that would have anchored the defenses of the town, most of whose other buildings would have been of wood. There is also the massive Cracow Gate in the ancient walls of the town.

The synagogue—dating back to the sixteenth century and one of the oldest synagogue buildings in Poland—is a large, blocklike structure with heavy buttresses on all sides and a crenelated roof. (Legend has it that it was founded by King Casimir the Great's Jewish lover, Esterka.) It was converted into a library and culture center in the 1960s; the arched and vaulted sanctuary was painted stark white and used as a games room and exhibit hall, though the Aron ha Kodesh was left intact. When I first visited, the only furniture was a Ping-Pong table and scattered chairs. The culture center was moved out after 1990 because of a lack of funds, and the building was left empty and abandoned.

*Szydlowiec (Szydłowiec)

Jews settled in this town in central Poland between Radom and Kielce in the late fifteenth century, and by the end of the eighteenth century, they made up ninety percent of the local population. Before the war, the 7,200 Jews in Szydlowiec still made up about eighty percent or so of the local inhabitants. They were active in the town's big leather and shoemaking industry as well as in quarrying the huge local sandstone deposits.

Today, Szydlowiec is a nondescript, rather anonymous town—except for what is one of the largest and most impressive remaining Jewish cemeteries in Poland. Easily visited, it is sited just off the main road from Radom on the way into town and has about 3,000 mazzevahs dating back to the late eighteenth century.

Tombstones with very elaborate carving crowd up against the main fence and locked main gate along the road, like people pressing their faces to a window; it is an impressive sight.

Szydlowiec—Gravestones in the large Jewish cemetery show vivid carvings of the Levite pitcher, a bookcase (denoting the deceased was learned), lions, and the Cohen's priestly hands.

The wall of the cemetery runs along the edge of a modern apartment building complex, and entry is from a smaller gate here, which seems to be kept open. Children run in and out, using the cemetery as a playground.

Many of the tombstones are very beautiful, and some still bear traces of polychrome decoration. There is a Holocaust memorial, and many of the stones are numbered, indicating conservation work.

*Tarnow (Tarnów) (Yiddish: Torne or Tarne)

This charming old town of 120,000 in southern Poland, about forty miles east of Cracow, has a large market square (Rynek) surrounded by highly decorative, pastel-colored buildings, a towered Renaissance town hall dating to the fifteenth/sixteenth centuries, and a late Gothic cathedral with magnificent tombs of the local Tarnowski family inside. There are ruins of a castle and several other striking churches, including one built of wood.

Jews settled here in the fifteenth/sixteenth centuries. Tarnow was a big Hasidic center, and the old Jewish section is right off the market square along winding ul. Zydowska—Jewish Street—lined with sixteenth- and seventeenth-century stone houses. This old section retains the antique medieval character of narrow streets and squares.

About 25,000 Jews lived in Tarnow in 1939, over forty percent of the town's population. The Nazis made it a ghetto, and by 1942 some 40,000 Jews were crowded there. Thousands more were herded into the ghetto later. Tarnow had been famous for its clothing industry and its tailors; the Nazis forced at least 3,000 Jews to sew clothing for the German army. All but a few hundred Jews from Tarnow's ghetto—including some people hidden by non-Jews—were deported to Auschwitz and Belzec.

On June 13, 1940, more than 700 Tarnow men, including some Jews, were dragged from prison to the Moorish-style mikvah (which still stands). The next morning, they were taken to the train station and deported to Auschwitz. This was the first transport of prisoners to Auschwitz, at that time a concentration camp for political prisoners and others. There is a monument across from the mikvah, on Plac Wiezniow Oswiecimia (Auschwitz Prisoners Square) commemorating them.

The haunting remains of the former Old Synagogue can be seen in a park on ul. Zydowska. All that's left are the four pillars of the central bimah, now covered by a recently erected protective roof and marked with a memorial plaque. Much of the present park was once taken up by the synagogue.

Nearby ul. Wckslarska, or Money-Changers Street, still bears a name harking back to the time it was the center for moneylenders and other Jewish-run financial activities. It's a broad, straight street built in the sixteenth century after a fire had destroyed earlier wooden buildings.

The Jewish cemetery on ul. Nowodabrowska, outside the town center, has thousands of distinctively carved stones dating back to the seventeenth century whose animal and plant motifs as well as Hebrew lettering have close links to native folk-art traditions. There is a monument to the Jews killed in the Holocaust. The cemetery is listed as a historic monument, and there have been recent efforts to tend and restore it.

Tomaszow Mazowiecki (Tomaszów Mazowiecki)

This drab industrial town of more than 60,000 is on the main Warsaw-Katowice highway southwest of Warsaw and has a very large, walled Jewish cemetery that has many finely carved tombstones, most of them from the nineteenth century.

Tomaszow Mazowiecki—A pile of broken gravestones is heaped up just inside the gate of the Jewish cemetery.

The big front gates were propped open by a rock when I visited on a chilly late-winter day. The first impression was that of devastation: Right inside the gate is a huge pile of uprooted tombstones and fragments of tombstones, all heaped up into a towering jumbled mass. One stone, I noticed, was Christian.

Beyond, a broad space was dedicated to mass graves of Holocaust victims as well as monuments to partisan and resistance fighters. I could see that flower beds were laid out, but in early March, everything was grim and gray—and some of the memorials had been vandalized.

Further back, row after row of towering tombstones, most with vigorous carved inscriptions, stretched into the distance, a thick forest of rock. Young saplings grew up among them; there were weeds, broken or toppled stones, and other evidence of vandalism.

*Treblinka

This village on the Bug River about fifty miles northeast of Warsaw was near the site of one of the Nazis' most infamous death camps. Between 1942 and 1943 as many as 800,000 Jews from all over Poland and other countries died here in thirteen gas chambers secluded in a forest near a railway station. Their ashes were scattered on surrounding fields.

Several hundred prisoners staged an abortive uprising in August 1943. One month later, the Nazis began to demolish the camp and eventually destroyed almost all traces of it, going so far as even to plow under the earth.

Today, the camp has been turned into a large monument in the form of a symbolic graveyard. Some 17,000 jagged, symbolic tombstones are ranged round a massive central pillar: Each stone represents a town whose Jews were killed in the camp.

One stone only commemorates a single person: Janusz Korczak (Dr. Henryk Goldszmit), the Warsaw teacher, writer, doctor, and social worker who ran a Jewish orphanage in Warsaw and voluntarily stayed in the wartime Warsaw Ghetto to care for the children. In July 1942, he was shipped to Treblinka with his orphan charges and was murdered along with them.

*Tykocin (Yiddish: Tiktin)

In 1522, ten Jewish families were invited to settle in this little village in northeast Poland near Bialystok by the noble family who owned the town. By the nineteenth century, there was a Jewish majority in the village, and on the eve of World War II about half the local inhabitants were Jewish.

The massive early baroque synagogue, built in 1642, has been beautifully restored inside and out and is used as a Jewish museum and local town museum. Cantorial music plays from tapes, and the brilliantly colored restored frescoes, including wall-sized texts of Hebrew prayers, are impressive.

The museum attached to the synagogue itself contains little on the Jewish history of the town, but there is a fascinating model of how the village once looked, with the settlement grouped around two poles: the synagogue and Jewish marketplace at one end and the Catholic church and Christian marketplace at the other. Most of the little wooden Jewish houses have disappeared, but otherwise the layout of the village is much the same as it was in past centuries.

In the tower of the synagogue are some Jewish exhibits, including a table laid as if for a seder, and in the wooden window frames of a house nearby you can still see a decorative Star of David. Next door, an art gallery is housed in the old Jewish study house.

Tykocin has an evocative Jewish cemetery: Most of the eroded gravestones are mere stumps, pushing up through a meadow where sheep often graze. Some still, however, preserve very fine carved decoration.

*Wlodawa (Włodawa) (Yiddish: Vlodavi)

Jews settled in this little town in eastern Poland near Lublin—today hard by the border with Belarus and Ukraine—in the latter part of the sixteenth century. The community was virtually wiped out during the Chmielnicki uprising massacres in 1648, but it quickly recovered. By the mid-nineteenth century, Wlodowa's 4,300 Jews made up more than seventy percent of the local population.

On the eve of World War II, the town's 5,600 Jews made up more than sixty percent of the local population. All of them, plus about 2,000 Jews brought here by the Nazis from elsewhere, were deported to Sobibor death camp, where all but a few perished.

Many former Jewish homes and other buildings still stand. Foremost among them is the main synagogue, built in 1764. Severely damaged by the Nazis and for decades used as a warehouse, it was beautifully restored in the 1980s and today houses the Museum of the Leczynsko-Wlodawski Lake District.

The building has a large central section with big arched windows and is covered by a typical high-peaked, multisloped Polish mansard roof. This is flanked by two smaller side elements with ground-floor arcades.

Inside the sanctuary, four columns supporting the ceiling vaulting mark where the central bimah was sited. There is a gorgeous, extremely elaborate Aron ha Kodesh in painted stucco work in neo-Gothic style that was constructed in the 1930s to replace the original wooden Ark destroyed by an earlier fire. Elements include winged lions, a menorah, twisted columns, and other symbolic imagery as well as inscriptions. Walls and ceiling vaults contain other frescoes and original stucco work.

Next to the main synagogue is a small nineteenth-century synagogue with some decorative elements intact. The former study house also remains. There are plans to restore both of the buildings as museums.

The Nazis destroyed all three Jewish cemeteries in Wlodowa, though the area where one of them stood is today used as a park. As elsewhere, the Nazis forced Jews to carry out some of the desecration of the cemeteries. In a memorial book about Wlodowa, survivor David Holzmann has described how he was forced to destroy his own father's tombstone for use as paving material.

Wodzislaw (Wodzisław)

The hulking ruin of a massive late sixteenth/early seventeenth-century synagogue crouches in a slight hollow near the center of this small village in southern Poland on the main road between Kielce and Cracow. Fenced off and posted with danger warnings, it is a magnificent, battered, very evocative wreck; huge buttresses support thick walls.

Wodzislaw was the birthplace of Simcha Bunam (c. 1762–1827), a lumber merchant and trained pharmacist who opened himself to Western culture and learning but who eventually turned inward and became an extremely influential Hasidic tzaddik in Przysucha after the death there of "The Jew." (See Przysucha.) Bunam was himself deeply influenced by the teaching of Rabbi Judah Loew ben Bezalel, the Prague rabbi who died in 1609 and was associated with the legend about the creation of the golem. He stressed study of the Talmud and also thought it would be a good plan for wealthy Jews to join together to purchase Palestine from the Turks.

A monument and the fenced-in remains of the Jewish cemetery are right on the main Warsaw-Cracow road outside of town.

*Wroclaw (Wrocław)

Jewish Community: ul. Wlodkowica 9. Tel. (71) 36401

For most of its history, Wroclaw, a major industrial city of over 600,000 people in the Silesia region of southwest Poland, was part of Germany, and Jewish history here parallels that of German Jews. In fact, in 1920, with a Jewish population of more than 23,000, the city, known in German as Breslau, had the third largest Jewish community in Germany.

Jews are known to have settled here in the twelfth century—the earliest known Jewish gravestone in Poland, that of a certain David ben Shalom who died in 1203, is here at the old cemetery.

Jewish life here followed the usual pendulum swing between persecution and prosperity. Jews were banished and readmitted to the town several times. In 1453, after riots instigated by the virulently anti-Semitic preaching of John of Capistrano in which many Jews were burned at the stake for blasphemy, Jews were expelled and not permitted to return officially for nearly 200 years.

Wroclaw was a Jewish intellectual center, and from the late eighteenth century, religious and intellectual life was marked by conflicts between Orthodoxy and the enlightenment, or Haskalah, the Reform movement that had originated in Germany.

Before World War II, there were at least a dozen functioning synagogues in Wroclaw, including a magnificent domed Reform temple, as well as various private prayer rooms. In 1938, little more than 4,000 Jews lived in the city; the population had dwindled from the high point in 1920 due to Nazi persecutions in the 1930s.

Today, Wroclaw is the second largest Jewish community in Poland after Warsaw, with several hundred—maybe as many as 1,000—Jews living in and around the city. The mostly elderly community worships in a prayer room at community headquarters, but there is also an active youth group.

Nearby, the only synagogue that remains standing today is little more than a ruin. Known as the Storch Synagogue, it was designed by Karl Friedrich Langhans and built in 1829 for the city's Orthodox congregation. The building's neoclassical facade is marked by tall, arched windows separated by flat, fluted Corinthian pilasters beneath the triangular pediment.

The Old Jewish Cemetery on ul. Slezna today is preserved as part of the city's Architecture Museum. Opened in 1856, the cemetery has about 12,000 gravestones and 300 big funeral monuments—some like miniature temples—ranged along the walls. Many are extremely elaborate with rich—at times sentimental—sculptural decoration.

Many of the tombs are fine examples of nineteenth-century German stonework and design. They reflect the prosperity and assimilation of Wroclaw's German Jewish community: The difference between this cemetery and the more traditional East European Orthodox Jewish culture evidenced in most other Polish Jewish graveyards is striking indeed.

Inscriptions are mainly in German rather than Hebrew, and gravestone decorations follow western European trends—most are not much different from Christian tombs of the same era.

Several notable people are buried in the Wroclaw cemetery, including early German Social Democratic leader Ferdinand Lassalle (1825–1864)—a friend of Marx and Engels—and the parents of Edith Stein, the Jewish convert to Catholicism who died in Auschwitz and was beatified by Pope John Paul II.

The cemetery was overgrown and badly damaged after the war: Many of the gravestones were toppled; metal decorative elements were stolen; stones were smashed. A handful of non-Jewish volunteers restored the cemetery during the 1980s, and it is now also used as a hands-on training laboratory for students of stone restoration and conservation.

There is another cemetery, very overgrown and in bad condition, on ul. Lotnicza on the other side of town.

*Zamosc (Zamość)

This unusual and extremely striking city of 60,000 was founded as a private town in 1580 by Polish chancellor Jan Zamoyski, who consciously designed it as an ideal Renaissance city. Its regular urban plan, centered on an impressive arcaded market square with pastel-colored buildings, was laid out by Italian architect Bernardo Morando, whom Zamoyski, who had studied in Italy, imported from Venice.

The town lay in a section of Zamoyski's huge estates, on one of the major trade routes between the Baltic and the Black seas. Zamoyski invited Sephardic Jews to settle in 1588, and within a few years there was a well-established little Jewish quarter on what is now ul. Zamenhofa. Ashkenazic Jews began arriving in the seventeenth century and eventually became the dominant, then the only, community.

Thousands of Jews sought refuge in the town during the Chmiel-nicki uprising in the mid-seventeenth century, and while Zamosc itself withstood the Cossack attacks, many Jews and other townspeople died of hunger and disease.

Zamosc became a center of Jewish scholarship and in the nineteenth century it became a vibrant focus of the Haskalah, or Jewish enlighten-ment movement. In the mid-nineteenth century Jews made up more than sixty percent of the population.

Yiddish writer I. L. Peretz (1851–1915), considered by many the fa-ther of Jewish literature, was born and brought up here and practiced law in the town for ten years. He worked passionately for the Jewish cause and the betterment of his people: Besides his literary work, he was deeply involved in educational and social activities aimed at helping modernize Polish Jews and bring them closer to Europe. Turn-of-the-century social-ist leader Rosa Luxemburg also came from Zamosc.

On the eve of World War II, the town's 12,000 Jews made up just under half of the local population. The Nazis renamed the town "Himmlerstadt" and began to deport the entire local population to make way for a planned colonization of the town and surrounding region by German settlers. They set up a Jewish ghetto in the town, and in 1942 deported the Jewish popula-tion to the death camp at Belzec.

Much of the former Jewish quarter, like the whole town itself, has re-mained intact. The massive, early seventeenth-century synagogue, with its decorative crenelations and black decorative outer painting, stands at the corner of ul. Zamenhofa and ul. Bazylianska. Rebuilt and reconstructed many times, today it is a public library. Much of the interior decoration is intact, including ceiling vaulting and walls highlighted by fine stucco work, a stone Aron ha Kodesh, and some traces of polychrome frescoes.

Down the street, at ul. Zamenhofa 3, is the building that once housed the mikvah. On ul. Mikolaja Reja, a nineteenth-century synagogue has been rebuilt as a kindergarten.

The Nazis destroyed both of Zamosc's Jewish cemeteries, but at the site of the New Cemetery on ul. Prosta, a striking Holocaust monument in the shape of a huge mazzevah was erected in 1950, built of gravestones the Germans had uprooted.

OTHER PLACES OF JEWISH INTEREST

(The province is in parentheses.)

Barczewo (Olsztyn)—Synagogue dating from the mid-nineteenth century; now a Museum of Weaving.

Bedzin (Będzin) (Katowice)—Cemetery dating back to the eighteenth century.

Biala (Biała) (Opole)—Large and extremely picturesque cemetery on a steep hillside with typical Polish Silesian-style gravestones. (See Osoblaha, Czech Republic.)

Biecz (Krosno)—Synagogue from the mid-nineteenth century; now a hotel.

Bierun Stary (Bieruń Stary) (Katowice)—Small cemetery with gravestones dating to the eighteenth and nineteenth centuries in a small town near Oswiecim (Auschwitz).

Bilgoraj (Biłgoraj) (Zamosc)—Hometown of Nobel Prize–winning author Isaac Bashevis Singer, many of whose stories are set in the area. The devastated nineteenth-century cemetery was restored in the 1980s, and a Holocaust memorial was erected.

Biskupice (Lublin)—Remnants of an eighteenth-century cemetery on a hill outside town. In town, a few gravestones used for paving by the Nazis are still in place.

Bochnia (Tarnow)—Cemetery dating to the latter part of the nineteenth century, local Holocaust memorial, local Jewish history in local museum; mid-nineteenth-century synagogue, now a warehouse.

Brzesko (Tarnow)—Cemetery dating to the nineteenth century, with ohel of tzaddik from the Halbersztam dynasty.

Buk (Poznan)—Nineteenth-century synagogue, now empty.

Bychawa (Lublin)—Mid-nineteenth-century synagogue with traces of interior decoration left; used as a fire station and warehouse; remnants of devastated cemetery.

Chelmno (Chełmno)—Site of the first Nazi death camp in Poland. A monument commemorates the roughly 310,000 people who died here.

Choroszcz (Bialystok)—Overgrown cemetery; numerous gravestones immersed in young forest.

Chrzanow (Chrzanów) (Katowice)—An overgrown cemetery with very fine, detailed carvings on gravestones dating back to the eighteenth century.

Ciechanowiec (Lomza)—Nineteenth-century synagogue, now a warehouse. Jewish gravestones removed from cemetery during the war are now set up outside the local Agriculture Museum.

Ciepielow (Ciepielów) (Radom)—Nineteenth-century synagogue, now a warehouse.

Cieszanow (Cieszanów) (Przemysl)—Nineteenth-century synagogue, now a warehouse.

Czudec (Rzeszow)—Nineteenth-century synagogue, now a library.

Dabrowno (Dąbrówno) (Olsztyn)—Early nineteenth-century synagogue, now a warehouse.

Debica (Dębica) (Tarnow)—Cemetery and synagogue (now used as a bargain-basement department store).

Dukla (Krosno)—Eighteenth-century synagogue, now a ruin; cemetery dating to the nineteenth century.

Fordon (Bydgoszcz)—Mid-nineteenth-century synagogue, now a cinema; one of the few surviving synagogue buildings in this part of central Poland.

Frampol (Zamosc)—Very interesting nineteenth-century cemetery with particularly fine carving on gravestones. There is a Holocaust memorial marking a mass grave.

Gliwice (Katowice)—Ruined late nineteenth-century synagogue; interesting cemetery with ceremonial hall.

Grodzisk Mazowiecki (Skierniewice)—A local committee was recently formed here to restore the devastated nineteenth-century Jewish cemetery, most of whose tombstones were uprooted and used by the Germans to pave a road.

Inowlodz (Inowłódz) (Piotrkow)—Nineteenth-century synagogue, now a library; remnants of cemetery dating to the nineteenth century.

Izbica (Zamosc)—Ruined cemetery; typical old shtetl buildings in the village.

Katowice (Katowice)—Cemetery with several dozen gravestones dating back to 1868.

Kepno (Kępno) (Kalisz)—Synagogue dating from 1814 near market square amid remnants of old Jewish quarter. Heavily damaged during the war, it is under reconstruction as a regional museum and culture center.

Klimontow (Klimontów) (Tarnobrzeg)—A fine late neoclassical synagogue built in 1851; used as a warehouse. The cemetery is around it.

Kolbuszowa (Rzeszow)—Synagogue built in 1825, now a local museum; cemetery dating to the nineteenth century.

Konin (Konin)—Nineteenth-century synagogue, now a library.

Kosow Lacki (Kosów Lacki) (Siedlce)—Nineteenth-century synagogue, now used as a flour mill. Some of the former ghetto setting remains.

Krasnik (Kraśnik) (Lublin)—There is a synagogue dating to the mid-seventeenth century on ul. Boznicza (Synagogue Street). Traces of interior decoration, including frescoes on walls and ceiling, are still visible. Next door is a nineteenth-century former study house. The local cemeteries were devastated by the Nazis. A handful of standing tombstones remain, along with a Holocaust memorial.

Kromolow (Kromołów) (Katowice)—Cemetery.

Krynica (Nowy Sacz)—Cemetery.

Krzepice (Czestochowa)—Very interesting ruined early nineteenth-century neoclassical synagogue. There is a fascinating cemetery with tombstones dating to the eighteenth century and over 100 iron grave markers.

Laszczow (Łaszczów) (Zamosc)—Jews here bought a ruined castle in the late eighteenth century and converted it into a synagogue and community house. Both still exist. The community house is now a cinema. There are plans to renovate the synagogue, which fell into ruin after the war.

Leczna (Łęczna) (Lublin)—The massive synagogue built in 1648 retains much of its intricate interior decoration. It is now used as a Jewish museum.

Lipno (Wloclawek)—Nineteenth-century synagogue, now a cinema; a twentieth-century synagogue, now a warehouse.

Lomza (Łomza)—Two cemeteries, one like the one in Tykocin, where the eroded stones just push through the meadow. The Old Cemetery on ul. Rybacka has thousands of gravestones.

Lowicz (Łowicz) (Skierniewice)—Cemetery whose earliest gravestone is from about 1830.

Lubaczow (Lubaczów) (Przemysl)—Very fine, large nineteenth-century cemetery.

Lubartow (Lubartów) (Lublin)—Remnants of early nineteenth-century cemetery, with Holocaust memorial.

Lubraniec (Wloclawek)—Nineteenth-century synagogue, now a cultural center.

Miedzyrzec Podlaski (Międzyrzec Podlaski) (Biala Podlaski)—Cemetery dating to the eighteenth century, with Holocaust memorial.

Miedzyrzecz (Międzyrzecz) (Gorzow Wlkp)—Seventeenth-century neoclassical synagogue, now a warehouse.

Mikolow (Mikołów) (Katowice)—Cemetery with gravestones dating to the eighteenth century.

Modliborzyce (Tarnobrzeg)—Synagogue, dating to 1760, devastated in the war and rebuilt as the local cultural center.

Muszyna (Nowy Sacz)—Cemetery dating to the nineteenth century.

Niebylec (Rzeszow)—Nineteenth-century synagogue, now a library.

Nowy Korczyn (Kielce)—Ruined eighteenth-century neoclassical synagogue, used as warehouse after the war and then abandoned.

Nowy Sacz (Nowy Sącz)—The main synagogue, built in 1746, is now an art gallery. There is a large cemetery.

Nowy Wisnicz (Nowy Wiśnicz) (Tarnow)—Cemetery in wooded area with some very beautiful gravestones dating to the eighteenth century.

Ostrowiec Swietokrzyski (Ostrowiec Świętokrzyski) (Kielce)—Cemetery, founded in the seventeenth century, with oldest preserved tombstone dating to 1743.

Ostrow Wlkp (Ostrów Wlkp) (Kalisz)—Synagogue from 1857, now a furniture warehouse.

Parczew (Biala Podlaska)—Mid-nineteenth-century synagogue, now a textile factory; early twentieth-century synagogue, now a kindergarten; early twentieth-century mikvah, now a cinema.

Plock (Płock)—Synagogue from 1810, now a warehouse.

Poznan (Poznań)—Synagogue from 1910, now a swimming pool.

Praszka (Czestochowa)—Nineteenth-century synagogue, now a cultural center.

Przemysl (Przemyśl)—Synagogue from 1890, now a garage; the 1910 Steinbach Synagogue, now a library.

Radymno (Przemysl)—Synagogue built in about 1910 in art deco style, now a warehouse.

Sandomierz (Tarnobrzeg)—The synagogue, built in 1758, retains interior decoration and is used as a library. There is a ruined Jewish cemetery with an impressive pyramid-shaped Holocaust monument built of gravestones.

Sanok (Krosno)—Cemetery; synagogue, now used as archives.

Sejny (Suwalki)—Very interesting synagogue built in 1860, recently restored for use as cultural center.

Siemiatycze (Bialystok)—Synagogue built in 1755, reconstructed as cultural center.

Sieniawa (Przemysl)—A very fine cemetery dating to the eighteenth century with several ohels to tzaddikim.

Skierniewice (Skierniewice)—Mid-nineteenth-century synagogue; a cemetery with a few gravestones.

Sobibor (Sobibór) (Chelm)—A monument marks the site of a Nazi death camp.

Sokolow Malopolski (Sokołów Małopolski) (Rzeszow)—Late nineteenth-century synagogue, now a cultural center; also an interesting cemetery.

Sosnowiec (Katowice)—Cemetery dating to nineteenth century.

Starachowice (Kielce)—Cemetery.

Starogard (Gdansk)—Synagogue from 1849, now offices; one of the few synagogues to survive in northern Poland.

Strzyzow (Strzyżów) (Rzeszow)—Late eighteenth-century synagogue, now a library.

Szczucin (Tarnow)—Cemetery.

Tarlow (Tarłów) (Tarnobrzeg)—Ruined synagogue from 1780.

Tarnobrzeg (Tarnobrzeg)—Nineteenth-century synagogue, now a library.

Tarnogrod (Zamosc)—Massive baroque synagogue, possibly dating to 1686. Some interior decoration, including the Aron ha Kodesh, survive.

Devastated during the war, it was later used as a warehouse. There are plans for restoration as a museum. The cemetery may date to the sixteenth century. It was devastated during the war but restored in the mid-1980s. There are Holocaust monuments.

Tomaszow Lubelski (Tomaszów Lubelski) (Lublin)—A few tombstones left in the ruined cemetery dating back to seventeenth century; the Nazis pulled up the rest for use as paving stones.

Turek (Konin)—Nineteenth-century synagogue, now a warehouse. In 1990, numerous fragments of brilliantly painted tombstones—their colors still bright—were unearthed. They were taken to the museum in Konin for conservation.

Ustrzyki Dolne (Krosno)—Late nineteenth-century synagogue, now a library.

Wielkie Oczy (Przemysl)—Nineteenth-century synagogue, now a warehouse.

Wojslawice (Wojsławice) (Chelm)—Synagogue built in 1890, served as a warehouse after the war; restoration as library planned.

Wrzeszcz (Gdansk)—Twentieth-century synagogue, now a music school. One of the few synagogues to survive in that part of northern Poland.

Zabno (Żabno) (Tarnow)—Cemetery with richly decorated gravestones dating to the nineteenth century.

Zarki (Żarki) (Czestochowa)—Early nineteenth-century synagogue, now a cinema; also an interesting cemetery dating to the eighteenth century.

Zyrardow (Żyrardów) (Skierniewice)—Interesting cemetery dating to the nineteenth century.

HOTELS/RESTAURANTS

Most major cities have at least one hotel, and more and more hotels and private pensions are being opened. In Warsaw and Cracow, be prepared to pay American prices in better hotels. In provincial towns it is possible to find a double room for $70 or often much less.

Many of the best restaurants are new, privately run local places.

WARSAW

Hotels

- Marriott Hotel, Al. Jerozolimskie 65-79. Tel. (22) 30-63-06; fax (22) 211290. American luxury, American prices in the center of town. Its half a dozen restaurants and snack bars are generally good and popular.
- Europejski, ul. Krakowskie Przedmiescie 13. Tel. (22) 26-50-51; fax (22) 261111. Old world, well located.
- Victoria Intercontinental, ul. Krolewska 11. Tel. (22) 27-80-11; fax (22) 279856. American-style, well located.
- Pension/Bed and Breakfast Apts-Agency Polonaise, ul. Swietojerska 4/10. Tel. (22) 635-5477; 635-0765.
- R&J Bed and Breakfast Agency, ul. Emilii Plater 30. Tel. (22) 29-29-93.

Restaurants

- Kosher Restaurant Menora, Plac Grzybowski 2. Opened in 1991 as the first kosher restaurant in Warsaw in thirty years.
- Bazyliszek, Rynek Starego Miasta 3/9. Tel. (22) 31-18-41. Famous restaurant with elegant decor right on the Old Town Square.
- Gessler Restaurant, Senatorska 37 (entrance from inside Saxon Gardens). Tel. (22) 27-06-63. "Polish nouvelle cuisine" and some Jewish specialties. A pleasant garden atmosphere.
- Ambassador, Matejki 2 (across the street from the American Embassy). Tel. 25-99-60. Almost elegant; good Polish cooking.
- Cafe Eilat, Al. Ujazdowskie. Some Jewish specialities. Cafe, sometimes offering entertainment, run by Polish-Israeli Friendship Society.

CRACOW

Hotels

- Cracovia, ul. Focha 1. Tel. (12) 82-86-66; fax (12) 21-95-86. Modern, fairly central.
- Forum Hotel, ul. Konopnickiej 28. Tel. (12) 66-95-00; fax (12) 66-58-27. Modern, near Wawel castle.
- Francuski, ul. Pijarska 13. Tel. (12) 22-51-22. Old world, central.

- Grand Hotel, ul. Slawkowska 5. Tel. (12) 21-72-55; fax (12) 21-83-60. Old-world elegance, perfectly located near Market Square. It has a good restaurant.
- Pod Roza, ul. Florianska 14. Tel. (12) 22-12-44. Old world; near Market Square.

Restaurants

- Staropolska, ul. Sienna 4. Tel. (12) 22-58-21. Old Polish cuisine.
- Wierzynek, Rynek Glowny 15. Tel. (12) 22-10-35. One of Cracow's most elegant, right on Market Square.
- Ariel Cafe, ul. Szeroka 17. Tel. (12) 21-38-70. Jewish-style food in the heart of Kazimierz.

RZESZOW

- Hotel Rzeszow, ul. Cieplinskiego 2. Tel. (17) 37441.

WROCLAW

- Hotel Orbis-Novotel, ul. Wyscigowa 35. Tel. (71) 67-50-51; fax (71) 67-52-75. Modern. Close to the Old Jewish Cemetery.
- Hotel Orbis-Monopol, ul. Heleny Modrzejewskiej 2. Tel. (71) 37041. Near the city center; originally built in 1894 in art nouveau style.

AUSCHWITZ (OSWIECIM)

- Center for Information, Meeting, Dialogue, Education, and Prayer, ul. Sw. M. Kolbego 1, 32-600 Oswiecim. Tel. (381) 31000; fax (381) 31001. Simple, inexpensive accommodations and meals in church-run interfaith study center.
- International Youth Meeting Center, ul. Legionow 11, 32-699 Oswiecim. Tel. (381) 32107. Inexpensive, youth-oriented accommodations.

THE CZECH REPUBLIC AND SLOVAKIA

Population: 17 million
Czech Republic: 11.7 million
Slovakia: 5.3 million
Jewish Population of Czechoslovakia before World War II: c. 225,000
(excluding Sub-Carpathian Ruthenia)
Jewish Population in 1994:
c. 3000 in Czech Republic
c. 3500 in Slovakia

A LITTLE HISTORY

In 1918, following World War I and the breakup of the Austro-Hungarian Empire, the Republic of Czechoslovakia came into existence, joining together the historic regions of Bohemia, Moravia, part of Silesia, and Slovakia, which had long been ruled by the Hapsburgs. Slovakia for many centuries was an integral part of Hungary.

On January 1, 1993, Czechoslovakia split peacefully into two independent states: the Czech Republic, comprising Bohemia and Moravia, and Slovakia.

Jewish presence here goes back 1,000 years, but the history of the Jewish communities in each region is somewhat different. Jews are believed to have lived in Bohemia and Moravia as early as the tenth century—Jewish slave traders are mentioned there at that time—and established communities are known to have existed in the eleventh century. By the thirteenth century, Jewish life had begun to flourish throughout all regions in centers such as Prague, Brno, Mikulov, Bratislava, and Trnava.

These medieval Jewish communities were fairly autonomous and well treated, but they counted on the royal protection of the king—rather than on local authorities—for their security. In 1254, for example, a historic decree by King Premysl Otakar II gave Jews in Bohemia and Moravia permission to carry out trade, moneylending, and pawnbroking; prohibited any violence against Jews or their property; prohibited forced baptism of Jews, disturbance of Jewish holidays, and desecration of synagogues and Jewish cemeteries; and granted Jews freedom to practice their religion and be autonomous in running community affairs. These rights were abused by the local rulers and revoked in 1356.

Conditions deteriorated in Bohemia and Moravia in the late fourteenth and early fifteenth centuries. There were restrictions, persecutions, and pogroms. In the middle of the fifteenth century, Jews were expelled from a number of major cities in Bohemia and particularly Moravia, where Jews consequently settled in villages, setting the pattern for Jewish development in Moravia for the next four centuries.

Bohemia, Moravia, and Hungary, including Slovakia, became part of the Hapsburg domains in 1526 with the ascension of Ferdinand I to the throne. Waves of anti-Jewish violence and expulsion orders paralleled the beginning of an exceptional burst of Jewish creative energy, especially in

Prague. This creative energy came to fruition under Emperor Maximilian II, who succeeded Ferdinand in 1564 and issued an imperial charter canceling expulsion orders, granting Jews freedom of trade and commerce, and promising them a permanent home in Prague. He, his wife, and courtiers even paid a formal visit to Prague's Jewish Town.

Under Maximilian—and even more so under his successor Rudolf II, who came to power in 1576—the Jews of Bohemia and Moravia enjoyed a golden age of cultural creativity, prosperity, and power. Outstanding Jewish personalities emerged in all fields, and the partial economic freedom, combined with better social conditions, particularly in Prague, led to a rapid expansion of the Jewish population.

The pendulum swung back somewhat in the seventeenth century, with new restrictions on Jewish economic activity and on where Jews could live, spawned in part by the waves of Jewish immigrants from Poland and the Ukraine following the bloody Cossack uprising there led by Bogdan Chmielnicki in 1648–1649. (See Poland.)

These restrictions culminated in 1726 and 1727 with the Familiants Law issued by Charles VI. This law limited the number of Jewish families allowed to live in Bohemia to 8,541 and in Moravia to 5,106. It also stipulated that only one son from any Jewish household could legally marry and start a family. Although not scrupulously enforced, these restrictions remained in effect until 1849 and prompted tens of thousands of Jews to immigrate to Poland and Hungary, particularly Slovakia.

Virulently anti-Semitic Empress Maria Theresa, who came to power in 1740, imposed a steep "toleration tax" on Jews for the privilege of being allowed to live in Bohemia.

Things began to look up again for Jews throughout the Hapsburg domain after Josef II assumed the imperial throne in 1780. His Edicts of Tolerance regarding Bohemia, Moravia, Hungary, and Galicia, issued between 1781 and 1789, removed most restrictions on Jewish economic activity and opened the doors of universities to Jews. The Edicts also included reforms that actively encouraged Jewish assimilation. Among these, for example, was the abolition of the judicial autonomy of Jewish communities and the 1787 order for all Jews to adopt German names.

Nonetheless, Jews were not officially granted full civil equality until the mid-nineteenth century, and it wasn't until the creation of the dual Austro-Hungarian monarchy in 1867 that Jews were fully emancipated. Freed finally from residency restrictions, Jews in great numbers began moving from small towns and villages into larger cities. Many rural communities disappeared altogether. A law was passed in 1890 formally abolishing Jewish community organizations in towns where few Jewish families still remained.

Meanwhile, from the beginning of the nineteenth century, conflicts began to emerge on the religious level between proponents of strict Orthodoxy and those supporting the Reform movement sparked by the enlightenment. Also in the nineteenth century, the influence of

Hasidic teaching began to be felt, particularly in eastern Slovakia, thanks to immigrants from Poland and the Ukraine.

As the nineteenth century advanced, Jews in Bohemia and Moravia tended to become more secular and assimilated into the mainstream population. There was much intermarriage and conversion. They also became embroiled in the growing parallel ethnic conflict between the German-speaking and Czech-speaking population of the region. Czech-Jewish and German-Jewish movements sprang up, with the Czech-Jewish allegiance eventually becoming dominant.

In Slovakia, traditional Jewish life was more widely followed; Orthodoxy and Hasidism were particularly strong in the east. At the same time, those Slovak Jews tending toward reform followed the Hungarian pattern and chose Hungarian as their language of emancipation—rather than Slovak, as the non-Jewish population did.

The Czechoslovak Republic, founded on October 28, 1918, was one of the rare experiments in democracy in East-Central Europe, and Jews contributed greatly to its economic and cultural development. (In addition to Bohemia, Moravia, and Slovakia, the republic, during its brief life between World Wars I and II, also included the region of Sub-Carpathian Ruthenia, to the east of Slovakia, now part of Ukraine.)

Zionist movements were important among Jewish communities all over the country. Tomas G. Masaryk, founder and first president of the Czechoslovak Republic, supported Zionism and was a forthright opponent of anti-Semitism—he lashed out publicly against Christian superstition during a notorious blood libel case in the town of Polna in 1899 and in 1927 visited Jewish settlements in Palestine.

Nonetheless, anti-Semitism bubbled under the surface, particularly in Slovakia.

Czechoslovakia became a sacrificial lamb to Hitler with the Munich Pact of September 30, 1938, when Czechoslovakia was forced to cede its frontier regions to Germany. Dozens of synagogues and Jewish cemeteries in this territory were destroyed by the Nazis during *Kristallnacht*, November 9–10, 1938, and thousands of refugees fled to the remaining parts of the country.

On March 14, 1939, Slovakia declared itself an independent state ruled by the Catholic priest Father Jozef Tiso, and Hungary occupied Sub-Carpathian Ruthenia. The following day, Nazi troops occupied the rest of Czechoslovakia and declared the formation of the "Protectorate of Bohemia and Moravia."

At the outbreak of the war, there were about 90,000 Jews in Bohemia and Moravia, of whom nearly 80,000 were killed in the Holocaust. Most either died in the ghetto of Terezin or were deported from Terezin to Auschwitz. It is a measure of the assimilated character of Bohemian and Moravian Jews that many are said not to have recognized their Jewish identity until they found themselves deported to Terezin. Of the 135,000 Jews in Slovakia before the war, all but about 15,000 perished.

Under the communists, Jews in Czechoslovakia continued to suffer persecution—as did members of other religious groups. Immediately after the communist takeover in 1948, the senior communist party leadership included many Jews—party secretary general Rudolf Slansky among them. This boosted anti-Semitism among the people. When anti-Semitism became official communist policy in the early 1950s, Slansky and thirteen other senior officials were put before a show trial. Eleven of the fourteen defendants were Jewish—eight Jews were executed. Hundreds of other Jews were arrested, dismissed from jobs, or sentenced to hard labor. "Anti-Zionism" gained ground; relations with Israel were broken after the Six-Day War in 1967.

There was a thaw and an attempt to right wrongs during the short-lived Prague Spring in 1968, but after the Soviet-led invasion, the Czechoslovak communist regime remained one of the most oppressive in Eastern Europe regarding all religious practice.

After the ouster of the communists in the winter of 1989–1990, Jewish life began to flower somewhat, particularly in Prague, Bratislava, and Kosice—the only cities with a sizable Jewish community. Young people in particular have become involved in learning about their cultural heritage. Diplomatic relations with Israel, broken after the Six-Day War in 1967, were reestablished, and Czechoslovak President Vaclav Havel was the first of the new, noncommunist East-Central European leaders to visit Israel.

The renaissance of Jewish life continued after the breakup of Czechoslovakia into the Czech Republic and Slovakia. By mid-1993, rabbis were serving in Prague, Bratislava, and Kosice, and active Jewish educational, cultural, and religious programs were under way in all three cities.

FOR THE TRAVELER

Where

The Czech Republic and Slovakia are in the heart of East-Central Europe, bordering Germany, Austria, Poland, Hungary, and Ukraine. Most of the country is hilly or mountainous.

When

Both the Czech Republic and Slovakia have a climate similar to that of the northeast United States, with four distinct seasons. Late fall and winter are cold and gloomy—the gloominess exacerbated by terrible smog and air pollution in some parts of the country.

How

There are frequent train connections from Vienna, Berlin, and other major European cities. Roads are generally good. Major international airlines regularly serve Prague and Bratislava. It is also convenient to fly into Vienna or Budapest.

Visas

Americans do not require visas for travel in either the Czech Republic or Slovakia.

Languages

Czech is spoken in the Czech Republic, and Slovak is spoken in Slovakia. They are closely related Slavic languages, and Czech and Slovak speakers can generally understand each other. German is widely understood, particularly in the Czech Republic. Russian and Hungarian are spoken in parts of Slovakia. Among younger people, English is also becoming widespread, particularly in cities.

Helpful Phrases

English	Czech (Pronunciation); Slovak Underneath
Synagogue	Sinagoga (Sinagoga)
	Sinagoga
Jewish cemetery	Židovský Hřbitov (Zhidovskee Shbeetov)
	Židovsky Cintorin (Zhidovskee Tsintoreen)
Yes	Ano (Ah-no)
	Ano
No	Ne (Ne)
	Nie (Nyeh)
Hello/Good day	Dobrý den (Dohbree den)
	Dobrý deň (Dohbree dyen)
Good-bye	Na Shledanou (Nah Skhled'ahnoh)
	Do videnia (Doh veedenya)
I don't speak Czech	Nemluvím česky (Nemlooveem chesky)
I don't speak Slovak	Nehovorím po slovensky (Ne hovoreem paw slovensky)
Please	Prosím (Proseem)
	Prosím
Where is . . .?	Kde je . . . ? (Kde ye?)
	Kde je . . . ?

English	Czech (Pronunciation); Slovak Underneath
Thank you	Děkuji (Dyekooyi)
	Ďakujem (Dyakooyem)
Entrance	Vchod (Vkhod)
	Vchod
Exit	Východ (Veekhod)
	Východ
Toilet	Toaleta; WC (Toaleta; Ve-Tse)
	Toaleta; WC; Záchod (Zah-khod)
Men	Muži, Páni (Moozhee, Pahnee)
	Muži, Páni
Women	Ženy, Dámy (Zhenee, Dahmee)
	Ženy, Dámy
Do you have a room free?	Máte volný pokoj? (Mahteh volnee pokoy?)
	Máte volnú izbu? (Mate volnoo eezbu?)
How much does this cost?	Kolik to stojí? (Koleek taw stoyi?)
	Koľko to stojí? (Kolko taw stoyi?)
One	Jeden (Yeden)
	Jeden (Yeden)
Two	Dva (Dvah)
	Dva
Three	Tři (Tzhi)
	Tri (Tree)
Four	Čtyři (Chteezhee)
	Štyri (Shteeree)
Five	Pět (Pet)
	Pät (Pet)
Six	Šest (Shest)
	Šesť (Shest)
Seven	Sedum (Seddum)
	Sedem (Seddem)
Eight	Osum (Awsum)
	Osem (Awsem)
Nine	Devět (Devyet)
	Deväť (Devet)
Ten	Deset (Desset)
	Desať (Dessat)

Money

In 1993, there were about 27 Czech crowns and 30 Slovak crowns to the dollar.

Kosher Cuisine

There are kosher restaurants at Jewish community centers in Prague, Bratislava, and Kosice.

If You Only Have a Few Days

See Prague, with its wealth of Jewish relics, above all. Places of Jewish interest within thirty to thirty-five miles of Prague include: Terezin, Libohovice, Budyne, Roudnice, Mlada Boleslav, Brandys nad Labem, Kolin, Rakovnik.

Elsewhere in the Czech Republic, try to see sites in Volyne, Mikulov, Trebic, Lomnice, and Holesov. In Slovakia, you can easily visit Malacky, Trnava, and Jur from Bratislava. In eastern Slovakia, Kosice, Presov, and Bardejov are near each other.

Possible Routes

The following sites are easily visited in side trips off the main Prague-Brno-Bratislava highway: Humpolec, Trest, Polna, Velke Mezirici, Lomnice, Ivancice, Dolni Kounice, Mikulov, Breclav, Hodonin, Straznice, Malacky.

The following sites are easily visited as side trips between Bratislava and Liptovsky Mikulas: Jur, Pezinok, Senec, Trnava, Beckov, Trencin, Zilina, Ruzomberok, Dolny Kubin.

Helpful Addresses

(The direct dialing code is 42.)

> **CEDOK** (National Travel Bureau)
> 10 East 40th Street
> New York, NY 10016
> Tel. (212) 689-9720

> **CEDOK**
> Na Prikope 18
> 111-35 Prague 1
> Tel. (2) 2127-111

> **Bratislava Information Service (BIS)**
> Laurinska 1
> Bratislava
> Tel. (7) 333-715

Wittmann Tours, specializing in Jewish interest travel. The director, Sylvie Wittmannova, also runs an informal prayer and study group on Friday evenings.
Uruguayska 7
120 00 Prague 2
Tel./fax: (2) 251-235

Society for the History of Czechoslovak Jews
Joseph Abeles, Treasurer
102-30 62nd Road
Forest Hills, NY 11375

U.S. Embassies
Trziste 15
Prague 1
Tel. (2) 2451-0847

Hviezdoslavova 4
Bratislava
Tel. (7) 335-932

Prague Jewish Museum (Offices)
Jachymova 3
Prague 1
Tel. (2) 2481-0099

Main Active Jewish Communities

The communities listed generally try to hold services at least on Friday nights and holidays (depending on whether a minyan is possible). Often a small prayer room is used, even if there is a synagogue still owned by the community in town. Big synagogues may only be used on main holidays. Contact the community offices for times and locations of services, local Jewish facilities, specific information (for example, whether kosher food is privately available), local records. I have always received a warm welcome.

Czech Republic

- Prague

  Local community and Federation of Czech Jewish Communities: Maiselova 18. Tel. (2) 2481-0130 (Federation)
      (2) 231-8664 (local community)

  Kosher Restaurant: Maiselova 18

  Regular services are held in:
      Old-New Synagogue
      Jubilee Synagogue, ul. Jeruzalemska

- Brno   Hybesova 14. Tel. (5) 4221-5710
- Ostrava   Revolucni 17. Tel. (69) 232-389
- Plzen   Smetanovy sady 5. Tel. (19) 357-419
- Usti nad Labem   Tel. (47) 22710

Slovakia

- Bratislava

  Local community and Federation of Slovak Jewish Communities:
    Kozia 21. Tel. (7) 312-167 (Federation)
    (7) 316-949 (local community)

  Synagogue: Heydukova 13-15

  Kosher Restaurant: Chez David, Zamocka 13.

- Galanta   Janasvermu 2. Tel. (707) 2004
- Kosice   Zvonarska 5. Tel. (95) 622-1047
- Lucenec   Moyzesove 56. Tel. (863) 3439
- Nitra   Gorazdova 3. Tel. (87) 26782
- Nove Zamky   Cyrila-Metoda 19. Tel. (87) 25704
- Presov   Svermova 32. Tel. (91) 31271
- Zilina   Holleho 9. Tel. (89) 42262

Local Jewish Interest Guidebooks

- *Jewish Sights of Bohemia and Moravia* by Jiri Fiedler, available in bookstores all over Prague, is an invaluable guide to Jewish heritage in the Czech Republic.
- *Old Bohemian and Moravian Jewish Cemeteries* combines photographs and historical information.
- Many new books and brochures on Prague's Jewish heritage are now available—you will find them on sale all over the city.
- A Slovak-language book on Jewish sights in Slovakia by Ludovit Dojc is available in Bratislava.

JEWISH HERITAGE IN THE CZECH REPUBLIC AND SLOVAKIA

Independent researchers, such as Jiri Fiedler, and staff researchers at the Jewish museum pioneered the systematic documentation of Jewish relics in the Czech Republic.

About 210 out of the estimated prewar 360 synagogues remain standing in one form or another. Many have been converted into Christian churches, museums, or other cultural centers, but most stand empty or are used as warehouses, or have been converted into dwellings, factories, schools, sports centers, and the like.

More than 300 out of the estimated prewar 430 Jewish cemeteries are known to still exist, although the large majority of them are in a derelict state. In addition, remnants of several dozen Jewish quarters in cities, towns, and villages remain. These range from extensive ghetto complexes, such as in Trebic and Boskovice, to individual streets with a few remaining Jewish houses, to small village ghettos.

Until recently, much less was known in a systematic fashion about what remains in Slovakia. Many, if not most, of the prewar hundreds of Jewish cemeteries remain, most in devastated or severely neglected condition. Even cemeteries still cared for by existing Jewish communities have suffered vandalism—not necessarily anti-Semitic in nature, however, but typically comprised of thefts of precious black marble tombstones for reuse.

Most remaining synagogues in Slovakia date from the nineteenth or early twentieth centuries, and many are in poor condition.

When traveling in the Czech Republic and Slovakia, get the most detailed road maps you can, as roads in both states are very poorly—and often very confusingly—marked.

THE CZECH REPUBLIC

PRAGUE

(Czech: Praha)

Jewish Community: Maiselova 18. Tel. (2) 231-8664

Kosher Restaurant: Maiselova 18

The "Golden City," capital of Czechoslovakia and ancient Bohemia—and now capital of the independent Czech Republic, Prague was historically one of the most important Jewish centers in Europe.

Prague today is the site of numerous exceptional Jewish relics and, in the Jewish Museum, the greatest collection of Judaica in all of Europe—a collection that ironically was largely put together by the Nazis, who gathered materials from 153 destroyed Jewish communities in Bohemian and Moravian towns, villages, and provincial cities for what they planned as a "Museum of an Extinct Race."

Prague—A gravestone in the Old Jewish Cemetery, where 12,000 graves are crowded together in the heart of the Old Jewish Town, shows a carving of two hands in priestly blessing, denoting that the deceased was a Cohen, or a descendant of Aaron.

Jews are believed to have settled in Prague in the tenth century. Eventually, the Jewish quarter became established on the low-lying right bank of the Vltava (Moldau) River, not far from the Old Town Square.

Jews on the whole flourished in Prague, but their fortunes were also marked by waves of persecution, depending on which ruler was in power.

At Easter 1389, nearly the entire Jewish population of the city—more than 3,000 people—perished in an attack on the Jewish quarter spurred on by local priests claiming the Host had been desecrated. One of the few survivors was Avigdor Kara, a chief rabbi, poet, and physician who lived on until 1439 and whose tomb is the oldest preserved gravestone in the Old Jewish Cemetery. Kara described the bloody attack and wrote a moving elegy on it that is still recited in Prague on Yom Kippur.

Jews were expelled several times from Prague over the centuries but were always allowed to return.

For hundreds of years Prague was ruled by the Hapsburg monarchy. A golden age for Jews extended for many decades after the death of Ferdinand I in 1564 and particularly during the reigns of Maximilian (1564–1576) and Rudolf II (1576–1612).

Jews were permitted a large measure of economic freedom, and at the same time there was a flowering of Jewish culture. The period produced some of the most notable figures in Prague and East-Central European Jewish history. These included revered rabbis such as Judah Loew ben Bezalel (c.1525–1609), a scholar and educator known as the Maharal ("most venerated teacher and rabbi"), who centuries later became celebrated in legends as a mystic miracle worker who created the golem—an artificial man made of clay and brought to life with a magic incantation in order to protect the Jews.

Other important figures included the mathematician, historian, and astronomer David Gans (1541–1613) and the dynamic financiers Jacob Bashevi (1580–1634)—the first Jew to be knighted under the Hapsburgs—and Mordechai Maisel (1528–1601), who served as mayor of Jewish Town and sponsored numerous Jewish organizations, activities, and construction projects, including the Jewish Town Hall and several synagogues.

Maisel, who has been compared to the Rothschilds, funded the building of the High Synagogue and a magnificent private synagogue, a public bathhouse, a ritual bath, and an almshouse. He also paved the streets of the Jewish quarter and donated numerous Torah scrolls to communities as far away as Jerusalem. In addition, he distributed food and clothing to the needy, provided dowries for poor young women, supplied loans to Jews in need, and carried out other acts of charity.

The pendulum swung back against the Jews in the eighteenth century, culminating with an expulsion from the city by Empress Maria Theresa between 1745 and 1748. Under Emperor Josef II (1780–1790), conditions improved so much that the Jewish Town was officially named Josefov—a name it keeps to this day—in his honor.

Throughout the nineteenth century, gradual emancipation took place. The ghetto was abolished in 1852, and Josefov simply became a district of Prague. By 1867, the year the Austro-Hungarian Empire was formalized, Jews enjoyed full equality. Many moved out of the Josefov quarter to other locations in the city and suburbs. Jews became prominent in the Prague business, cultural, and intellectual scene. Among the most famous internationally were the writers Franz Kafka, Max Brod, and Franz Werfel.

More than 55,000 Jews lived in Prague at the outbreak of World War II. At least two-thirds of them perished. Half of the survivors emigrated by 1950. Under hard-line communist rule between 1950 and 1964, emigration was impossible and Jewish life was stifled by official communist anti-Semitism. A new wave of emigration followed the Soviet invasion in 1968.

Today, slightly more than 1,000 people are affiliated with Prague's Jewish community, and the historic Jewish Town Hall is the center of an active Jewish cultural, social, and religious life.

Major Places of Jewish Interest in Prague

• Josefov—Prague's "Jewish Town"

Though the Josefov district, between the Vltava River and the Old Town Square, is famous today as the old Jewish Town of Prague, it bears very little resemblance to the way it looked to generations of Jews who lived there over the past 800 years.

After emancipation in the mid-nineteenth century, Jews were allowed to live wherever they wanted, and wealthier and upwardly mobile families moved to other parts of town. Josefov became something of a poorly maintained slum where mainly poor people (Jews and non-Jews alike) lived amid a welter of dank, narrow streets, tiny squares, dark passageways, and crowded courtyards.

The city swept almost all of this away at the end of the nineteenth and beginning of the twentieth centuries in a major urban renewal project that saw the complete redesign of the street network and demolition of almost every building in the neighborhood except a handful of ancient synagogues.

The old section was replaced by the handsome complex of turn-of-the-century buildings we see today, but some historians and art historians bemoan the fact that the wholesale destruction of the old ghetto—for whatever reason it was carried out—destroyed an important historic section of town.

At Maiselova 21 (across from the Old-New Synagogue), notice the Jews symbolized by the Star of David, money, and stereotype profiles in the decoration of the facade of the building.

At the corner of U Radnice and Maiselova, a life-sized bust in black bronze of writer Franz Kafka marks the place where Kafka was born July 3, 1883. Kafka, who died in 1924 and is buried with his parents in the New Jewish Cemetery on Nad vodovodem, lived in Prague most of his short life. His works were virtually banned under the communists, but since the democratic changes he has been taken to heart in his native city. In 1991, a Kafka museum was opened in the house where he was born, U Radnice 5. The exhibits include information on Kafka's life as well as on Jewish life in Prague.

• The Jewish Town Hall: Maiselova 18

This bright pink building, with its distinctive tower and big clock with Hebrew letters instead of numbers, is one of the landmarks of the old Jewish Town—and one of the few buildings to survive the urban renewal.

The structure, on a corner across a narrow alleyway from the Old-New Synagogue, dates from the 1560s, and its construction was partially funded by Mordechai Maisel. For centuries it was the seat of the local Prague Jewish community government and the council of the Jewish Community of Bohemia—and it still is the center of Jewish life in Prague today. It houses the offices, library, and function rooms of the present Jewish community, the seat of the rabbi, and the office of the community newsletter, as well as a kosher restaurant on the ground floor—a popular stop for tourists as well as a kind of a club for members of the local Jewish community.

Local Prague Jews are valiantly trying to carry on Jewish cultural and religious life, despite the rather fishbowl atmosphere of the Jewish Town. Tour bus groups can crowd the kosher restaurant in the summer season, and tourists sometimes regard local Jews as exhibits along with the medieval buildings and tombstones. I have had lunch with a local Jewish friend unpleasantly interrupted by a tourist with a napkin on his head barging up to our table and bombarding my friend with questions such as, "How can you still live here after all that happened?"

• The Jewish Museum: open daily except Saturday, 9 A.M. to 5 P.M.

Prague's Jewish Museum, originally established in 1906, contains the largest collection of Judaica in Europe. Most of the objects come from the provincial communities of Bohemia and Moravia destroyed by the Nazis.

The exhibits are displayed in the half dozen synagogues that were not torn down in the urban renewal: The historic buildings themselves form an important part of the museum, as does the unique Old Jewish Cemetery. Tickets can be purchased at the various entrances, and all museum exhibits are within a few minutes' walk of each other.

Prague—In Josefov (Jewish Town), the sixteenth-century Jewish Town Hall (right), with its distinctive tower and clock with Hebrew letters, and the Old-New Synagogue, built around 1270, the oldest synagogue in continuous use in Europe.

• The Old-New Synagogue: between Maiselova and Parizska on an alleyway called Cervena

The Old-New Synagogue is the oldest synagogue still in use in Europe,
and for centuries it has been a focal point of Jewish life in Prague. Built in
about 1270—and then known as the New Synagogue, as it was the second
synagogue to be built in the Jewish quarter—it got its present strange
name years later when a still newer synagogue was erected.

The compact Gothic building, with its high peaked roof and distinctive brick gables (added in the fifteenth century), stands slightly below
street level and is separated from other buildings in a space that once
served as a Jewish marketplace. Inside, its twin naves are surmounted
by striking Gothic vaulting. The support pillars in the center of the
small sanctuary define space for the central bimah, which is enclosed by

Prague—In the Old Cemetery is the tomb of Rabbi Judah Loew ben Bezalel (c.
1525–1609), who is revered in legend as the creator of the golem. Note the pebbles
and written messages on the ledge of the tomb.

a late-Gothic iron grille. Hanging above is a banner given to the Jews by Charles IV in 1358.

Over the centuries, many legends grew up about the Old-New Synagogue—including one story that Rabbi Loew hid the body of the golem in the synagogue attic after causing the artificial man to die, and that it remains up there to this day. Legend tells us that Rabbi Loew created the golem to defend the Jews, but if it is in the attic of the synagogue, why wasn't it brought to life again during later hardships? According to one legend, it is because the word used to bring him to life has been forgotten.

• The Old Cemetery: entrance from U Stareho Hrbitova

No single Jewish relic captures the imagination the way Prague's Old Jewish Cemetery does. In this small, irregular plot of land in the heart of the old ghetto district some 12,000 tombstones are crowded together.

Tilted over in crazy patterns, broken, eroded, sunk into the earth, and jumbled together in bizarre clumps, they make an unforgettable, ghostly sight—and represent probably the only space in Prague's old Jewish Town that fully preserves its historical character and aspect.

Founded at the beginning of the fifteenth century, the cemetery was in use until 1787. The oldest identified gravestone is that of Avigdor Kara, dating to 1439.

In the 350 or more years of the cemetery's use, lack of space caused graves to be placed on top of each other, layer after layer—possibly as many as twelve layers exist. This has caused the characteristic irregular hilliness of the terrain marked by clumps and clusters of gravestones.

Many of the gravestones are superb examples of carving and craftsmanship, both of epitaph inscriptions and symbols. They include some rare examples of human figurative representation, particularly the figure of a woman on graves of unmarried women.

Many famous Prague Jews are buried here, including Mordechai Maisel, David Gans, and noted rabbis, including the legendary Rabbi Loew himself. Visitors by the score from all over the world place pebbles on the tombs in remembrance and—particularly at Rabbi Loew's impressive tomb—leave written messages (called kvittleh) in many languages asking him to intercede to bring them good luck and blessing.

The cemetery's unique appearance has exerted a special appeal on artists over the years. Romantic and symbolic painters in the eighteenth and nineteenth centuries particularly loved to portray the haunting contrasts between the tumbled, crumbling stones and the lush vegetation growing among them.

• Ceremonial Hall: U Stareho Hrbitova 3

At the entrance to the Old Cemetery stands the ceremonial hall, built in pseudo-Romanesque style in 1906. It houses a very moving exhibition of materials from the Holocaust period, particularly from the Terezin Ghetto, including paintings, writings, photographs, and other relics of and by ghetto inmates. In particular, there is a collection of artwork, diaries, and poems by the children of the ghetto, who were educated in secret and who used their creativity to express fears, hopes, broken dreams, and the horrors of reality.

Few of these children survived the war.

• The Pinkas Synagogue: Siroka 3

This synagogue, at the edge of the Old Cemetery, was built in the early fifteenth century as a private synagogue for the wealthy Horowitz family. It was rebuilt several times over the centuries, partly because of repeated flood and damp damage due to its low-lying position.

A major restoration project—begun in the late 1960s—was largely completed in 1991, and the synagogue was reopened to the public for the first time in more than twenty years. Excavation during this project uncovered an ancient mikvah and well in dank subterranean rooms that were part of the synagogue complex.

The synagogue today has been stripped of the highly ornamental decoration it had during the nineteenth century, so that the simple lines of the building and its soaring vaulting can be appreciated.

Following World War II, the Pinkas Synagogue became a memorial to the 77,297 Jews from the Czech Republic who perished in the Holocaust. Their names, dates of birth, and dates of death were inscribed, one by one, on the walls of the sanctuary. The inscriptions were removed during the restoration work, probably at least in part because of the communist regime's anti-Zionist policy. Experts began reinscribing the names in August 1992.

• High Synagogue: on Cervena, between Maiselova and Parizska

The High Synagogue, across the alleyway from the Old-New Synagogue, was built by Mordechai Maisel in 1568 at the same time as the Jewish Town Hall, from which the synagogue was directly accessible. The sanctuary, on the second floor, is almost square, under a vaulted ceiling decorated by plasterwork.

In 1982, the Jewish Museum's precious exhibition of embroidered Jewish textiles was installed here.

• Klausen Synagogue: U Stareho Hrbitova 1

This baroque synagogue, near the entrance to the Old Cemetery, was built in the late seventeenth century and has been rebuilt and restored several times. The large, oblong sanctuary has a very lofty barrel-vaulted ceiling and tall arched windows flanking the Aron ha Kodesh.

In 1984, the Jewish Museum's permanent exhibition of Hebrew prints and manuscripts was installed in the synagogue. The collection includes centuries-old illuminated Hebrew manuscripts, some dating back to medieval times, as well as printed Hebrew works dating back to the early sixteenth century.

More recently, exhibitions on Jewish life were mounted in the hall.

• Maisel Synagogue: Maiselova 10

Built in the 1590s by Mordechai Maisel as a private prayer house, the Maisel Synagogue was the most opulent building in the Jewish Town. The original synagogue burned down, however, in 1689, and the reconstruction carried out two years later was much less elaborate.

Today, the Maisel Synagogue looks quite different even from that reconstruction, thanks to extensive rebuilding in the latter part of the nineteenth century that gave it a pseudo-Gothic aspect.

Since 1965, the building has housed the precious Jewish Museum collection of ritual silver objects.

• Spanish Synagogue: corner of Dusni and Vezenska

Built in the latter part of the nineteenth century, the Spanish Synagogue was constructed in an extravagant Moorish style with incredibly detailed, overwhelming interior decoration. Every inch of wall and ceiling space is covered by sinuous Islamic-style arabesques, fretwork, and colorful geometric designs highlighted by extensive gilding, but the synagogue has been closed for some years awaiting much-needed cleaning and repair work.

• New Cemetery: Nad vodovodem, at Zelivskeho Metro Station

This large cemetery, founded in 1890 next to a main Christian cemetery, is still used by the Jewish community and makes a very moving contrast to the Old Cemetery in Josefov. Laid out initially to encompass 100,000 graves, the New Cemetery was founded during one of the most prosperous and optimistic periods of Jewish life in Prague.

Most tomb inscriptions are in German or Czech, denoting a non-Orthodox community—like any Conservative or Reform community in the United States; and the names on the tombs, too, read like the membership list of any U.S. temple: Bacher, Beck, Ehrenfeld, Epstein, Katz, Kraus, Roth, Singer. They were, according to inscriptions, doctors, businessmen, lawyers.

The wealth and importance of the community can be seen in the many large and sculpturally elaborate family tombs and other monuments in styles ranging from neo-Gothic to classic to art nouveau.

As soon as a visitor walks through the gates, he finds arrows pointing the way to the simple white stone marking the grave of writer Franz

Kafka and his family. This includes a plaque commemorating Kafka's sisters, who perished in the Holocaust.

What is impressive and particularly haunting about this cemetery, however, is the way the tombs are already beginning to tilt and crack; the way trees and saplings and shrubs are already pushing their way up around them; the way many of the graves are overgrown and unkempt. The people who are buried here have no descendants to care for their graves.

- Zizkov Cemetery: Fibichova, in eastern Prague near Jiriho z Podebrad Metro Station

This very interesting cemetery opened as a graveyard for Jewish plague victims in 1680 and was the main Jewish burial ground in Prague between the closure of the Old Cemetery in 1787 and the opening of the New Cemetery in 1890. Unfortunately, only a small portion of the cemetery, including imposing monuments to leading personalities such as the influential Rabbi Ezekiel Landau, remains. Most of the cemetery was demolished in the 1950s to make way for a park, where the city's huge, futuristic-looking television tower was erected in the 1980s.

- Jubilee Synagogue: Jeruzalemska, near the main train station and Wenceslas Square

Built in 1906 from a design by Wilhelm Stiassny, this highly elaborate synagogue incorporates Moorish, Byzantine, and art nouveau elements. Its striped exterior facade features towers, numerous arches of all sizes, and a rose window in the form of a Star of David. It is still used as a synagogue and has regular services.

- Charles Bridge

The Hebrew words *Kadosh, Kadosh, Kadosh* (Holy, Holy, Holy) are affixed in gold letters on a big crucifix, one of the sculptures lining this famous bridge across the Vltava connecting the Mala Strana with Old Town. The story has it that in 1696 the Jewish community was forced to pay for these words to be affixed on the cross in punishment for the alleged desecration of a crucifix by a Jew.

Other Synagogues and Cemeteries

There are a number of other Jewish cemeteries and synagogue buildings still standing in various districts of the city. Some are the relics of centuries-old Jewish communities in villages not originally part of Prague. Others reflect the fact that many Jews moved out of Josefov to the suburbs and other neighborhoods after Jews were granted civic equality in the mid-nineteenth century.

- *Synagogue at Vitkova 13* (in the fairly central district of Karlin). Built in 1861 and now a Protestant church, it was remodeled on the inside and has no remnants of its Jewish origins. The entrance around the back leads to an eerie display room for funeral urns.

- *Synagogue in Liben district* (Ludmilina, near Palmovka Metro Station). Jews lived in this suburb (now well within the city) since the sixteenth century, and the first synagogue was built as early as 1592. It was replaced in the mid-nineteenth century by the current large, recently renovated neoclassical building, which is set in a small park and used as a storehouse.

- *Synagogue in Michle district* (U Michelskeho Mlyna). Neo-Gothic reconstruction of a possibly eighteenth-century building; today it is a Protestant church.

- *Synagogue in Smichov district* (corner of Plzenska and Stroupeznicky). Jews established a community in this suburb at the end of the eighteenth century. A neo-Romanesque synagogue was built here in 1863, but it was totally reconstructed in a modern style by architect Leopold Ehrmann in 1931. Today it stands empty.

- *Smichov/Radlice cemetery* (on U Stareho Zidovskeho Hrbitova—Old Jewish Cemetery Street—in southwest Prague). This cemetery was founded in 1759 and has many graves from the eighteenth century.

- *Uhrineves cemetery* (in the Uhrineves suburb in southern Prague). Jews settled here in the seventeenth century, and the cemetery dates from the early eighteenth century. It is totally overgrown and abandoned but has many fine carved gravestones. The former synagogue in Uhrineves, built in the mid-nineteenth century, is now used as the local laundry.

BOHEMIA

*Brandys nad Labem-Stara Boleslav (Brandýs nad Labem-Stará Boleslav)

This ancient double town of 16,000 people straddles the Elbe River and is only a twenty-minute drive north of Prague, making it a convenient (and worthwhile) side trip from the capital.

Jews settled in Brandys in the first half of the sixteenth century, and the cemetery, founded in 1568, contains some of the oldest gravestones in the country still in situ. Many stones have fascinating folk carving, including one with the highly unusual figurative representation of a woman. The carved script of epitaphs is also very beautiful, and some of the stones themselves have odd shapes—their tops crenelated like battlements or the tops of crowns, for example. The tombstones are arranged among hills and hollows in a striking manner, and near the entrance, several ancient stones are embedded in a wall.

Near the cemetery, not far from the town square, is a nineteenth-century former synagogue, recently restored and now used as a medical supply warehouse. It dominates remnants of a small former ghetto area.

*Breznice (Březnice)

Just off the main square of this small quiet town in hilly country about fifty miles southwest of Prague is an extremely well-defined and evocative old Jewish quarter and synagogue.

Jews first settled here toward the end of the fifteenth century and lived here until the Nazis wiped out the community in 1940. The picturesque old Jewish quarter consists of a small square giving onto a large square, in the middle of which, standing alone, is a fine eighteenth/nineteenth-century cube-shaped synagogue with a peaked red tile roof. As of late 1990, it was empty but in reasonably good repair, with much interior decoration, including ceiling frescoes, stuccos, and vaulting, intact.

The big square is rimmed by quaint old houses typical of old Jewish neighborhoods. Some of these are under reconstruction. One corner house has, on a corner under the eaves, dim fragments of frescoes—they appear to be of angels.

The town has long-term plans—or at least hopes—to restore the synagogue for use as a museum or gallery and also to restore the entire quarter, conserving the Jewish character.

The cemetery is easily reached and is about a mile outside town near the gas station on the way to Rozmital. Dating back to the seventeenth century, it is small, walled, well-maintained, and shaded by big oak and birch trees: a beautiful, quiet, meditative place with some extremely fine, centuries-old gravestones.

Budyne (Budyně)

This is a charming little town with a castle north of Prague where Jews lived from the early sixteenth century until the Nazis wiped out the community in 1940.

Two Jewish buildings remain. At Ostrovni 125 is the former synagogue dating from the eighteenth century; today it is semiruined and used as a warehouse, but some traces of the once-elaborate Baroque interior decoration can still be seen. Across the street is the former Jewish school, now empty.

The cemetery, also dating from the eighteenth century, sits like an overgrown, walled, secret garden in the middle of farmland a couple kilometers outside town near a Catholic cemetery. It has a ruined ceremonial hall, but you can only gain access by hacking your way through brush and climbing over the partially destroyed wall at the rear.

Much of the cemetery has been plowed up for use as a garden and orchard. The back section, where there are still gravestones, is extremely overgrown and wild, with tombstones looking like Inca monuments looming up in the jungle. It feels like another world. The carving of a deer on one tombstone—symbolizing the name Hirsch—seems almost alive.

There has been recent, obvious vandalism: graves dug up, apparently by people looking for gold.

The friend who came with me to visit the cemetery, a Czech non-Jew, carefully picked up a carved urn that had been toppled and set it upright in its original place.

"It's dangerous to rob graves," he said. "Bones and bodies can carry infection." He spoke in a way that almost suggested satisfaction: just deserts for desecrators of tombs.

*Dobruska (Dobruška)

This little town near the Polish border south of the crossing point at Nachod, in the foothills of the Orlicke Mountains, has a pretty main square with a Renaissance town hall.

Jews settled here in the sixteenth century, and there is a fascinating and historic Jewish cemetery, with tombstones dating from the seventeenth century. In the cemetery's ceremonial hall there is a small museum of the Jewish community, which was wiped out by the Nazis.

The fine carvings, particularly on the eighteenth-century tombs, are considered typical examples of a local northern Bohemian style also seen in other nearby cemeteries such as Vamberk, Zamberk, Jevicko, and Rychnov n Kneznou. The latter two towns also have former synagogues.

In Dobruska there is also a formerly Jewish street with an eighteenth century neo-Gothic synagogue, now used as a church.

*Golcuv Jenikov (Golčův Jeníkov)

This rather nondescript town of a few thousand people about fifty-five miles southeast of Prague has a remarkable old Jewish quarter and a fascinating centuries-old Jewish cemetery. Jews lived here from the end of the sixteenth century until the Nazis destroyed the community in 1940.

Rabbi Isaac Mayer Wise, the father of American Reformed Judaism, studied at the yeshiva that was once established in the town. Born in 1819 in the Bohemian village of Lomnicka, Rabbi Wise, one of the founders of Hebrew Union College, immigrated to the United States at the age of twenty-seven and settled in Cincinnati.

The old ghetto area, in a hollow in the town center on Pod Vy-sehradem, evokes the uncanny feel of a village from the last century. (Looking down one cobbled alleyway you can even see a nineteenth-century factory chimney in the distance.) It's like a village within a village, cut off from the rest of the town. There are dirt roads, grassy (and weed-choked) areas, narrow cobbled lanes, and a little bridge across a small stream. Though people live all around, it feels deserted, almost a ghost town.

Dominating the scene is the big neo-Romanesque synagogue with a flat facade, which was built around 1871 on the site of an earlier synagogue; it faces the former school building, which also probably housed the mikvah.

The synagogue served as a Protestant prayer hall after World War II. Partially restored in the 1970s, it now belongs to the Jewish Museum in Prague and is used as a storage area for the museum's precious textile collection. The interior features a very fine, ornate Aron ha Kodesh. Further restoration work was begun in 1990.

There is a fascinating cemetery, listed as a cultural monument, on the outskirts of town. It is walled and well maintained (get the key from Mr. Ronovsky in the last house before the cemetery on the unnamed street leading to it).

The earliest gravestones date from the late seventeenth century. Many of the older gravestones feature some very delicate carving—trees, flowers, palms, decorative borders. On some of the tombs, the forms of living vines and creepers eerily merge with those of the carving. The shapes of some mazzevahs are deliberately irregular or asymmetric, and many are inscribed in very decorative script, some with raised letters.

Hermanuv Mestec (Heřmanův Městec)

This small, quiet town sixty miles east of Prague has an abandoned synagogue that is now used as a warehouse, the remains of a typical ghetto, and a fascinating cemetery.

Jews lived here from the fifteenth century until the Nazis wiped out the community in 1940. In the nineteenth century, they were very active in the large local shoe industry.

The simple, boxlike synagogue, dating from the eighteenth/nineteenth centuries, stands closed and alone amidst the remains of the ghetto on Havlickova ulice, a few steps from the rather sleepy main market square near the church. A few panes of stained glass glint in the sun; inside, much of the decoration, including an ornate Aron ha Kodesh and busy wall frescoes, remains in good condition: It makes a sad backdrop for the piles of huge industrial spindles stored in the sanctuary.

Although there is much new construction nearby, one old Jewish street with typical low houses winds from the synagogue parallel to the main street. If you turn your back on the raw new apartment buildings, you can think you are in another century.

The cemetery, whose oldest gravestones date from the mid-seventeenth century, is about 200 yards away, off Havlickova.

When I visited, an elderly woman with one lone tooth in her mouth was living in a house crawling with cats and kittens at the edge of the cemetery grounds; entry into the graveyard was through her hallway. She put up a fuss, but not a terrible fuss; I had the impression that she complained about visitors just for the sake of talking, of easing her loneliness. After a minute or so she switched moods and became quite friendly. Maybe it was because I complimented her on her cats—or maybe it was the magic word "America" when she asked where I was from.

The cemetery was well worth the effort. Some of the crowded old gravestones feature extremely delicate carving; others have an almost clumsy, primitive design. There was recent evidence of considerable clean-up and clearing work, too.

Jicin (Jičín)

A district center of 17,000 people at the edge of stunning hill country northeast of Prague, Jicin was founded around 1300; Jews settled here not long after and lived in the town until the Holocaust. The writer Karl Kraus (1874–1936) was born here.

Today the town center, with its Renaissance/baroque castle and exquisite town square surrounded by arcaded baroque and nineteenth-century houses, is a protected architectural zone.

There is a very interesting Jewish cemetery, dating back to the seventeenth century, with finely carved gravestones employing sculptural relief elements and painstakingly executed Hebrew inscriptions. The ancestors of socialist leader Rosa Luxemburg (who was born in Zamosc, Poland) are buried here.

In the town, an old Jewish street remains, along with a seventeenth-century synagogue, the rabbi's house, and other former Jewish buildings. The synagogue has been used as a warehouse, but some interior decoration, including the Aron ha Kodesh, has survived.

*Kolin (Kolín)

A historic (and now industrial) town of 32,000 about thirty-five miles due east of Prague, Kolin has one of the country's most important complexes of Jewish relics, most centered near the very attractive main town market square and soaring early Gothic church of St. Bartholomew.

To get a good orientation, stop in at the local museum (open daily 9 to 4, except Mondays) across from the church, where there is a small exhibit of local Judaica as well as a model of the ancient old town center that clearly shows the Jewish quarter. The keys for the old cemetery and the synagogue are kept at the museum.

Kolin was founded in the thirteenth century, and Jews were already living here by the early part of the fourteenth century. In medieval Bohemia, Kolin's Jewish community was second only to that of Prague in size and importance, and a famous yeshiva was established in the town.

The extraordinary old Jewish cemetery, in use from 1418 to 1888, is one of the most historically and artistically important in the Czech Republic. The earliest surviving tombstones date from the late fifteenth century and constitute the oldest gravestones in situ in Bohemia outside the Old Cemetery in Prague.

Much of the cemetery is fantastically overgrown with ivy, trees, and bushes; tombstones and tree trunks alike are covered by carpets of vines—but this adds to the impressive sight and imparts a sense of timeless age quite different from that felt at the Prague Old Cemetery. In season, pear trees among the gravestones produce delicious fruit.

Many famous local rabbis as well as other prominent Jewish personalities are buried here, among them Rabbi Bezalel, son of the famous sixteenth-century Rabbi Loew (the legendary creator of the golem whose own tomb is in Prague), and Samuel, a nephew of the Prague financier Mordechai Maisel, who was murdered in Kolin in 1621. In the newer part of the cemetery are the imposing tombs of many nineteenth-century businessmen, industrialists, and community leaders.

The old Jewish quarter is near the main square, around Zlata and Karoliny Svetle streets. Until recently, the neighborhood was very rundown. Many poor Gypsy families lived in the dank, decrepit medieval houses. Restoration—in many cases gentrification—efforts began, largely due to the private initiative of young local activists and entrepreneurs, after the ouster of the communists made such activities possible.

The former Jewish Town Hall, with its overhanging upper story, is now an art gallery. Opposite stands a highly decorative building similar to those on Prague's Old Town Square that was the Jewish school. A simple doorway here leads into a courtyard where the massive late seventeenth-century synagogue stands. It has stood empty for years, but much of the ornate baroque decor, including lovely delicate frescoes of grapevines and bunches of grapes on walls and ceiling vaultings and a very ornate Aron ha Kodesh, has remained intact. Here, too, local people have carried out extensive restoration work.

*Libochovice

Jews settled in this nondescript little town near Terezin, north of Prague, in the fifteenth century and lived here until the Holocaust. When my Czech friend and I asked directions to the former synagogue from a youngish man drinking a large mug of beer in a cafe, the man did not know what we were talking about. "He doesn't know what synagogue means," my friend told me.

There does not, in fact, seem to be a remaining synagogue building anymore, although several people eventually tried to direct us to where it once stood.

The only physical relic of the Jewish population is the town's abandoned Jewish cemetery, whose oldest tombstone dates from the late sixteenth century.

The cemetery is on a low hilltop just outside town past the railroad tracks next to a brick factory. Garden allotments back up against the hill, and if you are lucky, someone will allow you to approach it through his gate. Otherwise, you must climb up the rough hillside. The cemetery contains some of the most unusual and finely carved stones I've seen in the Czech Republic, including one large rectangular stone with a vivid plant motif forming a sort of picture frame around the epitaph.

It also is one of the most devastated, overgrown, and totally abandoned cemeteries I've seen, and there are unfortunate examples of recent vandalism—stones toppled, broken, and chipped.

Libochovice, like Budyne and Roudnice, is quite near Terezin, site of the infamous wartime ghetto and concentration camp. I found that the ruined Jewish traces in these towns were just as telling memorials to the Holocaust as are the museum and formal monuments at Terezin.

Mlada Boleslav (Mladá Boleslav)

This is a major industrial town of 49,000—site of the big Skoda automobile works—northeast of Prague that despite the heavy industry retains a rather charming old center with some fine Renaissance and baroque buildings, including a castle that looks as if it is right out of a fairy tale.

Jews settled here in the fifteenth century and developed into one of the most important historic communities in Bohemia. In local folklore and humor, according to the *Encyclopaedia Judaica,* the townspeople had much the same reputation for being naive as did the townspeople of Chelm, in Poland.

There is a fascinating Jewish cemetery, dating to the sixteenth century, spectacularly positioned on a steep hill directly opposite the extraordinary twin-towered sixteenth-century castle, which looks like something the Wicked Witch of the West might live in. Flocks of blackbirds hovering around the towers add a spooky touch—are they birds or winged monkeys?

Until recently, the cemetery had some fine symbolic and folk-style carving on many old tombstones, but acid rain and other pollution have taken a heavy toll on the local sandstone. Most older gravestones are literally crumbling away: Run your finger across the surface and the entire

Mlada Boleslav—In the Jewish cemetery, the grave of an apparently happy husband and wife peeks through the foliage.

area turns to dust. Some mazzevahs seem simply to have collapsed in a heap. Even many newer tombs have already begun to erode.

Among the tombs is that of Jacob Bashevi (1580–1634), one of the most notable Jewish figures of his age. A financier, leader of the Prague Jewish community, philanthropist, and adviser to the Hapsburg rulers, he was named to the rank of Court Jew by King Matthias of Bohemia and, in 1622, was knighted by Emperor Ferdinand II—becoming the first Jew in the Hapsburg monarchy to be raised to nobility.

There is a large ceremonial hall worth seeing in the newer section of the cemetery. I had some trouble gaining entry into the cemetery. The elderly woman who once kept the keys had recently died, and it was necessary to find a neighbor whose garden backed on to a place in the cemetery wall where there was a breach big enough to crawl over. Since this neighbor wanted to sell her house and move away, it might be best to check in town with the CEDOK office or the local municipal hall for the key.

Plzen (Plzeň)

Jewish Community: Smetanovy sady 5. Tel. (19) 357-419

This industrial city of 175,000 (and famous brewery town—home of Pilsner beer) southwest of Prague still has a Jewish community of a few dozen souls.

Jews settled here as long ago as the early fourteenth century but were expelled at the beginning of the sixteenth century and barred from living in the city proper until 1848. During this period, Jewish communities developed in nearby villages and the Jewish population took part in the important Plzen fairs and markets.

Today, a huge, abandoned neo-Gothic/Moorish-style synagogue with two massive, highly decorative cupola-topped towers stands empty in the heart of the city center. Built between 1890 and 1893, it could seat 2,000 people; one of the largest synagogues in Europe, its size and opulence are an indication of the one-time prosperity of the local Jewish community.

The synagogue was seriously damaged during World War II and afterward used as a warehouse. The postwar Jewish community took it over again in the 1950s and used it for religious purposes until the 1970s, when lack of funds for maintenance forced them to abandon the building. Its condition has steadily deteriorated, although much survives of the ornate interior decoration.

Local civic authorities, as well as the Jewish community, hope to raise money to restore the building as a Jewish museum and Holocaust memorial whose sanctuary could be used for classical concerts as well as for religious services. There are also plans to restore a smaller synagogue and the Jewish community building at Smetanovy Sady 5.

The cemetery dates back to the nineteenth century.

*Rakovnik (Rakovník)

This is an industrial town of about 17,000 people thirty miles west of Prague where Jews settled in the early fifteenth century. They lived in town until the Nazis destroyed the community in 1941.

The ornate eighteenth-century synagogue has been painstakingly restored as a concert hall, retaining its full Jewish character and synagogue decor, including a fantastic rococo Aron ha Kodesh, stained glass windows, decorative stuccoed dome with raised cupola, and other rich ornamentation. It opens right off the rabbi's house next door, which has been restored and made into an art gallery: the Rabosova Galerie at Vysoka 123. Together the buildings form a magnificent local cultural complex.

There has been some talk that some of the ritual objects plundered from Rakovnik by the Nazis and now kept in the Prague Jewish Museum, may be returned to be exhibited in their original positions.

On the road heading out of town toward Beroun, an overgrown, walled cemetery, dating back to the seventeenth century and listed as a historical monument, straggles up a steep slope.

*Roudnice nad Labem

It was in the sixteenth century that Jews first settled in this currently run-down, but potentially beautiful little town on the Elbe River near Terezin, north of Prague. It is famous for the stunning but sadly dilapidated Lobkovic Castle, originally built in the thirteenth century and rebuilt in baroque style in the seventeenth century.

One long street of once-Jewish buildings remains, running beyond the big church with two towers below the castle, but the synagogue, now part of a school, is totally restructured and unrecognizable.

There are two abandoned Jewish cemeteries, both outside town near the gas station on the road to Budyne. The old cemetery was used from the seventeenth century to the end of the nineteenth century. It is completely overgrown, but it is worth the effort to push through the undergrowth, as you'll find some exceptionally beautiful old carved stones.

The new cemetery was almost totally destroyed by the Nazis, and within its broken walls are only the remnants of devastation. Its large, ruined Moorish-style ceremonial hall, victim of a fire, crumbles slowly but still has traces of Hebrew inscriptions.

Like nearby Libochovice and Budyne, I think it is worth it to visit Roudnice and its Jewish relics along with Terezin.

*Terezin (Terezín)

This small town thirty miles northeast of Prague was built as an Austro-Hungarian fortress at the end of the eighteenth century and named after the Hapsburg empress Maria Theresa. During World War II, the Nazis turned Terezin into the biggest concentration camp complex in Czechoslovakia.

The camp had two components: one was the concentration camp/prison, in the so-called Small Fortress, just outside town, which generally served as a transit camp for political prisoners; the other was the entire town of Terezin itself, which was turned into a Jewish ghetto.

About 150,000 Jews—mainly from Czechoslovakia but also from Austria, Germany, Holland, Denmark, and elsewhere—passed through Terezin between 1941 and 1945. Some 34,000 perished under the cruel conditions of the ghetto itself. Of the 87,000 deported to death camps, only 3,000 survived.

Whole families were interned at Terezin, including many children. Despite the hardships, there was a rich cultural life, and the internees placed much emphasis on education for the children, whose writings and drawings form a poignant exhibit at the Jewish Museum in Prague.

Cynically, the Nazis tried to pass Terezin off as "an exemplary Jewish settlement." At the beginning, many Jews believed (or hoped) they would be able to sit out the war in the ghetto there and escape being transported to the death camps in the east. In July 1944, the Nazis cleaned up the ghetto and created an entire false-front charade of Jewish life there in order to fool a visiting Red Cross commission investigating Nazi treatment of the Jews.

Today, Terezin is a sleepy little town of a few thousand people. The former concentration camp and other sites nearby are part of a national monument and memorial to Holocaust victims.

Sights in Terezin include:

- A museum/memorial to the Jewish Ghetto, opened in October 1991.
- The National Cemetery for thousands of Nazi victims, laid out in a rose garden at the entrance to the Small Fortress.
- The Small Fortress, maintained as a concentration camp museum, with the Nazi slogan *Arbeit Macht Frei* (Work Makes You Free) painted over the arched entryway.
- The Jewish Cemetery, where more than 10,000 prisoners were buried, mainly in mass graves. Today, this has been turned into a monument dominated by a huge, modernistic sculpture of a menorah surrounded by symbolic, nameless graves. Next door, a few old—prewar—Jewish tombstones remain in a small section of a Catholic cemetery, the Hebrew inscriptions juxtaposed with the crosses.
- A memorial on the bank of the Ohre River at the spot where the ashes of about 22,000 victims were thrown by the Nazis.

Velka Bukovina (Velká Bukovina)

This tiny village in eastern Bohemia, near Nachod between Ceska Skalice and Dvur Kralove nad Labem, is so small that it doesn't appear on most maps. The Jewish population disappeared in the late nineteenth century as Jews moved out to bigger cities.

Here, however, are the picturesque remains of an eighteenth-century ghetto with low wood-framed houses. Between the houses are the ruins of the synagogue—actually the place where the synagogue used to be. The building was demolished before World War I, and now all that remains are two granite portals with Hebrew inscriptions.

There is also a typical village cemetery. The oldest tombstone is that of one "Beila, daughter of Yokev," who was buried in 1737. Her gravestone is decorated with primitively carved tulips and rustic lettering. Many other mazzevahs are decorated with similar rustic-style floral and plant motifs. The latest identified gravestone is from 1890.

*Volyne (Volyně)

A small town about eighty miles south of Prague whose early nineteenth-century synagogue is now the local cinema. (Ask for directions to the *Kino*—or better, write it out, as the girl I asked couldn't understand my pronunciation.) Nothing original remains of the interior, but over the columned portal entrance there is still a Hebrew inscription and bold stucco work of lions supporting a crown—apparently once a clock.

Volyne has what is considered one of the most artistically important cemeteries in southern Bohemia. Jews settled here before the year 1500, and the cemetery's oldest surviving gravestones are from the mid-eighteenth century. Many of the stones are of white marble and are characterized by ornamental lettering and floral and plant motifs showing the influence of folk art.

The cemetery, on U Vodojemu, is surrounded by a big new wall and is very well maintained by a young family living in a house at the edge of the grounds, who have the key and can act as guides. They were allowed to purchase and remodel the house only on the condition that they provide free upkeep to the graveyard, a commitment they take seriously.

Vaclav, the young husband, was just going out when I knocked on the door, but he had no qualms about changing his plans, letting me in to wander around the cemetery, and inviting me in for a cup of coffee afterward. It turned out that he (like me) could speak Italian—he works as a travel agent arranging tours for Czechs to Italy, where he has relatives.

He and his wife bought the house on the edge of the cemetery in 1981 and took four years to restore it. Earlier, an elderly woman had lived there, but she was unable to care for the graves.

"What belongs to us stops at the front steps," Vaclav said. All the rest is the cemetery.

He keeps the grass cut and clears the grounds of fallen branches. His wife planted flower beds along the wall.

On the wall of their kitchen is a crucifix.

MORAVIA

*Boskovice

Boskovice, today a quiet town of about 10,000 people in fine wooded hill country north of Brno in central Moravia, is believed to have been one of the oldest Jewish settlements in what is now the Czech Republic. There was a Jewish community already in the early Middle Ages, and possibly as far back as the eleventh century. The site of a famous yeshiva, it also was one of the most important Jewish centers in Moravia between the seventeenth and nineteenth centuries.

In 1930, about 400 Jews lived in the town; the Nazis wiped out the entire community.

Boskovice today retains an extensive old Jewish quarter, one of the largest, best preserved, and most evocative in the Czech Republic. Just off the long main market square and stretched out below the local church, it features narrow lanes, little squares, and characteristic low houses. At least one recently restored house retains a Hebrew inscription.

Jews were forced to live in this ghetto as of the early eighteenth century, and at one end, at the beginning of Plackova ulice near the town's castle, the arched entryway into the ghetto area still remains. A gate or door here would have closed off the street.

The large abandoned synagogue on U Templu ulice, possibly dating to the seventeenth century, has an unusual iron balcony and some decorative upper windows. Quite a bit of the interior decoration, including baroque frescoes, vaulting, and the Aron ha Kodesh, remains intact.

The Jewish cemetery, near the ghetto, dates back to the seventeenth century and is registered as a historic monument. It's likely to be locked, but there is usually a note posted where to get the key. A campaign was launched in 1992 to restore the synagogue, cemetery, and ghetto houses.

I wandered through the old ghetto and the picturesque market square surroundings for the better part of a morning. It was a brilliant fall day, but there were no other foreign visitors in town. What I found typified the recent changes in the Czech Republic. The graceful square was lined with the usual holdovers from the communist era: run-down shops and horrible greasy-spoon type buffets serving sausages, beer, and weak coffee from the early hours of the morning. Only (alas) after having a snack at one of these places, did I suddenly come across what seemed to be a mirage—a tiny private cafe, spotlessly clean, serving espresso coffee, various cakes, and selling cute little souvenirs.

"Private?" I asked the proprietor after having an excellent coffee.

"Oh yes," he nodded. I bought one of the dried flower arrangements he had on display for seventy-five cents.

Breclav (Břeclav)

This rather drab town in southern Moravia, halfway between Brno and Bratislava, is just off the superhighway.

Jews are first believed to have lived here in the early fifteenth century; there was a well-established community a century later. Of the 600 or so Jews living in Breclav on the eve of World War II, none is believed to have survived the Holocaust.

A large, ruined, late nineteenth-century synagogue, apparently used for years as a warehouse, stands empty on a little square right in the center of town—only under the inefficient communist system could a ruin like this remain unrepaired (or undestroyed) on such prime real estate.

It is not a beautiful, historic, or architecturally important building, but with its blank windows and two charming little side cupolas, it is an eloquent, albeit bleak reminder of the past. The little square, now called

U Trziste, was formerly called Templova—Temple Street—because of the synagogue and the Jewish neighborhood around it.

Other abandoned, formerly Jewish buildings surround the synagogue, which has a few remaining panes of stained glass and some intact interior decoration. There is also a ruined cemetery.

Brno

Jewish Community: Hybesova 14. Tel. (5) 4221-5710

This ancient capital of Moravia, now a big industrial and trade fair center with a population of nearly 400,000, was heavily damaged during World War II, but it still has a historic Old Town center with many picturesque and important medieval and baroque buildings.

The Jewish community was established here in the thirteenth century and lived here in relative prosperity for awhile. A few Jewish tombstones from this medieval period are found in the local museum.

Jews were expelled from the city in 1454 and were not allowed to return until 1848, although a few (generally very wealthy) Jews, like banker Philip Gomperz in the early nineteenth century, did manage to get residency permits from time to time. After 1848, though, Brno—as one of the leading cities of the industrial revolution in the Austro-Hungarian Empire—became one of the places to which Jews migrated from villages and small towns. The Jewish population soared from a little over 200 in 1860 to more than 8,300 in 1900.

After World War I, many Jewish refugees from various parts of Eastern Europe settled in Brno, and in 1930 Jews made up about seven percent of the population.

There are two synagogues. One has been turned into a research institute, and the other, built in 1932 at Skorepka 12, is used by the community.

There is a large cemetery from the 1850s with a grand ceremonial hall and impressive tombs of wealthy nineteenth-century industrialists and businessmen, as well as tombstones dating to the seventeenth century brought from other old cemeteries.

Here, too, there is a plaque to the 11,000 local Jews deported to their deaths by the Nazis.

Dolni Kounice (Dolní Kounice)

Jews settled in this little town in rolling hill country south of Brno in the fourteenth century and lived here until the Holocaust.

The cemetery, whose oldest tombstones date to the seventeenth century, is lost in tall grass and weeds behind a sturdy low wall and decorative iron gate on which there is a plaque noting that it is a cultural

Dolni Kounice—The Jewish cemetery, dating back to the seventeenth century, is lost in tall grass and weeds on a hilltop overlooking this town in Moravia.

monument. Situated high above the town on a hilltop across the lane from the Christian cemetery, it looks out over the pastoral landscape and the cluster of red-roofed town buildings in the hollow below. Across the valley, a white church with a small steeple tops a hill in the distance.

In the town itself, the former synagogue, situated at the main bus stop, is undergoing extensive renovation. It is a large, barnlike masonry building, dating to the seventeenth century, with thick walls and round arched windows. Inside, there is a beautifully proportioned arched gallery and a few faint traces of fresco decoration. Over the entrance, there is some striking plant-motif carving on the stone portal.

*Holesov (Holešov)

Signposts point the way from the run-down main square of this central Moravian town to one of the most precious Jewish monuments in the Czech Republic, the so-called Schach Synagogue, originally built after a fire in 1560 and named for the famous seventeenth-century scholar Rabbi Shabtai ben Meir Kohen, known as Schach. (Like most road signs in the Czech Republic, though, they were confusing and I had to ask several people to clarify directions.) Rabbi Kohen originally came from Poland and served as rabbi in Holesov from 1648 to 1663.

Until the "Velvet Revolution," which ousted the communist authorities in 1989, the synagogue, restored and opened to the public in the early 1960s, was maintained as the only Jewish museum outside Prague and one of the few fully restored synagogues in the country.

Jews settled here possibly as early as the fifteenth century, and about 2,000 lived in the town before World War II. Almost all perished in the Holocaust.

The synagogue building itself is so understated you may walk right by it (though its compact solidity is in high contrast to the drab apartment block development surrounding it.) Inside, the walls glow with pastel-colored frescoes incorporating flowers, folk themes, and Hebrew inscriptions. There are also time-darkened wooden hangings bearing Hebrew inscriptions from the psalms and other sources. The central bimah has an elaborate wrought iron grille and top that includes a Torah holder enclosing a 200-year-old Torah.

The arched women's gallery upstairs has for years housed a tiny, inadequate exhibition of Judaica that showed little and explained less—I understand, however, that plans are being drawn up to expand this.

Nearby, directly across the housing estate and behind a bright orange ceremonial hall, is the very interesting cemetery, with gravestones dating from the seventeenth century to the twentieth century and many memorials to local victims of the Holocaust.

At the time of my last visit, it was overgrown and untended—surprising, given the quality of the care and upkeep of the synagogue. Paths were cleared, however, to the protected ohel of Rabbi Kohen.

Ordinarily the synagogue is open only in the mornings, except Mondays, from April to October. From November to March it is only open on Sundays. The phone number of the caretaker, for years an elderly woman living nearby, is posted on the door, and you can probably convince her to let you in at other times. She was very kind to me, and if you can speak German or Czech, she is a storehouse of information and rich, detailed memories.

Ivancice (Ivančice)

"How did you know I had the key?" asked the old man who lives across the street and cares for the historic Jewish cemetery in this small town south of Brno.

He wiped his hands on his faded jacket and came across the lane with me to open the big iron gate, nodding when I told him I had simply asked another neighbor.

Jews settled in Ivancice in 1454, and the cemetery is one of the oldest in the Czech Republic, its earliest preserved gravestone dating from 1552. It is large and parklike, shaded by trees and spread out on the steep slope of a hill behind an impressive baroque-style ceremonial hall that is now used by the elderly caretaker to store hay—probably the gleanings from when he cuts the grass.

He accompanied me as I wandered around the slope, occasionally throwing in a piece of sometimes erroneous information (the carvings of ewers on Levite tombstones, he said, showed that these were the graves of hotel keepers—in fact, the ewers, or ewers and bowls, symbolize the washing of the hands of priests carried out by Levites in their traditional role of priestly assistants).

Many of the most ancient gravestones are sunken into the turf; others are jammed together in tight rows. In the nineteenth-century section, where there are many imposing tombs of wealthy merchants and factory magnates (this was a textile center), there has been a lot of vandalism—tombstones toppled, metal letters and decorative elements stolen.

A few hundred yards away, in the rather run-down center of town, the synagogue still stands. A large Hebrew inscription runs across the wall, but, as if to overstate the message of how times change, the building has long been turned into a warehouse for clocks and watches.

*Lomnice

This exceptionally picturesque and unspoiled little town in the low, wooded mountains of central Moravia has many historic buildings and a very charming old ghetto area retaining a wonderful sense of its Jewish past. The town is one of the few in the Czech Republic with little or no evidence of new concrete construction or communist-era "modernization."

Jews settled here in the seventeenth century. The ghetto square, once named after writer Josef Uher but renamed Zidovske namesti (Jewish Square) after the ouster of the communists, features a massive yet austere synagogue dating to the eighteenth century. This synagogue forms an important part of the complex of buildings (including the yellow house that was once the Jewish school) ringing the parklike square, where a local cafe sets out benches in fine weather.

Children play under the many shade trees—mainly horse chestnut and linden—including a linden planted in 1968 to mark the fiftieth anniversary of the establishment of the Czechoslovak Republic.

A two-minute walk from the square, the ancient, overgrown cemetery, its oldest gravestones dating to the late seventeenth century, spreads out on a hillside with a great view of the town.

This is one of the most evocative and pleasant places I visited in all of the Czech Republic. The sympathetic atmosphere was emphasized when a local woman called me over and invited me into her spotless home between the ghetto square and the cemetery for a cup of coffee and delicious home-baked cake. What stories she could have told me if we had had a language in common!

*Mikulov

Picturesquely situated amid the orchards and vineyards of southern Moravia on the Austrian border and dominated by a medieval castle, this beautiful and ancient town was for centuries the center of Moravian Jewry.

Jews settled here in the fifteenth century or earlier and became active in the wine trade, transport, and commerce, and it was in Mikulov that the powerful chief rabbi (*Landesrabbiner*) of Moravia had his seat. The chief rabbi had the right of jurisdiction over Jews in both religious and secular affairs and was also head of two different councils of delegates from Jewish communities all over Moravia: the so-called Small Council, which met annually, and the Great Legislative Council, which met every three years. The Councils, formed around the end of the fifteenth century, lasted into the eighteenth century.

Many famous rabbis served as *Landesrabbiner*, including Rabbi Judah Loew ben Bezalel (the legendary creator of the golem buried in Prague's Old Cemetery), who served from 1553 to 1573, and famous mystic and cabalist Rabbi Shmuel Shmelke Horowitz, a legendary Hasidic master who was *Landesrabbiner* from 1772 to 1778. Another *Landesrabbiner*, Menachem Mendel Krochmal, who served from 1648 to 1661, began in 1651 the practice of collecting and publishing the acts passed by the Councils. A century later, the Hapsburg rulers had these translated into German as an official guide to regulation of Jewish life in Moravia.

The Jewish population seriously dwindled in the latter part of the nineteenth century as most local Jews moved to bigger cities.

Most of the old ghetto and all but one synagogue have been destroyed, but these relics are enough to make Mikulov a precious trove of Jewish heritage.

The remaining Old Synagogue, on Husova ulice below the town square and castle, is believed to date back to 1550, though it was totally rebuilt in 1723 after fire destroyed it and a good part of the surrounding ghetto. It features a high peaked roof, vaulted ceilings, and an elegant masonry four-pillared central bimah, beautifully integrated as central support for the ceiling vaulting. It recently has been painstakingly restored to become a Jewish museum.

Husova ulice itself includes what's left of the old Jewish quarter and has many fascinating old houses, some restored and painted in pastel candy colors.

Close by, you'll find the sprawling cemetery, one of the most impressive and historically important Jewish cemeteries in the Czech Republic—well worth a lengthy visit. Besides a wealth of strikingly decorated tombstones dating back to the seventeenth century and employing fine script and numerous floral and folk motifs, there are the tombs of several famous rabbis, including Menachem Mendel Krochmal (d. 1661), Mordechai Benet (d. 1829), and Shmuel Smelke Horowitz (1726–1778).

The artistic design of the tombstones from the seventeenth to the early nineteenth centuries is highly characteristic of tomb sculpture in southern Moravia, utilizing very vivid carving of Jewish symbols and geometric and plant motifs.

There are also later tombs, as well as a poignant, partially ruined monument to Jewish soldiers who died in World War I. "Oh, how the heroes have been cut down!" reads the memorial to Moriz Jung, Max Feldsberger, Heinrich Deutsch, Hans Kohn, and their comrades. There are also memorials to victims of the Holocaust.

Parts of the extensive, hilly cemetery have been cleared; parts are still overgrown with brush, weeds, and saplings. A disquieting sight is a retaining wall built out of old gravestones.

The nineteenth-century, pale blue ceremonial hall at the cemetery is a fine building, and there are long-term plans to restore it as an exhibition hall.

*Osoblaha

This remote village in the Czech part of Silesia is well off the beaten track near the Polish border north of Krnov, but if you manage to get there, you will find the remains of an artistically important cemetery, unique in the Czech Republic because of the strong influence of Polish/Silesian-style gravestone art.

Osoblaha, settled by Jews in the fifteenth century or earlier, was an important Jewish community in the Middle Ages, but the population declined sharply in the nineteenth century as people moved out to bigger cities. By the 1930s, the community had virtually ceased to exist.

The cemetery dates from the late seventeenth century or earlier, and the remaining tombstones contain some of the most vivid carving found in Czech gravestone art.

The Polish/Silesian influence is seen in the exaggerated semicircular top part of the mazzevahs, where there is a rich concentration of ornamental relief based on plant motifs combined with vivid renditions of Jewish symbols and inscriptions. There are identical gravestones in cemeteries just across the border in Poland.

*Polna (Polná)

This small, quiet town just off the Prague-Bratislava superhighway about eighty miles southeast of Prague is infamous in modern Jewish and Czech history as the scene of an ugly blood libel case that touched off a wave of anti-Semitic violence and is sometimes compared to the Dreyfus affair in France. This was the so-called Hilsner affair.

In 1899, Leopold Hilsner, a twenty-two-year-old Jewish shoemaker, was arrested after Anezka Hruza, a nineteen-year-old local seamstress, was found murdered outside the village just before Easter. He was accused of murdering her with the complicity of the Polna Jewish community in order to drain her blood to make Passover matzo. After a trial rife with anti-Semitic rhetoric, he was condemned to death.

Tomas G. Masaryk, who later founded and became president of the Czechoslovak Republic, became involved in the case and wrote an eloquent appeal for the verdict to be reversed. In it he stressed he was not defending Hilsner against the murder charge per se but had to speak out against the superstition and backwardness underlying the accusation of ritual murder. He also pointed out numerous legal errors and judicial bias.

Masaryk's appeal prompted sharp reaction against him. The Hilsner case itself was so heated that it sparked riots in some towns and encouraged a wave of anti-Semitism in Europe. Hilsner's sentence was commuted to life in prison, and he was eventually amnestied in 1916. He died in poverty a few years later.

Today, Polna, where Jews settled in the sixteenth century, is a sleepy little town but has some fine relics of the Jewish past. There is a large, well-preserved, triangle-shaped old Jewish square, called Karlovo namesti. This leads onto a much smaller square dominated by a ruined seventeenth-century synagogue with massive buttresses and Gothic windows. Local officials want to turn it into a Jewish museum.

This old Jewish quarter, entered through narrow alleyways, feels very cut off from the rest of the town.

Outside town, across some rather marshy fields, there is a very fine cemetery whose oldest gravestones date from the seventeenth century. In the autumn, the play of afternoon light hitting the carved gravestones and reflecting off fallen bright yellow leaves can be breathtaking.

*Straznice (Strážnice)

This small town on the border of Moravia and Slovakia about thirty-five miles southeast of Brno has a very interesting and evocative synagogue, cemetery, and ghetto complex on and around Bzenecka ulice.

Jews settled here in the sixteenth century. In the seventeenth century, Shabtai ben Meir Kohen (Schach) served as rabbi here before he went on to become famous as rabbi of Holesov.

The early nineteenth-century synagogue, long used as a warehouse, is a big, barnlike building of red brick, partially hidden by crumbling plaster, that has a sundial on its front and a Hebrew inscription over the entrance. Some interior decoration remains. This is one of the few synagogues that actually sits on the edge of a cemetery, a well-maintained graveyard listed as a cultural monument and dating back to the seventeenth century. A local woman tends the graves. Ivy trails among the gravestones, which date into the twentieth century, and the effect is reminiscent of a church surrounded by an old village churchyard. Wild plum trees shade the area.

Next to the synagogue is a picturesque old house, which a plaque identifies as having been the house of the grave digger, and in front is the former Jewish school. Many of the other quaint houses in the immediate area also were once part of the old ghetto area.

Straznice is worth visiting to see the Jewish element within the context of local village life. A couple hundred yards from the old ghetto area is a very fine Skansen, or open-air village museum, where numerous homes, workshops, wineries, and other typical local buildings have been transferred. Many show characteristic brightly painted floral folk decoration. Nearby, too, is a display of folk art and ethnography in the local castle.

*Trebic (Třebíč)

This historic town of 40,000 in the southern Bohemian-Moravian highlands, on the Jihlava River about eighty miles southeast of Prague contains the most extensive and best preserved old Jewish quarter in the Czech Republic—perhaps in all Central Europe. Local officials would like to see the entire complex of buildings preserved as a historic precinct.

Trebic grew up around the magnificent late-Romanesque Basilica of St. Procopius, founded in 1101, a church and monastery complex partly rebuilt as a castle in the sixteenth century. It now houses the West Moravia Museum.

Jews, many involved in trade, settled in Trebic before the year 1410, and the community remained vibrant until the late nineteenth century, when people began moving out to larger towns and cities. Part of the family of the late Austrian chancellor Bruno Kreisky came from this town, and Kreisky used to spend vacations here as a child.

The Jewish quarter, stretched out alongside the opposite bank of the river from the elongated market square, includes a wide range of houses and other buildings dating from the Renaissance to the nineteenth century. There is a fascinating juxtaposition of narrow alleys and broad thoroughfares; little courtyards and arched passageways; sagging low houses and the quasi-mansions of the well-to-do.

Jews became active in the leather and other industries when Trebic became a footwear manufacturing center in the latter part of the nineteenth century, and at the edge of the old ghetto there is still a nineteenth-century factory that once belonged to Jews.

Two former synagogues are in the old quarter. One, dating from 1639, was rebuilt in the nineteenth century in neo-Gothic style and today is a Protestant church. There is a plaque inside memorializing the Trebic Jewish

Trebic—This former synagogue, built in 1639, stands in the vast old ghetto area of Trebic. The synagogue is now a Protestant church.

community. The young English-speaking pastor, a tall, bearded man, values the legacy. He expressed heartfelt support for both Israel and the Jewish people.

The other synagogue, dating to the early eighteenth century, stood empty or was used as a warehouse for years but recently was undergoing restoration. It is a massive building with a vaulted roof and a few faint traces of frescoes and Hebrew wall inscriptions.

On a hill above the ghetto area there is a very fine and extensive cemetery, well maintained by Mr. Pavlik, a sprightly man in his eighties. There is a pretty ceremonial hall, and tombstones dating from the sixteenth to the twentieth century spread out on rolling terrain under the trees.

Velke Mezirici (Velké Meziříčí)

This industrial town is a major exit on the Prague-Bratislava superhighway, roughly halfway between the two cities, and its Jewish relics are worth a stop.

There are two former synagogues in totally different styles standing almost right next to each other on Novobranska ulice, a main artery not far from the little oval-shaped town market square. One, probably built in the sixteenth century (shortly after Jews first settled here) is among the oldest synagogue structures in the Czech Republic, a massive masonry building with a high peaked roof, fine stone portal, and big iron doors, both with Hebrew inscriptions. Almost next door is a striking, neo-Gothic synagogue in red brick with green trim, built in 1867 to a design by architect August Prokop.

Both were long used as warehouses, and almost all Jewish interior elements were destroyed. In 1992, the neo-Gothic synagogue was converted into a department store (called the Templ) and some of the original interior painting was revealed and restored. The older synagogue is now a ceramics workshop.

The ancient cemetery, whose oldest gravestones date to about 1680, has many mazzevahs featuring the finely carved floral and folk motifs typical of Moravia.

SLOVAKIA

*Bardejov

This town of 31,000 in the mountainous far northeast corner of Slovakia near the Polish border is a center of industry but is also considered the best preserved medieval town complex in Slovakia. Its large, oblong town square, edged by Gothic and Renaissance houses, is at the heart of an architecturally protected pedestrian zone surrounded by the remnants of the ancient town walls, bastions, and moat.

Jews settled here in the seventeenth and eighteenth centuries, many coming from Moravia and Galicia, and developed into a thriving community on the main trade route between Hungary and Poland. Many local Jews were at one time active in exporting wine to Poland.

All but a few of the more than 4,000 local Jews perished in the Holocaust. In 1992, only three Jews lived there: Meyer Spira, a retired kosher butcher who had catered to the needs of observant Jews all over Slovakia, his sister, and her husband.

Mr. Spira, at Komenskeho 20, has the keys to the Jewish cemetery and synagogues, but he was out of town the first time I visited. Instead, an elderly gentile man I asked directions of went out of his way to guide me around. He walked me through what once had been the extensive Jewish quarter, where most of the houses had been razed and replaced by new construction, including the town theater.

Our goal was the nearby impressive but largely ruined complex of several important Jewish buildings, including a large synagogue built in the eighteenth century and an imposing ritual bathhouse. The buildings are still owned by the Jewish community, but they are used by a plumbing supply company.

The synagogue, with a Polish-style four-pillared central bimah, is used as a warehouse for pipes and bathroom fixtures. It still, however, has traces of beautiful red- and blue-colored frescoes featuring stars and floral designs on its lofty arched, domed, and vaulted ceiling. There are Hebrew inscriptions over the Aron ha Kodesh niche and a very lovely inscribed tablet with raised, oriental-style letters over the door.

"This was a beautiful church," the old man sighed.

He mourned the vanished Jewish community. "They were—how do you say it?—they were killed here. Men, women, and children. Young and old."

In 1992, memorial plaques to the Holocaust victims were placed both on the old synagogue and on the ritual bathhouse.

On a later visit to Bardejov, Mr. Spira was home and took me to visit a second synagogue in town, a small prayer house on Klastorska, a few steps from the beautiful large market square. The building has tall Gothic windows and a Hebrew inscription on its outer wall. Mr. Spira told me it was an old building that was only converted to a synagogue in the 1920s. Inside, the little sanctuary is fully intact, just as it was fifty years ago, although the gilded lions over the Ark had been stolen. Mr. Spira goes there every day, he said, to pray.

*Beckov

A massive ruined Gothic castle atop a craggy hill dominates this quaint little village in western Slovakia south of Trencin. On the slope beneath the spectacular ruins are two devastated Jewish cemeteries, both of them overgrown and showing signs of much destructive vandalism. The scene is extraordinary, tragic, and unforgettable.

The lower cemetery, clearly older and dating to the late eighteenth or early nineteenth century, is choked by woods. The upper one, dating from the nineteenth century, is a scene of utter abandonment set against the hulking mass of the castle: Tombstones are tipped over and broken, pedestals are bare.

Who, I wondered, had been Rosa Reif, whose name was all that was left on a broken chunk of marble?

Beckov—A devastated nineteenth-century Jewish cemetery on the slope below the massive hilltop ruins of a Gothic castle.

*Bratislava

Jewish Community Offices: Kozia 21. Tel. (7) 312-167, 316-949

Synagogue: Heydukova 13-15

Kosher Restaurant: Chez David, Zamocka 13. Tel. (7) 313-824

A city of nearly 500,000 on the Danube River, Bratislava, the capital of Slovakia, is a contrast between rococo splendor and communist concrete. For centuries under Hungarian administration, it served as the capital of Hungary for about 250 years when Budapest was occupied by the Turks. There is still a jewellike Old Town, but communist-era urban renewal projects have destroyed much of the historic center.

About 1,000 Jews live in the city today, and the offices of the Council of Slovak Jewish Communities are here. There's also an active Jewish cultural association, a kosher restaurant, and a new Jewish museum. Contact the community in order to attend the lively evening sessions of the cultural organization.

Jews probably lived here during the reign of the Roman Empire and later settled here in the early Middle Ages, forming one of the oldest Jewish communities in the area. The early community engaged in money lending and the wine trade. As the community grew it suffered numerous ups and downs, including expulsion orders, depending on the local rulers. Eventually, however, Bratislava developed into one of the most important Jewish centers in the region. Well over 15,000 Jews lived here before World War II.

As in many cities of what was then Hungary, the Bratislava community suffered deep internal conflicts between Orthodox and Reform Jews in the nineteenth century. Before World War II, there were strong communities of both types, each with its own synagogue, cemetery, and other institutions.

The Moorish-style twin-towered Reform synagogue, once a city landmark, was destroyed when a new bridge and crosstown highway were built in the 1970s. A partly ruined street called Zidovska (Jewish Street) runs right alongside the highway and is all that is left of this historic Jewish neighborhood.

After the ouster of the communists in 1989, young people painted a big picture of the Reform synagogue on the pavement next to the highway where it had stood, with the indignant words, "Here there stood a synagogue!"

There is one remaining synagogue today, at Heydukova 13-15. It is a striking, if austere, building of reinforced concrete designed by Arthur Szalatni in 1923 for the Orthodox community. The synagogue's exterior is defined by seven big columns; the interior is decorated with fixtures and trim in artificial stone. There are regular services here on Shabbat and holidays. Before a rabbi took up his post in Bratislava in 1993, worshipers—maybe as many as two dozen on Friday nights—drifted in at sunset and began praying on their own. Every now and then the beautiful, almost cantorial, voice of one of the elderly congregants would soar up over the general murmur of devotions.

The most remarkable Jewish monument in Bratislava, and still a place of pilgrimage, is the underground mausoleum of the revered eighteenth/nineteenth-century rabbi and sage Chatam Moses Sofer and other local rabbis.

Chatam Sofer (1763–1839) was one of the most famous Jewish scholars and educators, as well as one of the most authoritative Orthodox rabbis of his time. His influence as an exponent of strict Orthodoxy spread far and wide at a moment when Orthodox Judaism was being challenged by reformers.

Sofer was buried in a centuries-old Jewish cemetery that was almost entirely destroyed in a wartime urban renewal project. The only section that survived was a small plot around Sofer's tomb, which was preserved underground and covered over by a roadway.

Today, access is down a narrow flight of stairs from a small glass booth next to a bus stop near where trams exit a tunnel along the Danube. (Contact the Jewish community office for access.)

The dank underground tomb is an eerie sight. A walkway rings a raised plot of earth on which Sofer's tomb and other tombs still stand. Around the edges of the room, dozens of other mazzevahs line the walls.

In October 1990, on the anniversary of Sofer's death, a steady stream of pilgrims descended the narrow steps to pray at the sage's tomb. Some were Hasidim come from abroad; some were local members of the Jewish community. Bearded men dressed in black rocked back and forth in prayer, casting eerie shadows. Tears streamed unchecked from the eyes of two young women as they, too, recited prayers.

On the hilltop above the mausoleum, on Zizkova ulica, the vast Orthodox cemetery, still in use, spreads out over the slope and into the distance, guarded by a barking dog. The Neolog (Reform) cemetery is nearby.

In the cemetery of the huge high-rise Petrzalka suburb across the Danube there is a monument to 500 Hungarian Jews massacred at a concentration camp there in the spring of 1945.

Dolny Kubin (Dolný Kubín)

This town of 20,000 in mountainous north-central Slovakia is near the Polish border in the heart of a popular tourist area. Jews from Holesov, in Moravia, settled here around 1700. In October 1990, a Holocaust monument was dedicated in the eighteenth-century former synagogue on the main square. President Václav Havel himself unveiled the wall tablet inscribed with the names of the ninety-three Jewish families deported from the town during the war.

"When for whatever reason a society is disappointed, frustrated, and disillusioned, searchers for scapegoats appear and point at presumed culprits," Havel said during the ceremony.

*Jur

This village is just a few miles north of Bratislava and has a fascinating ruined complex of eighteenth/nineteenth-century synagogue, courtyard, rabbi's house, and ghetto street.

It is reached by following a narrow dirt alley that runs alongside a ditch opposite the bright yellow church. You can see a Star of David on the synagogue building, and the surrounding scene has the feel of an old Jewish quarter.

Today, the dilapidated synagogue is used as a storage area and barn by descendants of the family that bought it and the surrounding buildings in 1947. A Hebrew inscription is still over the door. When I visited, broken bits of pitchforks and other farm implements were heaped in the niche where the Aron ha Kodesh used to be. Wooden rakes hung on the wall alongside.

At first, eight families of relatives lived inside the old synagogue. Eventually, the rabbi's house was totally remodeled and modernized and now the daughter of the people who bought the complex lives there. She told me the original purchase contract stated that the synagogue could be destroyed but should that occur no building destined for entertainment— like a restaurant—could be erected in its place.

"We are believing Catholics," she said. "I know that Jesus was a Jew. This building was a temple and we don't want to tear it down, but we don't have money to repair it, either."

*Kosice (Košice)

Jewish Community: Zvonarska 5. Tel. (95) 622-1047

The biggest city in eastern Slovakia, Kosice somehow has the restless, rough-and-ready feel of a frontier town in the Old West (despite its 800-year history and the ornate architecture around its elongated central square). A center of trade, industry, and communications near the Hungarian, Polish, and Ukrainian borders, this city of 240,000 has one of the largest and most active Jewish communities in Slovakia.

Jews weren't allowed to settle here until the mid-nineteenth century, but by the eve of World War II the community numbered at least 12,500 Jews. Today there are about 1,000.

The Jewish community offices and facilities are centered in two courtyards surrounding a big nineteenth-century synagogue at Zvonarska 5. The communist authorities took over this synagogue and turned it into a book repository after they came to power in 1948. Under new legislation following the ouster of the communists in 1989, the synagogue is now being returned to the Jewish community. It is in shabby condition but has some lovely frescoes.

The courtyards—with their balconied buildings housing community offices, the kosher restaurant, kosher butcher shops, a new mikvah, a newly renovated prayer room, a kindergarten, meeting rooms, and other facilities—make a rare, unified Jewish complex highly reminiscent of prewar Jewish life.

On the cold winter day when I first visited, a weather-beaten old man from a village forty miles away had driven all the way into Kosice with a trunk full of homegrown poultry to be killed and koshered. One of the turkeys was found to be dead on arrival, and thus not fit to eat.

"Ah, it's hard to be a Jew," he sighed in Yiddish, recounting the episode.

The kosher restaurant, open for lunch and patronized by old and young alike, serves excellent home cooking in a family-style atmosphere very different from the impersonal, tourist-packed kosher restaurant in Prague.

In the summer, regular services are held in the big Orthodox synagogue, designed by Hugo Kabos in 1935, nearby at Puskinova 3. It is almost fortresslike, and its design, incorporating stylized battlements, has a medieval as well as slightly Middle Eastern flavor.

Not far away, there is a big, domed former Neolog (Reform) synagogue, dating from the late 1920s, that has been converted into a concert hall.

Today, a metal harp tops the dome. The big Star of David that used to rise there was removed when the building was converted and now stands as a monument to Holocaust victims in the Neolog cemetery. Both the Neolog and the nearby Orthodox cemetery are extensive and cared for by the community.

A new rabbi took up his post in Kosice in September 1992.

*Liptovsky Mikulas (Liptovský Mikuláš)

In the center of this northern Slovakian town of 32,000, picturesquely situated on the Vah River between the ridges of the Low and West Tatra mountains, looms an impressive nineteenth-century neoclassical synagogue. Surrounded by parking lots, modern construction, and a few lingering remnants of the old Jewish quarter, the synagogue is a magnificent building that was undergoing full restoration in 1993. Four tall pillars support the porch, and inside much remains of the interior structure and decoration, including the elaborate Ark and decorated galleries. This interior was designed by the prolific Hungarian synagogue architect Lipot Baumhorn, who carried out a renovation of the building in 1906.

Jews from Holesov, Moravia, settled in Liptovsky Mikulas in the early eighteenth century. Jews and Catholics got along well in the town— a Jew, Isaac Diner, even was elected mayor. About 1,000 Jews lived here on the eve of World War II—most perished in the Holocaust.

Lucenec (Lučenec)

Jewish Community: Moyzesova 56. Tel. (863) 3439

This textile town of 31,000 not far from the border with Hungary is one of the places where awe mixes easily with tears and anger.

Jews settled here in the late eighteenth and early nineteenth centuries, and in 1938, when the town was ceded to Hungary along with surrounding territory, the community numbered 2,200—about fifteen percent of the local population. Almost all perished; only a handful of elderly Jews live in the town now.

The former synagogue, designed in the 1920s by the prolific Hungarian synagogue architect Lipot Baumhorn (see Hungary), is an immense domed structure rising up next to an ugly modern hotel. Though it seems generally intact from the outside, it is a huge ruin, its vast interior reaching upward into the lofty dome—a scene of overwhelming devastation. The sheer size of the building accentuates everything: the gutted fixtures; sagging, broken planks; crumbling walls. In the failing light of dusk, when I saw it, it struck me as a nightmarish vision.

The agony of the building—and what that agony represents—is brought into sharper focus by comparing it to the Baumhorn synagogue at Szeged, Hungary, which it supposedly once rivaled. The exterior of Lucenec is much less elaborate than Szeged, but the dome and vast interior may have approached it in size and beauty.

"It *was* a fantastic place, one of the greatest synagogues in Central Europe," recalled one Holocaust survivor from the town.

There are two Jewish cemeteries. The old one dates from the eighteenth and nineteenth centuries and is not far from the synagogue. The new one, from the nineteenth and twentieth centuries, is very large and has a neoclassical ceremonial hall recalling a Greek temple.

*Malacky

In this town of 18,000 just off the motorway about twenty miles north of Bratislava, there is a lovely, ornate nineteenth-century synagogue, designed in Moorish style by Wilhelm Stiassny, that is in almost perfect condition despite being used as a primary school.

With its orange- and brick red-striped exterior, two side domes topped with Stars of David, and bright blue Moorish decorative detail, the building looks wonderfully cheery but totally out of place: an exotic structure against the drab setting of parking lots and grimy modern construction around it.

Inside, virtually all the interior decorative detail is in fine condition, despite the fact that the building has been converted into a school. There is a particularly beautiful carved and painted ceiling and an elaborate Ark with a decorative motif featuring clusters of grapes.

Pezinok

This is a famous wine-producing center of 21,000 people twelve miles northeast of Bratislava at the foot of the Little Carpathian Mountains. There is a well-known winery and restaurant in the centuries-old castle, and the town also boasts a wine museum and study center.

Though the modern Jewish community originated only in the mid-nineteenth century, Pezinok was a major Jewish center in medieval times and was the scene of an infamous trumped-up blood libel case in the sixteenth century. In 1529, a local nobleman who was in debt to Jewish creditors faked the abduction of a child and charged local Jews (including his creditors) with having killed him to use his blood for rituals. Some thirty Jews were burned at the stake after confessing under torture; others were expelled from the town. The child eventually turned up alive.

Today, in a most unsettling fashion, the remains of the Jewish cemetery form the backyard of a suburban house at Vitazneho Februara 8, off the road leading from Pezinok to Modra near the Christian cemetery. The gravestones poke up amid fruit trees and garden sheds, as if they are taking the place of more customary yard ornaments like plaster gnomes or reflecting balls on pedestals. One is even used as a bench.

*Presov (Prešov)

Jewish Community: Svermova 32. Tel. (91) 31271

This ancient town of 90,000 north of Kosice in eastern Slovakia is an industrial and educational center and also has a pleasant Gothic and Renaissance Old Town around its elongated market square.

Jews first settled here in the early nineteenth century. Some 6,000 Jews were deported from Presov and neighboring villages during the war; today only sixty mostly elderly Jews live here, keeping the faith.

Jewish relics in Presov are centered on and near a courtyard just outside the old town walls. The centerpiece is a magnificent synagogue with sumptuous interior decoration, built in the 1890s. It is fairly well maintained but needs some urgent repair work on its walls. A small prayer room is attached to the main sanctuary for regular use, and a new Jewish museum is also in the building. (For years, to the consternation of local Jews, a Jewish community in California has made repeated requests to transport this enormous synagogue to the United States!) Facing the synagogue across the grassy courtyard is the ruin of a smaller synagogue, heavily damaged by a recent fire.

Community offices are upstairs in a building, forming one side of the courtyard, that also once housed several kosher butcher shops. Across the courtyard is the old Jewish school, now a state school.

In the middle of the courtyard is a new monument to the 6,000 victims of the Nazi deportations: an obelisk leaning inside an iron cage. When I first visited Presov, community leaders were trying to find money to erect the monument and showed me the planned inscription. I found the translation into English by local Jews very moving:

> In the years 1942–1945, the Jews from Presov were burnt to ashes in the fire of fascism which had not occurred in the gravest moments in history. Dear descendants! Tell your children and the children to their children that this memorial tablet . . . is a symbol for you to remember, and never forget

the poor and unhappy co-believers and their families chased to death through concentration camps by fascist murderers who performed this work of destruction and disaster only because they belonged to the people of Israelites.

Just outside the courtyard, there is a small, twentieth-century synagogue and study house, today used as an office, which still has a window with menorah grillwork and a Hebrew inscription on its outer wall.

There is an Orthodox and a Neolog cemetery on the outskirts of town near the Catholic cemetery. Despite care by the community, both cemeteries have suffered vandalism, particularly the theft of precious black marble gravestones.

Samorin (Šamorín)

An empty nineteenth-century synagogue stands poignantly near the center of this small, rather nondescript town southeast of Bratislava near the Hungarian border. Its interior decoration, including intricate ceiling frescoes, is relatively well preserved despite the fact that it has been used as a warehouse. Keys may be obtained from the local municipal hall.

A couple of hundred yards away there is a devastated cemetery behind a broken wall next to the Catholic cemetery.

Trencin (Trenčín)

This town of 58,000 in hill country on the Vah River in western Slovakia dates back to ancient Roman times, when it was the site of the Roman military outpost Laugaritio, the northernmost in Central Europe.

Jews, many of them traders and merchants, lived here in the Middle Ages, but they then were banned from the town proper in the early sixteenth century. In the seventeenth and eighteenth centuries, many refugees from restrictive laws in Moravia found a home here.

A big, domed synagogue, built in 1912 to a design by the architectural firm of Fuchs and Nigrais, dominates a bustling downtown square off Vajanskeho ulica. It is a marvelous building, a combination of Moorish and art nouveau styles—similar to some of the designs by Hungarian architect Lipot Baumhorn. The large green dome is surrounded by squat towers topped by smaller domes.

The building, which has been designated a historic monument, is currently used as an exhibition hall and museum; much of the interior structure and decoration is intact, and there is a memorial plaque in an outer courtyard to 1,573 local Jews deported to their deaths during the war.

Trencin itself is dominated by a breathtaking Gothic castle, originally built in the eleventh century, crouched on top of a crag overlooking the town. From certain angles, the view of the castle looming up on the hill behind the synagogue is like a telescopic vision of past and present.

Trnava

Jewish Community: Kollarova 6. Tel. (805) 22402

The Roman Catholic Primate of Slovakia has his seat in this historic town of 70,000 people thirty miles northeast of Bratislava. It is an important center of industry and education, and traffic is barred from much of the town's historic heart—a collection of wide squares, Gothic cathedral, baroque churches, and the seventeenth-century Italian-style university complex.

Jews settled here in the fourteenth century in one of the earliest Jewish settlements in what was then Hungary. In 1494, sixteen Jews were killed in the aftermath of a blood libel accusation. The entire Jewish community was expelled in 1539 and did not return to live here until the eighteenth century. About 2,500 Jews lived in Trnava before the Holocaust; only a handful of mostly elderly Jews live here today.

Two abandoned synagogues loom over Havlikova ulica near the town center, both of them built around the turn of the century. One, the Orthodox shul, has a simple neoclassical design. There are plans to restore it for use as an art gallery. The other, a Status Quo (Reform—see Hungary) synagogue is churchlike, with two towers, and is a portrait of desolation and disrepair.

The cemetery, right on the main road into town from the superhighway, is still in use and is very well maintained; its tombstones are crowded together edge to edge in closely laid-out rows. The ceremonial hall was recently restored to pristine condition.

OTHER PLACES OF JEWISH INTEREST

Batelov (Moravia)—A small village ghetto area, baroque synagogue, and cemetery dating to the eighteenth century.

Bechyne (Bechyně) (Bohemia)—A cemetery here dates to the seventeenth century, and the nineteenth-century synagogue houses a local museum of firefighters.

Bzenec (Moravia)—A shady, meditative cemetery dating to the seventeenth century.

Caslav (Čáslav) (Bohemia)—There is an ornate, Moorish-style synagogue built in 1899 by architect Wilhelm Stiassny that is now used as an art gallery.

Ckyne (Čkyně) (Bohemia)—The nineteenth-century synagogue is now a dwelling/storage house. (There is some talk of making it a Jewish museum.) On a hillside beyond the railway line just outside town there is an interesting wooded, walled, well-maintained cemetery.

Drevikov (Dřevíkov) (Bohemia)—A typical walled village cemetery and the remnants of a Jewish street are well signposted as part of a Skansen, or open-air village museum.

Gabcikovo (Gabčíkovo) (Slovakia)—A small, well-maintained remnant of a cemetery in the backyard of a local house.

Galanta (Slovakia)—Old cemetery; small community.

Hlohovec (Slovakia)—Old cemetery.

Hodonin (Hodonín) (Moravia)—Half a dozen historical gravestones have been set up as a Holocaust monument on the main road opposite a huge factory.

Horazdovice (Horaždovice) (Bohemia)—New cemetery with interesting stones placed there from old cemetery.

Hranice (Moravia)—Seventeenth-century cemetery; nineteenth-century synagogue; former Jewish street.

Hroznetin (Hroznětín) (Bohemia)—A cemetery dating to the seventeenth century hidden deep in a woods near Karlovy Vary in western Czech Republic.

Humenne (Humenné) (Slovakia)—A lonely, meditative cemetery with a spectacular view from a hilltop outside town.

Humpolec (Bohemia)—Cemetery dating to the early eighteenth century; late eighteenth/early nineteenth-century synagogue with some decorative elements intact (now a Protestant church) dominating an old ghetto area.

Jindrichuv Hradec (Jindřichův Hradec) (Bohemia)—Very interesting, large cemetery originally laid out in the fourteenth century, but the oldest gravestones now date from the eighteenth century; ceremonial hall; mid-nineteenth-century neo-Gothic synagogue (now a church); small former ghetto area.

Kamyk (Kamýk) (Bohemia)—Cemetery dating to seventeenth century.

Karlovy Vary (Bohemia)—The famous spa town also known as Carlsbad. There's a mid-nineteenth-century cemetery with some impressive tombs and a memorial to Jewish soldiers who died in World War I.

Kasejovice (Bohemia)—Charming, highly decorated eighteenth-century synagogue has been turned into the local museum. There's a cemetery dating to the eighteenth century on a hill above town.

Kojetin (Kojetín) (Moravia)—Cemetery founded in the sixteenth century with gravestones from the seventeenth century; sixteenth-century synagogue now a church; rabbi's house.

Kolodeje (Koloděje) (Bohemia)—Small seventeenth-century cemetery in what once was a largely Jewish village.

Komarno (Komárno) (Slovakia)—A Holocaust memorial was recently erected in this town on the Danube. Small, active community.

Kosova Hora (Bohemia)—Eighteenth-century cemetery; nineteenth-century synagogue; old ghetto area.

Ledec (Ledeč) (Bohemia)—Seventeenth-century cemetery; eighteenth-century synagogue with vaulted ceiling.

Lipnik nad Becvou (Lipník nad Bečvou) (Moravia)—A former Jewish street with a synagogue (now a Protestant church), probably originally built in the sixteenth-century; cemetery.

Lostice (Loštice) (Moravia)—Interesting sixteenth-century cemetery; early nineteenth-century synagogue.

Luze (Luže) (Bohemia)—A baroque eighteenth-century synagogue, used as a leather works, has some fine interior decoration. There is a cemetery dating to the seventeenth century.

Milevsko (Bohemia)—Very interesting synagogue built between 1914 and 1918 in neoclassical style, now a Protestant church. There's also an eighteenth-century cemetery.

Mirotice (Bohemia)—Large seventeenth-century cemetery with a small ceremonial hall at its gate.

Myslkovice (Bohemia)—Very interesting cemetery, well maintained by a young caretaker, in what was once a mainly Jewish village.

Nitra (Slovakia)—Synagogue in use by the local community; cemetery.

Nova Cerekev (Nová Cerekev) (Bohemia)—Seventeenth/eighteenth-century cemetery; very striking neo-Romanesque synagogue on the outskirts of town; old ghetto area.

Nove Zamky (Nové Zámky) (Slovakia)—Synagogue in use by local community.

Novy Bydzov (Nový Bydžov) (Bohemia)—Large, overgrown cemetery with richly decorated gravestones; synagogue (now a church) built originally in the sixteenth century, remodeled many times—most recently in art nouveau style.

Osek (Bohemia)—Nineteenth-century cemetery with grave of Kafka's grandfather. The town has a Jewish street with the house of Kafka's grandfather that is the birthplace of Kafka's father. Nineteenth-century synagogue rebuilt as dwelling.

Pisecne (Písečné) (Bohemia)—Eighteenth-century cemetery with distinctive, strikingly carved gravestones; old ghetto area.

Prerov (Přerov) (Moravia)—Nineteenth-century cemetery and synagogue in a town where Jews settled in the fourteenth century.

Prostejov (Prostějov) (Moravia)—Large nineteenth-century cemetery with many fine tombs of the wealthy bourgeoisie in this former textile center; two former synagogues—one an art gallery, one a church.

Radenin (Radenín) (Bohemia)—Eighteenth-century cemetery; old ghetto area.

Rousinov (Rousínov) (Moravia)—Remains of a ghetto, with a synagogue (now a Protestant church) probably built in the sixteenth century. Also a fine cemetery dating to the seventeenth century.

Ruzomberok (Ružomberok) (Slovakia)—Nineteenth-century synagogue with brilliant red trim; crumbling remains of an old ghetto street.

Safov (Šafov) (Moravia)—Very fine cemetery on the Austrian frontier; old ghetto area.

Senica (Slovakia)—Unusual round cemetery with mound in the middle on which are tombs of rabbis.

Skalka (Bohemia)—Atmospheric eighteenth-century cemetery.

Slovenske Nove Mesto (Slovenské Nové Mesto) (Slovakia)—Small, compact synagogue with a high peaked metal roof is now a Catholic church—the only example of a synagogue being turned into a Catholic church in Slovakia. (See also Satoraljaujhely, Hungary.)

Surany (Šurany) (Slovakia)—Barnlike former synagogue and cemetery.

Susice (Sušice) (Bohemia)—Two cemeteries: one from the seventeenth century, inside the town; the other, later, outside.

Trest (Třešt) (Moravia)—Striking, probably seventeenth-century synagogue (now a Protestant church) with overhanging arcade. Also a large cemetery dating to the eighteenth century.

Turnov (Bohemia)—Very fine eighteenth-century cemetery and early eighteenth-century synagogue, now used as a warehouse.

Uherske Hradiste (Uherské Hradiště) (Moravia)—Fairly ornate nineteenth-century synagogue, now a library.

Uhersky Brod (Uherský Brod) (Moravia)—Large, seventeenth-century cemetery shaded by trees. There is a big ceremonial hall and a Holocaust monument in the cemetery.

Usov (Úsov) (Moravia)—Seventeenth-century cemetery; eighteenth-century synagogue (now a church); old ghetto area.

Vetrny Jenikov (Větrny Jeníkov) (Moravia)—Very impressive eighteenth-century cemetery in a valley outside the village near a lake.

Zatec (Žatec) (Bohemia)—The two-towered synagogue, built in 1872 and now used as a warehouse, was used in the movie *Yentl*. There is also a late nineteenth-century cemetery.

Zilina (Žilina) (Slovakia)—The former synagogue, built in 1931 to a design by Berlin architect Peter Behrens (chosen over a design by Lipot Baumhorn in a design competition), is considered a fine example of modern synagogue design. Today it is a technical high school. Only the outer appearance remains intact.

Znojmo (Moravia)—In this town on the Austrian border, the oldest known existing tombstones in the Czech Republic, dating to the fourteenth century, are preserved in the local museum at the castle.

HOTELS/RESTAURANTS

Prague has long had a shortage of hotel rooms during the tourist season. There is some new construction going up and new private accommodations are also opening up, but the situation during the summer months will probably remain tight for several years.

Prague hotels tend to be expensive, with better hotels costing American prices (at least $150, and often much more, for a double).

Outside Prague prices are much cheaper. In most provincial towns, hotels can be found for under $50 for a double. Prices are likely to increase, however, as the free-market economy takes hold.

PRAGUE

Hotels

- Alcron, Stepanska 40, Prague 1. Tel. (2) 245-741. Grand Old Hotel near Wenceslas Square. Good restaurant with interesting decor.
- Intercontinental, nam. Curieovych 43/5, Prague 1. Tel. (2) 231-1812; fax: (2) 231-0500. Impersonal, modern, expensive, but two steps from the Jewish ghetto area.
- President, nam. Curieovych 100, 11688 Prague. Tel. (2) 231-4812. Right next door to the Intercontinental, but considerably less expensive, it is perfectly located for Jewish Town sight-seeing.
- Palace, Panska 12, Prague 1. Tel. (2) 235-9394; fax 235-9373. Luxurious art nouveau hotel near Wenceslas Square. Its restaurant has a good salad bar.
- Prague Suites (private accommodation). Melantrichova 8, Prague 1. Tel. (2) 2422-9961; fax (2) 2422-9363.

Restaurants

- Kosher Restaurant, in the Jewish community building at Maiselova 18. Can be indifferent food, with poor service at lunch. More relaxed quality in the evening.
- U Fleku, Kremencova 11, Prague 1. Tel. (2) 292-436. Famous old beer hall.
- U Golema, Maiselova 8. Tel. (2) 261-898. Atmospheric tavern in Jewish Town.
- Obecni Dum, nam. Republiky. Tel. (2) 2481-1057. A choice of restaurants whose art nouveau decor is unforgettable!
- U Stare Sinagogy, Parizska. Plain, inexpensive, rather rough-and-ready restaurant next door to the Old-New Synagogue.
- U Sixtu, Celetna 2. Tel. 236-7980. Atmospheric restaurant in medieval cellar just off Old Town Square.

BRATISLAVA

Hotels

- Forum Hotel, Mierove ulica. Tel. (7) 34814. Far and away the best and most luxurious hotel in Bratislava. It also has good restaurants.
- Hotel Devin, Riecna 4. Tel. (7) 330-851. Modern.
- Chez David, Zamocka 12. Tel. (7) 313-824; fax 312-642. New pension (and Kosher restaurant) associated with the Jewish community.

Restaurants

- Chez David Kosher restaurant, Zamocka 13. Tel. (7) 313-824.
- Vegetarianska Jedalen, Laurinska 15. Inexpensive vegetarian lunch restaurant.
- Rybarsky Cech (Fishermen's Guild), Zizkova 1, along the Danube. Tel. (7) 313-049. Fish specialties.
- Stara Sladovna (Old Malthouse), Cintorinska 32. Tel. (7) 562-371. Huge beer hall with good, inexpensive food.

KOSICE

- Slovan, Hlavna 1. Tel. (95) 27378. Functional modern but comfortable, with a decent restaurant.
- Centrum, tr. Sovietskej armady 2A. Tel. (95) 760-301. Modern. Near the Slovan, but less expensive.
- Kosher Restaurant, Zvonarska 5. Very good home-cooking lunch service in pleasant atmosphere at Jewish Community headquarters. I had one of my tastiest meals in Slovakia here.

Hungary

Population: 10,700,000
Jewish Population before World War II: 650,000
(in Great Hungary, about 800,000)
Jewish Population in 1994: c. 100,000

A LITTLE HISTORY

Flat, fertile Hungary, cut north and south by the Danube and the Tisza rivers, is the geographical heart of East-Central Europe and for millennia has been a crossroads of competing tribes and empires.

Jews lived in Hungary in ancient Roman times, well before the arrival of the conquering Magyar (Hungarian) tribes from the east in the ninth century, but more modern Jewish history began with the immigration of Jews from Bohemia, Moravia, and Germany in the eleventh century.

During the next few centuries, Jews established several major communities in present-day Hungary and in Hungarian lands surrounding today's borders. Christian rulers and church leaders imposed tough restrictions on Jews, but they were often ignored. In 1092, the church banned intermarriage between Christians and Jews and work on Sundays and Christian holidays—penalizing Jews with a day of enforced idleness in addition to their own Sabbath. Several medieval decrees ordered Jews to wear special identification—generally either a yellow patch on their clothing or a high, pointed hat. In 1251, though, King Bela IV welcomed Jewish settlers and guaranteed them legal rights.

Jews were first expelled from Hungary in the mid-fourteenth century after the Black Death plague. The following centuries were marked, as in the rest of East-Central Europe, by pendulum swings from persecution to prosperity, from expulsions to toleration.

A relatively long period of stability for Hungary's Jews began when the more tolerant—at least more tolerant to Jews—Muslim Turkish forces defeated Hapsburg armies in the early sixteenth century, incorporating most of Hungary into the Ottoman Empire by 1541.

As elsewhere in the Ottoman Empire, Hungarian Jews were relatively well treated under the Turks. The empire had long been a refuge for Jews expelled and persecuted in Western, Christian countries. Tens of thousands of Jews expelled from Spain in 1492, for example, were welcomed by the Turks, who valued their skills as doctors, merchants, and artisans. Jews were often used as translators and interpreters, and several even were sent as Ottoman ambassadors to foreign governments. Jews were allowed to practice their religion and carry out any trade, and there were virtually no expulsions from the towns in which they lived.

The recapture of Hungary by the Hapsburgs in the late seventeenth century was marked by brutal anti-Semitic terror and mass expulsions of Jews from cities. Jews were barred from most trades. Many Hungarian Jews fled south and east with the retreating Turkish forces, and by the early eighteenth century only a few strongholds of Jewish life still remained, primarily on the western fringes of the country.

During the eighteenth century, particularly during the reign of the vehemently anti-Semitic Maria Theresa (1740–1780), widespread persecution marked the lives of the Jews, who were forced to pay enormous so-called "toleration taxes" for the privilege of living in Hapsburg lands.

At the same time, however, Hungary's Jewish population was bolstered by a great migration of Jews from Moravia and Poland—it was these migrants, settling in provincial towns and villages, who formed many of the Jewish communities that thrived until the Holocaust.

The situation of Hungarian Jews gradually improved after the death of Maria Theresa and the succession of her son Josef II, whose Edicts of Tolerance eased restrictions on where Jews could live and granted them some other civil rights.

In 1797, there were an estimated 81,000 Jews in Hungary. Their numbers continued to swell with immigration from other countries, mainly Poland. By 1850, there were an estimated 340,000 Jews in Hungary.

Throughout the first half of the nineteenth century, restrictions on Jewish life were gradually removed, and by the 1860s most restrictions on Jewish professions or residence were gone. Full, formal emancipation came in 1867. Reveling in their new freedoms, Jews quickly stepped in to play vital roles in the development of Hungarian industry and capitalism, in the growth of agricultural production, in the expansion of transport and communications, in business and finance, and in culture, the arts, and the professions.

Before World War I, forty-two percent of Hungarian journalists and forty-nine percent of Hungarian doctors were Jewish. More than fifty-five percent of Hungarian merchants were Jews, and powerful Jewish capitalists ran great shipping, textile, lumber, railway, grain, flour-milling, sugar-refining, cement, petroleum, and many other commercial empires.

From mid-century until World War I, the Hapsburg rulers raised 346 Jewish (or formerly Jewish) families to the nobility—many of these were wealthy capitalists, but they also included religious leaders, such as Ignac Hirschler, chairman of the Neolog (Reformed) congregation in Pest, who became a member of the House of Lords in 1885.

Despite legal emancipation, however, anti-Semitism was on the increase as a political ideology, particularly from the latter part of the nineteenth century. Anti-Semitic agitation culminated with a blood libel case in the village of Tiszaeszlar, in northeast Hungary near Tokaj, in which a local Jew was accused of carrying out a murder in order to drain the victim's blood for ritual purposes. The Jew was acquitted and Christian leaders condemned the superstition behind the accusation, but the affair sparked off anti-Jewish riots in several towns.

Meanwhile, Hungarian Jews themselves were facing internal conflicts that ultimately led to a religious schism in 1869–1870. This resulted in the formal division of the Jewish population into three distinct communities: Orthodox, strictly adhering to traditional observance; Neolog, similar to today's Conservative or Reformed Jews; and Status Quo Ante communities affiliated with neither.

A key Orthodox leader was the early nineteenth-century Rabbi Chatam Moses Sofer in Bratislava, a city now in Slovakia but until 1918 part of Hungary. (See Bratislava.)

Pioneers in the Reform movement were the influential Rabbi Lipot Loew (see Szeged) and others, such as Aaron Chorin (1766–1844), a rabbi in Arad in Transylvania, now just over the border in Romania. Chorin was deeply influenced by the intellectual enlightenment sweeping western Europe and fought to modernize Jewish ritual, including substituting the German language for Hebrew in most parts of the service. (This was equivalent to today's Reform Jews using English instead of Hebrew.) Eventually, Neology became the dominant form of Judaism in Hungary as Jews assimilated into mainstream life. Mixed marriages were common, and there were increasing numbers of conversions to Christianity.

In northeastern Hungary, there was a very strong Hasidic influence, introduced from the east in the early nineteenth century, and several great Hasidic courts were established in towns and villages like Olaszliszka, Satoraljaujhely, and Bodrogkeresztur in present-day Hungary and Satu Mare and Sighet, which are now part of Romania.

Despite emancipation and Jewish assimilation, anti-Semitism grew in the twentieth century. As many as 3,000 people died in anti-Jewish violence following the defeat of a communist revolutionary government that took power briefly after World War I. That government was led by a Jew, Bela Kun, and many other Jews held senior positions. Anti-Semites in Hungary today still point to this "early example of Jews bringing communism to Hungary" as one reason for their prejudice.

In 1920, a law was passed restricting the number of Jewish students in universities to only five percent. Further restrictive anti-Jewish laws were passed in the late 1930s as the world moved toward war.

Hungary allied itself to the Axis powers and was rewarded by annexation of parts of Slovakia, Transylvania, Yugoslavia, and Sub-Carpathian Ruthenia—much of which had belonged to Hungary before World War I. More than 800,000 Jews lived in this "Great Hungary" in mid-1941.

During the war years, Jews in Hungary suffered persecutions, violence, terror, humiliation, deportation into forced labor brigades, and mass murder. But it was not until 1944, when the Germans occupied the country, that the full-scale extermination of Hungarian Jewry began. Until then, the Hungarian government had refused mass deportation of Jews to death camps.

Starting in April 1944, under the orders of Adolf Eichmann, over 400,000 Jews in provincial towns, cities, and villages were rounded up and forced into ghettos. Beginning in mid-May, they were deported to Auschwitz.

Budapest's more than 200,000 Jews were forced into a ghetto, too. Tens of thousands also were deported to Auschwitz or sent on death marches toward Austria, but the Soviet army reached the capital before all Budapest Jews were killed.

In all, out of more than 800,000 Jews in Great Hungary before the war, at least 550,000 perished. Most Jewish communities in the provinces were virtually wiped out, but about half of Budapest's Jews survived.

Today, the Hungarian Jewish population of about 100,000 is the largest in East-Central Europe. More than ninety percent live in Budapest.

FOR THE TRAVELER

Where

Hungary lies in the heart of East-Central Europe, bordering Austria, Slovakia, Ukraine, Romania, Slovenia, Croatia, and Yugoslavia (Serbia). Most of the country is fertile, flat plains, but there are rolling hills in the northern and western border areas.

When

Hungary's climate is temperate, similar to that of the northeastern United States, with long, cold winters and hot summers. Spring and early fall can be very beautiful, but after November, wet, wintry fogs are common.

How

Hungary's airline, Malev, and many international carriers fly to Budapest. There is fast, comfortable train service from Vienna and also international train service from other neighboring countries. One of the most pleasant ways to reach Budapest is by taking a steamer or hydrofoil down the Danube from Vienna. Hungary has only a few four-lane superhighways, but its two-lane roads are well maintained and comfortable to drive.

Visas

Americans do not need visas for Hungary.

Languages

Hungarian is a unique language originating in Asia and unrelated to any other European language except Finnish. Most people you are likely to meet speak at least some German. Hotel and tourism personnel generally speak English, as do an increasing number of young people. Menus in most restaurants catering to tourists will also be written in at least German, if not other languages.

Helpful Phrases

English	Hungarian (Pronunciation)
Synagogue	Zsinagóga (Zhee'na-go-ga)
Jewish cemetery	Zsidó Temető (Zhee'-doh Tem'-e-too)
Hello/Good day	Jó napot (Yoh' naw-poht)
Please	Kérem (Keh'-rem)
Thank you	Köszönöm (Ku'-su-num)
Yes	Igen (Ee'-gen)
No	Nem (Nem)
Good-bye	Viszontlátásra (Vee'sont-lah-tahsh-raw)
Where is . . . ?	Hol van . . . ? (Hawl vawn)
How much does it cost?	Mennyibe kerül? (Men'-yi-be ker'-ewl)
I don't speak Hungarian	Nem tudok magyarul (Nem too'-dawk moh'-jawr-ool)
Toilet	Toalet, WC (Twal'-et; Veh'-tseh)
Men	Férfiak (Fair'-feeawk)
Women	Nők (Nuk)
Entrance	Bejárat (Bay'-yar-awt)
Exit	Kijárat (Kee'-yar-awt)
One	Egy (Edge)
Two	Két (Kate)
Three	Három (Hah'rom)
Four	Négy (Naydge)
Five	Öt (Ut)
Six	Hat (Hawt)
Seven	Hét (Hate)
Eight	Nyolc (Nyohlts)
Nine	Kilenc (Kee'lents)
Ten	Tíz (teez)

Money

The Hungarian currency is the forint. There are about 70 forints to one U.S. dollar.

Kosher Cuisine

There are kosher restaurants run by the Jewish communities in Budapest, Debrecen, Miskolc, Szeged, and (during the summer) Balatonfured.

If You Only Have a Few Days

Hungary is a small country and you can see a lot in a few days. Budapest has the richest collection of Jewish sites. If possible, try to see Sopron, Szeged, Baja, and Apostag, as well as the fascinating old cemeteries and synagogues in northeast Hungary near Mad and Tokaj. I am particularly fond of the synagogue in Koszeg.

Helpful Addresses

(The direct dialing code to Hungary is 36.)

IBUSZ, Hungarian National Travel Agency
650 Fifth Avenue
New York, NY 10110

There are IBUSZ offices in virtually all Hungarian towns and an IBUSZ desk at many top hotels. The main office in Budapest is:

Tanacs Krt 3/c
Tel. (1) 1222-252
or
Felszabadulas ter 5
Tel. (1) 1186-866

In addition to IBUSZ, there are dozens of other new, regional, and private travel agencies in Hungary, with offices all over the country. One specializing in Jewish tours is:

Chosen Tours
Jewish Cultural Tours
Konyves Gy. utca 5
Budapest 1114
Tel. (1) 1226-527

Additional addresses:

Tourinform (Tourist information for foreign visitors)
Suto utca 2
Budapest 5
Tel. (1) 1179-800

Biblical World Gallery (Good-quality Judaica items)
Wesselenyi u 13
Budapest VII

U.S. Embassy
Szabadsag ter. 12
Budapest
Tel. (1) 1124-224

Main Jewish Communities in Hungary

Some provincial communities have only a few remaining members. Check
with them to find out when and where services are held.

Budapest	Sip utca 12. Tel. (1) 142-1335
Debrecen	Bajcsy-Zsilinszky ut. 26. Tel. (52) 315-861
Gyor	Buda ut. 28. Tel. (96) 16217
Kaposvar	Berzsenyi ut. 14. Tel. (82) 319-867
Miskolc	Kazinczy ut. 7. Tel. (46) 315-276; 44884
Nagykanizsa	Lenin ut. 6. Tel. (93) 311-435
Nyiregyhaza	Martirok tere. 6. Tel. (42) 310-565
Pecs	Furdo ut. 1. Tel. (72) 315-881
Szeged	Gutenberg ut. 20. Tel. (62) 311-402
Szolnok	Majus 1 ut. 33. Tel. (56) 311-239; 30819
Szombathely	Batthyany ter. 9. Tel. (94) 312-500

Local Jewish Interest Guidebooks

- *Magyarorszagi Zsinagogak (Hungarian Synagogues)*. This hardback book,
  available in Budapest bookstores and beautifully illustrated with color
  pictures, maps, and drawings, is a must, both as a souvenir and as a
  very helpful guide in touring the country. Even if—like me—you don't
  speak a word of Hungarian, the maps and pictures are very helpful as
  orientation and in planning a trip.

- *The Jewish Museum of Budapest* by Ilona Benoschofsky and Alexander
  Scheiber. A lavishly illustrated guide to the museum collections, with
  lots of historical material in the introduction. It is available at most
  bookstores.

- *Itt Van Elrejtve* by Peter Wirth. This beautiful photograph album on the
  Jewish cemeteries of northeastern Hungary, by one of the country's
  leading experts on synagogue architecture, is only in Hungarian. It may
  be hard to find but is worth buying. The Hungarian text, by scholar
  Alexander Scheiber, the late head of the Rabbinical Seminary, tells the
  history of the towns.

- *. . . Es Beszeld El Fiadnak* by Tamas Fener, with text by Alexander
  Scheiber. This photograph book with pictures of Hungarian Jewish life
  at one time was available in several languages. You will be lucky to find
  it now in Hungarian.

- *Magyarorszag Zsido Emlekej, Nevezetessegej*, by Ferenc Orban. Unfortunately for foreign visitors, this comprehensive little guide to Jewish monuments in Hungary is only available in Hungarian, though foreign-language editions may be forthcoming.

JEWISH HERITAGE IN HUNGARY

Around the country, there are more than 100 remaining synagogue buildings and about 1,300 cemeteries, most of them abandoned and in poor repair; some are comprised of only a few broken gravestones.

Many cemeteries, however, and many remaining synagogue buildings, even when put to secular use, have prominent memorials to local Jews who perished in the Holocaust. Often these consist of plaques or inscriptions listing the names of all the deported. Some are imposing sculptural monuments.

Most remaining Hungarian synagogues date from the nineteenth and early twentieth centuries, and many of the architects are known.

One of the most important synagogue architects was Lipot Baumhorn, whose career flourished in the late nineteenth and early twentieth centuries. Baumhorn designed about two dozen synagogues all over Hungary (including former Hungarian territories in Slovakia, Romania, and the former Yugoslavia). Many of his synagogues are extremely ornate and stand as monuments to the prosperity and optimism of turn-of-the-century Hungarian Jewry.

BUDAPEST

Federation of Jewish Communities: Sip utca 12. Tel. (1) 122-6478

Jewish Community: Sip utca 12. Tel. (1) 142-1335

Kosher Restaurant: Hanna, Dob utca 35

Hungary's capital, Budapest, spreads out on both banks of the Danube River, which curves through the town center, dividing the hilly Buda section to the west from the broad, flat neighborhoods of Pest.

There has been a settlement here for thousands of years, but the city of Budapest as we know it today was officially formed in 1873, when what were until then three separate towns—Buda, Pest, and Obuda, north of Buda itself—were joined together. Today, the city's more than two million people make up a fifth of the entire country's population, and the Jewish population of 80,000 or more makes it the biggest Jewish city in East-Central Europe (outside the former Soviet Union).

History is written in the streets of Budapest, from the medieval section in Buda and the nearby castle looming up from a crag over the river, to the gorgeous and slightly wacky art nouveau extravagances in Pest. Bullet holes from the abortive 1956 Hungarian uprising against the communists still mar the facades of many houses, and memorials to Jewish victims of the Holocaust are found in several parts of the city.

Jews, mainly merchants, shopkeepers, and craftsmen, already lived here in early medieval times. A certain Comes Henel, king's chamberlain and bailiff of the mint in Esztergom, is believed to have established the first Jewish community in Buda after moving there from Vienna in the mid-twelfth century. Wealthy Jewish delegations, led by members of the influential Mendel family, wearing turbans, carrying silver swords and other ornaments, and bearing banners decorated with the Star of David took part in both the coronation ceremonies for King Matthias in 1464 and ceremonies marking his marriage to Beatrice of Aragon in 1476. Nonetheless, there were anti-Jewish riots in the early sixteenth century.

Except for about a fifteen-year period before the final Turkish conquest of Buda in 1541, Jews lived fairly peacefully in the city until the Austrian reconquest in 1686. Sephardic immigrants from the Balkans and Turkey swelled the population, and under Rabbi Ephraim ben Jacob ha-Kohen the Buda community became one of the strongest in the Ottoman Empire in the seventeenth century.

Jews in what is now Budapest suffered greatly under Hapsburg rule after the Turks were driven out. There were expulsions, violence, and restrictive legislation. No Jews were permitted to live in Pest, the riverbank commercial center, for a century after the 1686 conquest. Jews were not even allowed to spend the night there in an emergency. The Buda community was driven out in 1746.

During this period, many Jewish families expelled from Buda and Pest settled in Obuda, where they developed into a large, prosperous community under the protection of Countess Erzsebet Zichy, wife of the local Count Peter Zichy, on whose huge private estate Obuda was built. Here, Jews engaged in trade and commercial activities and developed into skilled craftsmen. Silversmiths from Obuda became particularly famous—in Obuda they were free to carry out this trade, unlike in other cities in the Hapsburg domains.

Jews were allowed to move back into Pest and Buda after the reforms introduced by Josef II in the 1780s. The Pest community was reestablished in 1787, and throughout the nineteenth century the Jewish population of the city grew rapidly.

In the nineteenth and twentieth centuries, following full Jewish emancipation in 1867, half of Hungary's Jews—over 100,000 in 1890 and more than 200,000, or more than twenty-three percent of the population, in 1910—lived in Budapest, and the community achieved great heights of cultural, professional, political, and commercial achievement.

Jews were a driving force behind Hungary's late nineteenth-century industrial boom. With their new freedoms, Jewish families—most based in Budapest—were able to build commercial and industrial empires in many fields: from railway construction to flour milling, from cement processing to sugar refining and textile and porcelain production. Before World War I, Jews comprised more than half of Budapest industrial managers. They were also bankers and financiers, journalists and publishers, doctors, merchants, lawyers, professors, and the like.

In recognition for their services, the Hapsburg rulers raised nearly 350 Jewish or once-Jewish families, most involved in commerce or industry, to the nobility in the seventy years before the outbreak of World War I. In his 1972 book, *Jewish Nobles and Geniuses in Modern Hungary,* historian William O. McCagg paints a fascinating picture of these early capitalists: families like the tobacco, sugar, and railway magnates, the Schossbergers; the Kohners, who started as poor traders and eventually became wealthy from real estate, oil, rail, flour, and other investments; and the Poppers, who built up a huge lumber industry.

Most of this capitalist elite, as well as most middle-class Hungarian Jews, turned to Neolog Judaism and assimilated into mainstream Hungarian culture. Several leaders of the Neolog congregation, including Zsigmond Schossberger, Zsigmond Kornfeld, and Karoly Svab, became barons or entered the Hungarian House of Lords around the turn of the century.

Budapest Jews also became active in the arts. Ede Telcs (1872–1948) was a popular sculptor famous for portrait busts and public monuments. Sculptors such as Fulop O. Beck, as well as noted architects, were influenced by art nouveau. The Jewish Hospital at Amerikai ut. 53 is a striking example of art nouveau architecture designed by Bela Lajta and built in 1910–1911.

The Nazis set up a large ghetto in Budapest in June of 1944, several months after they occupied Hungary and following the ghettoization and deportation of virtually all Jews living in the provinces. The city's 220,000 Jews were ordered into 2,000 houses, each marked with a yellow star, centered around Klauzal ter in the Pest neighborhood near the river, which then, as now, was the center for Jewish life. Conditions were very severe. In October, the Hungarian fascist Arrow Cross Party began carrying out an orchestrated program of anti-Jewish violence.

Preparations were being made for full-scale deportation of Budapest's Jews when Soviet troops reached the outskirts of the city in early November. Still, tens of thousands of Budapest Jews were forced into a death march toward the Austrian border. At the same time, within the city the Arrow Cross squads continued bloody attacks on the Jewish population; many people were shot to death and thrown into the Danube. The carnage only stopped when Soviet troops occupied the city on January 18, 1945. An estimated 120,000 Budapest Jews were saved.

Before World War II, Jews worshiped at some 125 synagogues and prayer rooms scattered around Budapest. Today, there are about a score of places where regular services are held. Several synagogues stand empty or are put to secular use.

Budapest Jews enjoy all the Jewish facilities and services of any major Jewish city in the West, and there has been a renaissance of Jewish life and cultural activities since the ouster of the communist regime. Given the importance of the Jewish community over the last 150 years, traditional Jewish dishes, like sholet (or cholent)—the traditional Shabbat dish of beans, barley, and meat cooked all Friday night in the warmth of a sealed oven—have become part of Hungarian cuisine. Canned sholet, kosher schnapps, and braided challah bread can be found in ordinary grocery stores all over the city, and sholet (including distinctly non-kosher sholet made with pork!) is a Saturday standby in many downtown restaurants.

Major Places of Jewish Interest in Budapest

• Medieval Synagogue: Tancsis utca 26

Excavations in the mid-1960s uncovered the remains of a Gothic synagogue here dating from the early to mid-fifteenth century. Surrounded by an apartment building in the Old Town of Buda, the synagogue was restored in 1966 to reveal its vaulting and frescoes and is now part of the Jewish Museum. Unfortunately, like the Jewish Museum itself, it is only open between May and October, but even when closed, much can be seen through the windows. In the entryway is a display of Jewish gravestones dating back to the thirteenth century.

Ruins of another fifteenth-century synagogue have been found nearby at number 23 of the same street.

• Main Old Jewish Neighborhood

Contemporary Jewish life in Budapest centers around the old Jewish section in Pest, a somewhat run-down district of nineteenth-century buildings not far from the Danube. Here, at Sip utca 12, are the busy offices of the Federation of Hungarian Jewish Communities, the Budapest Jewish community, and other Hungarian and international Jewish organizations, including the World Jewish Congress and the American Jewish Joint Distribution Committee.

In the surrounding streets are found several of the main synagogues, an Orthodox mikvah, the Jewish Museum, a striking Holocaust memorial, kosher restaurants, Jewish gift shops, a kosher sausage factory, kosher grocers, a kosher wine merchant, and three Jewish schools. Trendy little Jewish souvenir shops and even falafel bars have been springing up here, too.

English-speaking members of the community are generally available at the Sip utca offices and can give up-to-date information on the hours and location of services.

Visitors may purchase a *Luach*, or calendar booklet, that lists the addresses and phone numbers of all the more than twenty active synagogues

Budapest—A Holocaust memorial, erected in 1990, next to the Dohany utca Synagogue. In the shape of a weeping willow tree, it was designed in granite and steel by sculptor Imre Varga.

and five cemeteries in Budapest, main Jewish communities around the country, and kosher shops, schools, and other Jewish offices and facilities.

• Dohany utca Synagogue: Dohany utca

This immense, richly ornate, twin-towered synagogue was inaugurated in 1859 in the heart of the Jewish quarter of Pest. The Moorish-style design by Vienna architect Ludwig von Forster won a competition and eventually influenced the design of other Hungarian synagogues.

Budapest—The Dohany utca Synagogue, the largest in Europe, designed by Ludwig von Forster and inaugurated in 1859. The Jewish Museum is housed in the wing to the left, which was built in the 1920s as an extension of the synagogue and stands at the place where Zionist pioneer Theodore Herzl was born.

Seating about 3,000 people, it is the largest active synagogue in Europe today. A massive full-scale restoration of the synagogue, partly funded by the government, was begun in 1992.

The outer walls are of red brick, inlaid in decorative patterns and set off by ceramic trim. Inside, the sense of size is breathtaking, and the once-magnificent decor is striking. All attention is directed to the extremely elaborate Aron ha Kodesh and bimah, set off from the sanctuary by a wrought iron grille and backed by a mighty organ.

During the war, the synagogue was fenced off and it and its grounds were used as a concentration camp where Jews were massed before their deportation. In the synagogue courtyard, enclosed by arcades, are the mass graves of thousands of victims of the wartime Budapest Ghetto.

Next to the synagogue on Wesselenyi utca is the so-called Heroes Temple, a domed structure built between 1929 and 1931 in the same style as the synagogue as a memorial to the thousands of Jewish soldiers who died in World War I.

In a courtyard opening on the street alongside is a recently dedicated memorial to all Hungarian victims of the Holocaust in the form of a

weeping willow tree, designed in granite and steel by Hungarian sculptor
Imre Varga.

• Orthodox Synagogue: Kazinczy utca 27

Built in 1913, the Orthodox Synagogue is still in regular use, despite being
in poor repair. It's an interesting building with a flat, brick face set at an
angle to the narrow, crooked street.

Visitors may be (as I was) profoundly moved at the contrast between
the broken windows and shabbiness of the interior and the intensity of
the prayers during services.

The courtyard behind the synagogue was once a focus of bustling
community life and is still one of the best-preserved traditional Jewish
courtyards in Hungary. There are the foundations of an outdoor *Chuppah*
(wedding canopy) just behind the synagogue, and in the building to the
rear is a kosher restaurant, Hanna: a rough-and-ready place where you
can sit elbow to elbow with ancient rabbis in beards and sidelocks, eager
young students, furrow-browed intellectuals, classic chicken soup–sipping
"Yiddishe mammas," and foreign Jewish visitors.

• Rumbach utca Synagogue: Rumbach utca

Built between 1869 and 1872, the Rumbach utca Synagogue was one of the
first major projects by influential turn-of-the-century Vienna architect
Otto Wagner. Its flat, vaguely Moorish-style facade broken by tall, arched
windows and topped by two slim turrets resembling truncated minarets
opens through a vestibule into what was a striking octagonal sanctuary in
which metalwork was used both in structure and decoration. Each side of
the octagon featured a lofty, oriental-style arch supported by thin iron
columns over a raised gallery. Walls, doors, and other surfaces were covered with intricate, oriental-style floral and geometric designs.

The synagogue was empty and in extremely bad condition until
restoration work began in 1990. As of this writing, the new function for
the building had not yet been decided, but it was unlikely that it would
serve a Jewish purpose.

• Rabbinical Seminary: Jozsef Korut 27

Throughout the communist period, Budapest's Rabbinical Seminary
was the only Rabbinical Seminary in Eastern Europe. A famous seat of
Jewish scholarship since the turn of the century, the seminary includes a
priceless Jewish library of more than 150,000 volumes, many of them
centuries old.

• Obuda

In the Obuda section of town there is a handsome, neoclassical synagogue building designed by Andras Landherr and built in 1820 to 1821 at Lajos utca 163. Today, the building is owned by Hungarian television, and only the exterior, with its distinctive front porch supported by six Corinthian columns, remains as it was. The portico is still topped by the tablets of Moses, and a Hebrew inscription still runs across the front.

• Jewish Cemetery: Kozma utca

The vast main Jewish cemetery, where hundreds of thousands of Budapest Jews are buried, is an awe-inspiring testament to the size, vigor, and importance of the Budapest community before the war.

Near the huge ceremonial hall there are numerous ornate family tombs, many of them designed in the art nouveau style by leading turn-of-the-century architects, such as Odon Lechner, Bela Lajta, and Arthur Wellisch, who employed sinuous lines and brilliant mosaic decoration. Turquoise and gold gleam in the sun in evocative displays of opulence on such tombs as the Schmidl family mausoleum, built in 1903.

Most of the huge expanse of the cemetery, even where it is still used for interments, is overgrown with shrubs and weeds, but it is possible to wander for hours among the paths. Many of the tombstones are fine examples of nineteenth-century cemetery art; many are very sentimental, with somber sculptural detail, mournfully drooping floral motifs, sad portraits, and epitaphs carved as if in handwriting and incorporating pet names and sad farewells.

One section of the cemetery has been given over to a large Holocaust memorial. The names of thousands of Budapest Jews who died at the hands of the Nazis have been inscribed on walls surrounding a symbolic tomb. Poignantly, friends and relatives have written in by hand in pencil or ink the names of others whose names were somehow left out of the stone inscriptions.

• Jewish Museum: Dohany ut. 2, Tel. (1) 1428-949. Open May through October

The museum is situated right next to the Dohany utca Synagogue, in a building constructed between 1921 and 1931 as a new wing of the synagogue building itself, precisely at the site of the house where Zionist leader Theodore Herzl was born.

Unfortunately only open between May and October because of the lack of heating, the museum encompasses the whole sweep of Jewish history in Hungary in a collection of thousands of documents, photographs,

	1919	HELFER MIKLOS	1918
	1918	HOFFMANN GYÖRGY IMRE	1914
...RGY	1914	HOLLÓS GYULA	1911
...SZLÓ	1911	HOLLÄNDER TIBOR	1912
	1914	ISZÁK MÁRTON	1901
...S	1906	KALLÓS LÁSZLÓ	1908
...TVÁN	1897	KERTÉSZ SÁNDOR	1909
	1919	KOSÁLY ÖDÖN	1893
	1902	LANTOS SÁNDOR ÉS TIVADAR	
...Z.ROMÁN MÁRIA		LÖFFLER SÁNDOR	
	1901	LÖWY LÁSZLÓ	1920
...NOS	1910	MENYÁSZ ARTUR	1904
...NDOR	1902	PÁSZTOR ISTVÁN	1906
...VÁN ENDRE		PÁSZTOR PÁL	1902
		POLLÁK JÓZSEF	1912
	1913	PREISMANN GYÖRGY	1916
	1920	STERN MÁRTON	
...LÁSZLÓ	1920	BRÜLLER GYÖRGY	
...ÁNDOR		REISNER ÖDÖN	1904
...S	1905	SCHÖNFELD LÁSZLÓ	1916
...Ö	1905	SIMON VILMOS	1888
...DRÁS	1922	SIMON LÁSZLÓ	1918
...REICH MARGIT		SINGER FERENC	1889
...ZTÁV	1896	SPATZ LÁSZLÓ	1911
	1913	SPRINGER IZSÓ	1902
	1913	SUSCHNY JENŐ	1900
...OR	1904	SZÁSZ HUGÓ	1911
	1902	FODOR JÓZSEF	1895
...MANN PIROSKA	1912	DE SZÉKELY LÁSZLÓ	1901
...ZA		SZILASI BÉLA ÉS ENDRE	
	1912	TIBOR ISTVÁN	1909
...ÁN	1907	TOLCSINER SÁNDOR	1901
	1911	VAJDA GYÖRGY	1912
...STVÁN	1918	VÉG JÓZSEF	1913
...LORÁND		WEBER ANDOR	1917

Budapest—Close-up of the Holocaust monument in the main Jewish cemetery that lists the names of Budapest Jews who were known to have perished in the Holocaust. Here, survivors have written in by hand the names of people whose names were left out.

and relics of Judaica. The oldest exhibit is a Jewish tombstone dating from the third century found at Esztergom. It is incised with the picture of a menorah.

Collections include beautiful silver ritual objects, ceramics, richly embroidered textiles, illustrated manuscripts, and painting and sculptures by modern Jewish artists. (Unfortunately, many priceless objects were stolen in a burglary in 1993.) The historical section, which includes Holocaust material, is particularly interesting for its wealth of documents and photographs.

The museum grew out of a small Jewish exhibit prepared by the community for the great Millennial Exhibition staged by Hungary in 1896 to celebrate 1,000 years of the Hungarian state. Miksa Szabolcsi, editor of a weekly newspaper, suggested that the little Jewish exhibit should be kept together and expanded as a museum and urged Budapest Jews to contribute heirlooms and antiques to such a collection. The project got off the ground in 1910, and the museum was officially opened in 1916 in a small private apartment. It moved into its present premises in 1931.

• Wallenberg and Lutz Monuments

A sculptural monument to Raoul Wallenberg was dedicated in 1987 on Szilagyi Erzsebet Fasor in Buda, honoring the Swedish diplomat who saved thousands of Budapest Jews from the Holocaust by providing them with "Wallenberg passports"—Swedish certificates of protection. The memorial is in the form of a sculpture of Wallenberg placed between two massive stone walls.

Wallenberg was sent to Budapest by the Swedish Foreign Ministry in July 1944 with instructions to do what he could to help the Hungarian Jews who had survived the mass Nazi deportations that spring. The young diplomat became a legendary figure, issuing thousands of Swedish identity documents to Budapest Jews in order to protect them from Nazi deportation. Legations from other neutral states also issued such papers, and Wallenberg worked closely with Swiss consul Charles Lutz and representatives of the Portuguese and Spanish legations in setting up "protected" houses and a "protected" ghetto for the Jews with the foreign identity papers. These courageous men helped save more than 30,000 Jews.

Wallenberg, thirty-two, was last seen just after the Soviet army liberated the city on January 17, 1945; he was being driven toward the Soviet border under the escort of a Soviet officer. No one for sure knows his fate. The Soviets claimed he died soon after the war ended; other reports said he had been seen alive in a Soviet prison camp long afterward.

In 1991, a sculptural monument honoring Charles Lutz was dedicated near the Dohany utca Synagogue.

Elsewhere in Hungary

*Abony

Abony is a quiet town of 15,000 people about fifty miles southeast of Budapest. Jews first settled here in the mid-eighteenth century, and by 1851 more than 900 Jews, mostly engaged in trade and crafts, lived in the town. The Jewish population dwindled during the nineteenth century, and by World War II fewer than 500 Jews lived in Abony. Some 470 were deported to death camps by the Nazis; only 16 returned.

To my mind, the former synagogue here is one of the most moving Jewish relics in all Hungary; a physical symbol of loneliness and mourning that I found painful to look at. It is not the most ruined synagogue building in Hungary nor the most beautiful or most ravaged. Somehow, however, it reminds me of a living creature; a wounded animal, perhaps; an abandoned pet. It seems to feel and actually to mourn, as if it were alive.

The building, a beautifully pure, serenely classical structure in crumbling yellow and orange stucco with four Corinthian columns supporting a portico over the main entrance, dominates the immediate neighborhood. Built by architect Andras Landherr in 1825, today it is a warehouse, utterly gutted inside except for a few flaking fragments of frescoes on the ceiling high above.

Several other former Jewish buildings also still stand, including the former Jewish primary school, which still functions as a state school.

The cemetery, on Highway 4 en route to Szolnok, just outside town opposite the Christian cemetery, is just as forlorn as the synagogue; it is almost completely abandoned and suffocatingly overgrown with weeds and bushes.

*Apostag

In this out-of-the-way farming village of 2,300 people on the Danube about forty miles south of Budapest is one of the most beautifully restored of Hungary's former synagogues, an award-winning example of what can be done and a monument to community involvement in saving a valuable treasure from the past.

Jews probably lived in Apostag in the seventeenth century, but the major wave of Jewish settlement took place around 1760. Farmers, artisans, merchants, and scholars, the Jewish community amounted to 321 by 1851. In the latter part of the nineteenth century, the population dwindled after restrictions on where Jews could live were lifted and many Jews moved away to bigger cities.

By the outbreak of World War II, only 150 Jews still lived in the village. All were deported to death camps in 1944: Only six survived, none of whom settled again in the town.

The synagogue, a large, rectangular structure with a peaked roof whose simple exterior hides jewellike interior form and decoration, was built in 1822 to replace an earlier one that had burned down in 1820. Looted, ransacked, and seriously damaged during and after World War II, the abandoned building was considered a historic monument but was used as a warehouse.

By the early 1980s, its condition was so bad that local authorities wanted to pull it down. Peter Wirth, an architect and monuments preservation expert, was called to the scene and became convinced that the building must be saved. He recalls to this day how an elderly local peasant said he could still remember from his childhood, the "mysterious building with an ornamented ceiling, beautiful like the starry sky."

Wirth inspired village leaders with his own enthusiasm. In a rare example of such cooperation, local and county community members and officials pitched in on the total restoration, which eventually won an international award, the Europa Nostra Prize, in 1988—an award granted both to Wirth himself and to the entire village of Apostag "for the excellent restoration and appropriate cultural reuse of the fine neoclassical former synagogue."

Today, the synagogue, built around a Polish-style four-pillared central bimah, serves as a local library and culture center. The classical and late baroque ornamentation has been restored as closely as possible to what it was originally, including decorative stucco reliefs, frescoes, and the ornate Aron ha Kodesh surrounded by a beautifully conceived fresco of drawn-back curtains.

The space immediately outside the synagogue has been turned into a park, at the end of which is the overgrown cemetery that local residents hope to restore. There are also plans to erect a Holocaust monument and perhaps a small museum or Jewish exhibit. The library, housed in the women's gallery, already has a section on Judaica.

*Baja

Jewish Community: Sarkantyu utca 4

This charming town of 40,000 on the Danube about seventy miles south of Budapest provides another textbook example of the restoration and use of a former synagogue.

Jews settled here around 1725. Baja, with its beautiful, big central plaza right on the river, was a major stop along the Danube trade route and a vital commercial center. The Jewish community, many of its members involved in trade, grew rapidly throughout the nineteenth century. At its height, around 1910, the Jewish community of more than 2,000 made up nearly twenty percent of the local population.

The neoclassical synagogue, designed by architects Karoly Gerster and Lajos Frey and built in the mid-nineteenth century, was restored in 1985 virtually to its original appearance, maintaining all its Jewish character, including Stars of David rising from the peaked roof, a Hebrew inscription over the pillared entryway, and the ornate Aron ha Kodesh framed by a frescoed curtain, where three Torahs are kept to this day.

It is now used as the town library, but the reconstruction—which won the Hungarian Architects' Prize for Restoration—was carried out in such a sensitive way that the books seem to fit naturally into the setting.

The design also includes a large Holocaust memorial in the library garden: A corner, arched arcade protects wall inscriptions of the names of each of the approximately 3,000 Jews from Baja and surrounding communities who were deported to death camps and perished. Each year on May 28, the anniversary of the deportation, a memorial service is held in the synagogue.

At the end of 1990, only twelve Jews still lived in Baja. The community center is around the corner from the library on a street full of old Jewish houses. There is a prayer room but not enough men in town anymore for a minyan.

Ferenc Lichter, a sweet-faced man in his eighties and president of the community, invited me in to his nearby home for coffee. He talked proudly of his son, who had emigrated to Canada and become a civic leader in Nova Scotia.

Mr. Lichter came to guide me through the large Jewish cemetery, dating to about 1750. It is mostly overgrown, but there are plans to clean it and also to erect a small museum there concentrating on cemetery art.

"Look at this," Mr. Lichter said, beckoning me to follow. Inside the former ceremonial hall, now used as a workshop, was a century-old horse-drawn hearse. "This will be the main exhibit in the museum."

Bodrogkeresztur (Bodrogkeresztúr)

This small town, little more than a village, in the northeastern corner of Hungary near Tokaj was a renowned Hasidic center, and pilgrims still come to pay their respects at the tomb of Rebbe Saje Steiner (1851–1925) in the hilltop cemetery overlooking the town.

Jews moving south from Poland settled here in the early part of the eighteenth century. Later immigrants from Poland probably brought Hasidism with them; northeastern Hungary (along with former Hungarian territory now just over the border in Romania) is the only part of the country where Hasidism really took a deep hold.

Bodrogkeresztur is in wine-producing country and also is on a major north-south trade route. Jews took part in most areas of trade, including wine production and innkeeping, and also owned local quarries. No more than several hundred Jews ever lived in the town, but by the time of the deportations in 1944, they made up about twenty percent of the local population.

There is a barnlike former synagogue, built in 1906, on Kossuth utca; today it is used as a school sports hall.

The main place of Jewish interest is the hilltop cemetery. It can be seen high above the town from down below, but it is difficult to reach on rainy days due to the muddy road. Along with Steiner's tomb, there are some very fine old tombstones carved with folkloric designs.

Steiner's house, at Kossuth utca 65, may also be visited. Here, visitors may leave a donation for the proposed paving of the road to the cemetery and the creation of a little museum.

*Bonyhad (Bonyhád)

This small, rather nondescript town of 15,000 people lies in southern Hungary about seventy miles south of Budapest.

Jews, mainly from Germany, were invited to settle here in the mid-eighteenth century by the local landowners, the Perczel family, who granted them protection and encouraged them to carry out trade and commerce. The Perczel mansion still stands in the town.

The Jewish community grew quickly, and by 1851 more than 1,500 Jews lived in the town. The more than 1,000 Jews living here before World War II represented about fifteen percent of the local population.

The synagogue, built in 1795 after a devastating fire destroyed the Jewish quarter and earlier synagogue, now serves as a warehouse. It is a simple, early neoclassical building with a peaked roof, one of the few Hungarian synagogues—like those in Mad or Apostag—built around a Polish-style four-pillared central bimah.

Some important features of the interior decor remain, including the bimah and the Aron ha Kodesh, which is framed by columns and the faded fresco of a drawn-back curtain. There are traces of delicate frescoes on the vaulted ceiling.

The synagogue stands in the evocative remains of the old Jewish quarter on Martirok tere. The former yeshiva building, its exterior in poor condition, is still used as a state school. Nearby, on a side street on the other side of Rakoczi utca, another synagogue, built in 1924, has been totally rebuilt into a modern-looking warehouse; all traces of Jewish origin have been removed.

There are two adjacent cemeteries, a well-maintained one for the Orthodox community and a totally overgrown and almost impenetrable one for the Neolog (Reform) community, both entered down a lane alongside the eye-catching art nouveau high school on Kossuth utca.

I found the Orthodox cemetery a rather amazing and somewhat uncomfortable sight. The elderly peasant couple who live on the edge of the cemetery grounds and maintain the graveyard have taken such meticulous care that the ground between the mazzevahs looks as if it had been shaved. Many of the tombstones themselves are of bright pink marble, and some have their inscriptions emphasized in black paint. This House of the Living seemed rather dehumanized. (But then again I also feel uncomfortable in the homes of people who keep everything squeaky clean and rigorously in place.)

Debrecen

Jewish Community: Bajcsy-Zsilinszky utca 26. Tel. (52) 315-861

Kosher Restaurant: Bajcsy-Zsilinszky utca 26

Founded in the fourteenth century and today boasting a population of more than 210,000 people, this city in eastern Hungary is important as an economic, cultural, and university center as well as the centuries-old stronghold of Hungarian Protestantism—it was long known, in fact, as the Calvinist Rome. Jews were only allowed to settle here after 1840, when a decree permitted Jews to live in royal towns, but from the mid-nineteenth century on it was a major center of Jewish life. Today it still is one of the most important Hungarian Jewish communities outside Budapest, with several hundred, mostly elderly, Jews in the city.

More than 10,000 Jews lived here before the war, worshiping in several important synagogues as well as numerous tiny Hasidic study houses scattered throughout the Jewish quarter in the heart of town, not far from Calvin Square with its imposing Calvinist church.

During the war, many young Jews were deported to labor camps in the Ukraine, and in May 1944 the Nazis rounded up Jews from the surrounding area and herded them into the Debrecen Ghetto. In two days in late June of that year, some 7,500 were deported to Auschwitz.

Today, only two synagogues remain in regular operation. Both are in the old Jewish quarter, between Simonffy utca and Hatvan utca.

The small Orthodox synagogue on Pasti utca has a simple interior and an austere brick and stucco facade marked by three massive arched doorways and a decorative false arcade along its peak. Built in 1913, it is in good overall repair but shows neglect. From outside, a tantalizing hoard of dusty, deteriorating books can be seen through the upper-story windows.

Half a block away in a peaceful, shady garden, the Kapolnas utca or Status Quo (Reform) synagogue, built in 1909, also is in regular use. The low, cream-colored stone building with two decorative arches over three central doors is in fairly good repair. Elderly congregation members who attend noon services usually go together afterward for a meal at the kosher canteen in the community offices around the corner at 26 Bajcsy-Zsilinszky utca. (A young, English-speaking rabbi took up the post here in late 1992.)

"We *daven* [pray] every day, but it is often difficult to get a minyan," said Ludwig, an elderly member of the congregation who lives in a spacious apartment in the Jewish quarter. The high-ceilinged rooms were crammed with heavy wooden furniture; framed paintings, many darkened by time, covered the walls. A piano stood in one corner, and a violin, closed in its case, rested on a sideboard.

Ludwig was eager to welcome unexpected Jewish visitors and, in a mixture of Yiddish and German, talked about his life.

"I'm all alone now," he said. He gestured to framed photographs displayed on a cabinet, first pointing to a black-and-white portrait of a stern-faced man with a long gray beard. "This was my grandfather, a famous rabbi."

He showed another picture, that of an attractive young woman. "This was my sister. She died in Auschwitz." Ludwig held up his fingers—one, two, three, four—his family members who died along with his sister. On the wall was a picture of a magnificent, twin-towered synagogue. That, too, has vanished.

Gyor (Győr)

Jewish Community: Buda utca 28. Tel. (96) 16217

This historic city of 127,000 people halfway between Budapest and Vienna is called "the city of four rivers," as it lies at the point where the Marcal, the Raba, and the Rabca rivers join with the Mosoni Duna (Little Danube), a tributary of the Danube River a few miles from where the Danube forms the border between Hungary and Slovakia. The city has many baroque buildings and other monuments in its picturesque Old Town.

There has been a Jewish presence here since at least the late fourteenth century, and probably earlier. For centuries, though, local laws forced the Jewish community to be isolated on an island in the river near town, and only after reform laws were passed in the mid-nineteenth century were Jews permitted to settle within the city limits. On the eve of World War II, the city had a Jewish population of more than 7,000, all of whom were deported to Nazi death camps in 1944. Less than 100 Jews live in the town today.

Driving in from Vienna, just before you enter town, there is a good view to the left of the big gray dome of the synagogue on Kossuth utca. The building, designed in 1866 by Karoly Benko, has a striking, rather oriental design, with a large central dome surrounded by four squat domed-topped towers. There is some lovely, intricate decorative stonework on the exterior.

The octagon-shaped sanctuary under the lofty dome is empty and in poor condition, but some of the elaborate detailed interior decoration is still visible, including tiers of galleries, frescoes, and a bimah with a distinct Middle Eastern flavor.

Though the synagogue, sold by the community in 1969, has been left abandoned, the former Jewish school and community buildings attached to it have been restored and are in use as a public school. I found the contrast between the dilapidated grandeur of the massive synagogue and the busy modernity of the school disquieting.

*Janoshalma (Jánoshalma)

Time almost seems to have stood still in this small farming town, little more than a village, about seventy miles south of Budapest.

Jews settled here in the eighteenth century, and the community never amounted to more than a few hundred.

The peeling little yellow synagogue, built in the mid-nineteenth century and rebuilt in 1920, sits inside a walled courtyard at the corner of Rakoczi utca and Petofi utca, giving the impression of having stood empty and untouched, like a time capsule, since the end of the war. It is, in fact, important for historians as one of the few remaining village synagogues in Hungary where interior and exterior are fully intact.

Inside, the simple interior furnishings are in good condition but are neglected and dusty, as if when the Jews were deported everything else simply remained to decay, like meals left half-eaten on the kitchen table in a mystery story where a family has disappeared without a trace. There is a pile of ancient books in one corner, and on the bimah I found brittle palm fronds (*lulav*) left from the Sukkoth holiday—the Sukkoth just past or a Sukkoth from years ago? A small paperback exercise book on the bimah serves as a guest book; from time to time someone has signed the flimsy pages. Most visitors were former Hungarian Jews now living in Israel.

Outside, the walled courtyard has been given over to plots of Brussels sprouts and other vegetables planted by the families now living in what used to be Jewish community buildings. On the outer wall of the synagogue is a large monument listing the names of local Holocaust victims, about 300 people.

The small cemetery outside town off Jozsef Attila utca gives the same impression as the synagogue: It is fenced and isolated in the middle of fields far off the road, as if in a slightly different dimension.

Kecskemet (Kecskemét)

The pleasant center of this otherwise rather ugly agricultural and market city of 100,000 people fifty miles southeast of Budapest contains some extraordinary examples of Hungary's fanciful turn-of-the-century art nouveau architecture.

Many of these colorful buildings are centered around the tree-shaded main square, one of whose landmarks is also a big Moorish-Romantic former synagogue painted gleaming white and topped by a distinctive lotus bud–shaped dome on its central tower, which was designed by the ubiquitous Lipot Baumhorn to replace the original round dome after it was dislodged in a major earthquake in 1911.

Designed by architect Janos Zitterbarth and built in 1864 to 1871, the synagogue was transformed into the national headquarters of the Union of Technical and Natural Science Associations in 1974. Almost nothing is left of the once sumptuous interior. Instead, there are lecture halls, a conference center, a bar/cafe, and a gallery housing copies of sculpture by Michelangelo.

Jews were barred from living here until the end of the eighteenth century. The first community was formally established in 1801, and the first synagogue was built in 1818—it is a neoclassical building that still stands in a courtyard area directly behind the big white synagogue on the square. Only part of the old synagogue's facade has survived intact; the building is now used as a food-processing center. A third synagogue, dating from the early twentieth century, also still stands on Katona Jozsef ter. It has recently been turned into a photography museum.

About 2,000 Jews lived in Kecskemet before World War II; they were all deported to Nazi death camps in 1944. Only a handful of elderly Jews live in the town today.

The well-cared-for Jewish cemetery, dominated by a large Moorish-style ceremonial hall, is right on the edge of town on the main road to Budapest.

Keszthely

A resort town of 22,000 people at the southwest end of Lake Balaton, Keszthely has a fine collection of eighteenth- and nineteenth-century buildings—foremost of which is the magnificent mansion of the Festetics family, the noble landowners who owned the town from the beginning of the eighteenth century until 1945.

Jews settled here in the eighteenth century. They obtained special permission to settle on the main street of town (now called Kossuth Lajos utca) in 1810 and established a complex of Jewish buildings that remains to this day.

The neoclassical synagogue, built in 1852, is at the end of a deep, tree-shaded courtyard lined with arcaded baroque buildings, painted bright yellow, that have been restored to pristine condition. Above the entrance to the courtyard, at Kossuth utca 22, is a plaque to Jewish composer Karoly Goldmark, a cantor's son, who was born here in 1830. Goldmark, who died in 1915, is most famous for his opera *The Queen of Sheba*.

Still owned by the Jewish community—a few Jews still live in town and have a community office and prayer room in one of the other buildings of the courtyard—the synagogue, with a flat facade marked by three tall arched windows behind a decorative railing, is in good condition. Its delicate interior decoration, including a large chandelier, wall paintings, and ritual objects, also is well maintained.

In front of it is a black obelisk memorial to the 829 local Jews deported and killed in the Holocaust.

Kiskunhalas

Jewish Community: Petofi utca 1

Near the center of this lace-making town of 31,000 in southern Hungary is a well-restored and -maintained synagogue, painted white, that backs onto downtown Petofi utca but faces into a walled, gated garden.

Built in 1858, the synagogue, with its high, deep porch and a charming but rather austere interior, is one of the few provincial synagogues still in use by the small local Jewish community. It and the other buildings enclosed in the grassy garden form a traditional courtyard around which Jewish life in the town once flourished.

Jews settled here in the late eighteenth century and established a formal community in 1826. About 700 Jews lived here in the prewar decades of this century. On an outer wall of the synagogue is a memorial plaque to the hundreds of community members deported and killed in 1944.

*Kisvarda (Kisvárda)

The ruins of a huge castle built in the fifteenth/sixteenth centuries as a defense against the Turks dominate this town of 16,000 people in the far northeast corner of Hungary. One of the most imposing, more modern buildings is the large, rectangular, yellow brick former synagogue, built in 1901, which today serves as a local museum—one of the rare local museums that actually has an exhibition of local Judaica, including many old photographs.

Jews settled in Kisvarda in the eighteenth century with the permission of the great local landlords, the Esterhazy family. At that time, the town was a major marketplace on important international trade routes. By 1784, there were 118 Jews in the town. By 1941, Jews numbered 3,770 and made up twenty-five percent of the local population. All were deported to Nazi death camps; only about 800 survived, and by the late 1980s only a tiny handful of elderly Jews lived in the town.

In converting the synagogue into a museum, much of the original interior decoration was lost, but it still retains some of the original synagogue decoration, including a multicolored painted gallery and some detailed, very delicate ceiling frescoes as well as stained glass windows in the Star of David motif and wrought iron gates in the form of a menorah. Inside the entryway is a large Holocaust memorial listing the names of all the local victims of the Nazi deportations.

Next door is a small prayer house, which though closed tight and not used for years, was at least until the late 1980s still furnished with books and ritual objects, including piles of prayer shawls and tefillin once used in the large synagogue.

A large, well-maintained Jewish cemetery with many tall gravestones in pink marble is located near the town's Christian cemetery.

*Koszeg (Kőszeg)

This enchanting little town of 14,000 people on the border with Austria is nestled in the foothills of the Austrian Alps and has one of the best preserved complexes of medieval and baroque buildings in Hungary. The abandoned, nineteenth-century synagogue, too, is one of the most beautiful in the country.

Jews originally settled here in the Middle Ages, having been granted permission to live in the town by King Sigismund in 1395. The community suffered various persecutions and expulsions over the years, and Jews did not return to establish a permanent settlement until the eighteenth century. Two Jewish families lived in Koszeg in 1788, and the Jewish population never amounted to more than 300.

The synagogue, built in 1859, is a charming, beautifully proportioned building that remains a particularly evocative monument both to the vanished local Jewish community and the optimistic future that seemed open to Hungarian Jews in the nineteenth century.

The red brick building, with twin ramparted towers protecting a low, flat dome, is set back from the street in a long, narrow yard and is flanked by buildings constructed at the same time as part of a Jewish complex. On one side was the Jewish school, on the other, the home of the *shammas*, or sexton. (Ring the bell at the gate at Varkor utca 38 for entry.)

Construction of the complex was financed by Philip Schey, a wealthy Jewish philanthropist born in 1798 who had grown rich as a textile merchant during the Napoleonic Wars and later became a banker for the Hapsburgs. In 1859, Emperor Franz Josef raised him to the Hungarian nobility—he was the first Jew to receive this honor and took the title Philip Schey von Koromla.

Schey carried out many good works, particularly in the field of education. In the Romanian city of Satu Mare (once part of Hungarian Transylvania), I was presented by Jewish community leaders with a Hebrew book printed in Vienna in 1886. A full printed page in the front of the book noted that it had been published in Schey's memory.

The Koszeg synagogue has stood empty for years. Both the exterior and interior are very haunting and ghostly. Structurally the synagogue is in good condition; inside, the emptiness and dilapidation create an indefinable spiritual atmosphere.

The recessed Aron ha Kodesh is surmounted by a huge, filagreelike wrought iron Star of David; the bimah is set off by a delicate wrought iron grille; and the graceful women's gallery, set on slim iron pillars, encircles three-quarters of the sanctuary. A few stained glass panels remain in windows. Walls and the domed ceiling bear traces of delicate frescoes—some of them resembling Watteau landscapes. On the inside of the cupola, the following legend is written in German in fancy script: *"Zur Ehre Gottes erbaut von Philip Schey von Koromla"*—For the Honor of God, this was built by Philip Schey von Koromla.

Outside, there is a plaque placed in 1988 in memory of local Jews who died in the Holocaust.

The small, walled cemetery is on Temeto utca (Cemetery Street), and the key is available at the Catholic cemetery down the road. Near the entrance there is a memorial to 2,000 Jews from Koszeg and nearby villages deported by the Nazis. The cemetery is very overgrown, with many big trees, and much of it is impenetrable.

*Mad (Mád)

In this quaint (and in the rainy season muddy) little wine-producing village in the stunning hills of northeast Hungary near Tokaj is one of Hungary's Jewish treasures, an impressive baroque synagogue, built in 1795, that stands next to the unique, arcaded, L-shaped former Jewish school and rabbi's house, forming one of the best preserved complexes of Jewish buildings in Hungary.

Jews from Poland settled here in the early eighteenth century and became very active in the wine industry and trade. There was also a famous yeshiva. At its height, the Jewish community numbered about 800. All Jews in the village were deported to Nazi death camps in 1944.

The synagogue, a big, white-painted building atop a hill, dominates the former Jewish quarter. In fact, it and the two Christian churches, built at around the same time, dominate the entire village and illustrate the former religious balance.

The synagogue, one of the few in Hungary constructed around the Polish-style four-pillar central bimah, is kept locked, but a neighbor living in the left-hand house at the bottom of the lane leading up to the synagogue has the key. Much of the important interior decoration is intact, if in poor condition. There are some fascinating detailed carvings, particularly around the Aron ha Kodesh, as well as the remains of some lovely

Mad—This splendid baroque synagogue was built in 1795. It dominates the former Jewish section of this wine-making village in northeast Hungary. Much of the interior decoration, including the Polish-style four-pillar bimah, remains intact but in need of repair.

frescoes. There is also a memorial plaque listing the hundreds of Jews from Mad who died in Nazi camps.

Mad also has an extremely interesting old cemetery on a hillside outside town surrounding the ruins of a fortresslike ceremonial hall topped by battlements. The gravestones feature some exceptionally fine carving, and some are still highlighted by traces of polychrome decoration.

The view of the cemetery from the street is impressive—but don't fail to get the key from the jolly old peasant woman next door so you can look more closely at the carved tombs.

Mateszalka (Mátészalka)

This town of 20,000 people in the far northeast corner of Hungary near the Ukrainian and Romanian borders is very strange. It seems to have no center, no heart; it is almost completely a confusing assembly of modern construction of all types.

Jews were invited to settle here by the local landowners, the Karoly family, in the eighteenth century. In 1753, there were ten Jewish families, but by the early decades of this century there were well over 1,000 Jews in town. Their numbers were further swollen by a big wave of immigrants from Poland in the 1930s. A very few Jews live in the town today.

The synagogue is on Kossuth utca, one of the few streets to have escaped total rebuilding. Built in about 1857, the synagogue is in fairly good condition and most of its interior furnishings and decoration are still intact. This includes pews, decorative pillars, the Aron ha Kodesh, the women's gallery with fine grillwork, and very fine, elaborate ceiling frescoes.

Virtually all the rest of the once extensive Jewish quarter—the hometown of the father of actor Tony Curtis—has been destroyed.

Not far away from the synagogue is the walled Jewish cemetery. Parts of it are farmed, but the remaining tombstones, including an older section of pink marble mazzevahs, are well maintained.

Miskolc

Jewish Community: Kazinczy utca 7. Tel. (46) 315-276; 44884

Kosher Restaurant: Kazinczy utca 7

With a population of over 211,000, Miskolc is Hungary's main center of heavy industry and is undergoing difficult economic changes. It lies in the northeast of the country on the Szinva River at the foot of the Bukk Hills.

Miskolc is also an important commercial and transport center; Jews, mainly merchants and other people involved in trade, settled here in the eighteenth century. Jews eventually made up about twenty percent of the population. They were known among other things for the excellent Jewish educational system, which included three yeshivas, elementary and secondary schools, and a women's teacher-training college. The first Hungarian Jewish commercial school was established here, too.

As the community grew during the nineteenth century, it was bitterly split, like major Jewish communities all over Hungary, by the conflict between Orthodox and Reformed Judaism. The decision to build a choir loft in the synagogue, for example, touched off a furious reaction in the tradition-minded Orthodox community. As elsewhere, Miskolc Jews eventually split into two separate communities.

Some 10,500 to 12,000 Jews lived here on the eve of World War II; many were sent to forced labor camps. The rest were deported to Auschwitz; only 105 returned from the Nazi deportations, but the community swelled to more than 2,000 after the war's end when Miskolc became a center for Jews returning from concentration camps. Today, the 400 Jews in Miskolc make up one of the most lively Jewish communities outside of Budapest.

Though in some disrepair, the synagogue at Kazinczy utca 7 is still used by the community, whose offices (and a kosher restaurant) are at the same address. There is also a kosher butcher shop and a Talmud Torah class: Meeting just one afternoon a week, it is a pale shadow of the once famous Jewish educational system.

The synagogue was built between 1856 and 1863 to a design by Ludwig von Forster, the same architect who designed the Dohany utca Synagogue in Budapest. The outside is rather austere, but the inside decoration is marked by graceful thin columns supporting lovely vaulting, and walls and ceiling are completely covered by very busy, Moorish-style geometric designs.

The overgrown cemetery, founded in 1759, sprawls over Avas Hill above the city and has beautifully carved tombstones. The extraordinary view overlooks a vast expanse of pollution-belching industry.

*Nagykanizsa

Jewish Community: Lenin utca 6. Tel. (93) 311-425

This rather drab commercial city of 55,000 in southwest Hungary near the border with Croatia is a center of transport, trade, and the oil industry. Jews were invited to settle here in the early eighteenth century by the local landowning nobility, the powerful Batthyany family, whose former palace is now a town museum.

There is a big, early nineteenth-century neoclassical synagogue inside a Jewish courtyard off Lenin utca (a street name sure to be changed) through a gate marked by a Star of David. The beautifully restored, arcaded courtyard next door used to be filled with Jewish-owned shops. The building that once served as a Jewish middle school is behind the synagogue.

During the war, the Nazis used the synagogue as a stable. At the door today, there is an obelisk to the 3,000 local Jews deported to Auschwitz in 1944; 2,700 of these deportees perished. There is also a monument to Jewish soldiers who died in World War I.

The synagogue is no longer used and serves now as a storeroom for furniture, old pictures, and other dusty bits and pieces. Its interior is largely intact, however, with much of the furnishings—including pews and the gilded wooden Aron ha Kodesh—in place. Decoration includes false marble, remains of gilding on the two-level gallery, and a deep blue arched and domed ceiling studded with gold stars.

The Nagykanizsa community, under the influence of pioneering re-
formist Rabbi Lipot Loew, who served the community between 1841 and
1846, was one of the early adherents of the Hungarian Jewish Reform
movement. The synagogue in 1845 became the first in Hungary to have an
organ, and it also had a choir—both unknown in Orthodox congregations.

"When you see this you want to cry; it used to be so beautiful," said
a woman from the local Jewish community, whose offices are in the same
courtyard. "Here there was a wonderful Jewish community," she recalled.
"I was sixteen when I came back from Auschwitz. I was in the first transport. I was the youngest member of the community when I returned." She
rolled up the sleeve of her beautifully tailored leather jacket to show the
number on her arm. "How many Jews are here today? It's hard to say—
very few. My daughter is married to a non-Jew. She has two daugh-
ters . . . what are they?"

The labyrinth of rooms used by the Jewish community includes a
small prayer room for weekly services and a larger prayer room, with lovingly cared for Torahs, for use on the holidays.

There is a large, walled, tree-shaded cemetery outside town where
there is an Auschwitz memorial, numerous somber black marble obelisks,
and many sentimental nineteenth-century tombs featuring mournful
carved figures and floral motifs. Ivy trails among the graves. The big,
neoclassical ceremonial hall is crumbling amid the ivy and is now used as
a woodworking shop.

*Olaszliszka

A wine-producing village of about 2,000 people in the hilly northeast corner of Hungary near Tokaj, Olaszliszka was one of the most important centers of Hasidism in Hungary.

Like many villages in the area, the town was settled in the eighteenth century by Polish Jews who became active in wine production and
trade. Originally, the wine business had been in the hands of Italians—in
Hungarian, Olasz means Italian—who were brought in to settle here because of their wine expertise in the thirteenth century. No more than
about 400 Jews ever lived in the village.

The synagogue was built in the mid-nineteenth century under the
Hasidic tzaddik Zvi Hirsch Friedmann (1808–1874), a disciple of the great
Moses Teitelbaum of nearby Satoraljaujhely, who brought the Hasidic way
of life to the town.

It was a comparatively large building in order to accommodate the
rebbe's followers, who would flock to Olaszliszka to pray with him. Today
it is a total ruin: just one remaining wall with a couple of vacant windows
standing alone in a debris-strewn lot in the middle of the village. Every

Olaszliszka—The one remaining wall of the ruined synagogue in the village of Olaszliszka. At the center is the niche for the Ark.

time I see it, it has crumbled further. Hungarian filmmaker Andras Jancso made a very moving short documentary about the ruin.

Friedmann was an ascetic man; he refused all but a token salary of one florin a week. Like many tzaddikim—intense spiritual leaders whose followers regard them as holy men with sometimes miraculous powers and a direct channel to God—he incorporated symbolic actions in everyday life. For example, the last stone was never laid in the synagogue building in order to recall the destruction of the temple in Jerusalem by symbolizing that the local synagogue, too, was not complete. He also had his own house constructed without a foundation to symbolize the temporary character of the Jewish Diaspora in Hungary.

Friedmann is buried in the local Jewish cemetery, one of the most fascinating in Hungary. Hasidic followers from Israel have constructed an ohel for his tomb and have surrounded the cemetery with a tall, fortresslike wall topped with barbed wire. (The key is kept by a neighbor.)

Inside, besides the tomb of the tzaddik, are old, very weathered, but beautifully carved tombstones, many of which are rare examples of mazzevahs still retaining traces of brilliant red and blue polychrome decoration.

Oroshaza (Orosháza)

This town of 36,000 in the southeast corner of Hungary, a center of the food-processing industry, has a small synagogue, flush against the road

leading out of town to the northeast, with a simple, flat white facade surmounted by two slender towers topped by bulbous metal cupolas. The
door and two front windows are decorated with Moorish-style arches.

If the side fence is open, you can walk back behind to take a look at the
interior. The synagogue is used as a warehouse for kitchen appliances; its
ground floor is filled with boxes containing refrigerators and washers, all
stacked neatly amid the decorative pillars, which hark back to earlier days.

Unlike most other synagogues used as warehouses, however, a false
ceiling has protected the upper part of the building, which you can see
from outside through the upstairs windows. The barrel-vaulted upper
floor seems intact, its frescoed ceilings still bright and its big chandeliers
still hanging, as if waiting somehow to be lighted.

Jews from western Hungary settled here in the eighteenth century,
and a formal Jewish community was established in 1830. Most of the Jewish population prospered as merchants. About 800 Jews lived in the town
before World War II; all were deported to death camps.

The Jewish primary school, opened in 1850, still stands near the
synagogue building. It is used as a music school today, and local officials
hope to eventually restore the synagogue as a concert and exhibition hall
attached to the school.

Papa (Pápa)

This industrial and commercial town of 34,000 in western Hungary, about
twenty miles south of Gyor, was almost totally rebuilt in the eighteenth century and retains the appearance of a typical baroque Hungarian settlement.

Jews were granted special rights to settle here in the early eighteenth century by the local landowning noble family, the Esterhazys, who
issued a declaration guaranteeing them the right to sell kosher wine, set
up kosher butcher shops, and so on. The town soon grew to be an important Jewish center and the site of one of Hungary's most noted yeshivas.
Jews averaged around twenty percent of the local population. Already by
1851 there were nearly 3,000 Jews in the town, and about 2,500 Jews lived
here on the eve of World War II; more than ninety percent of them perished in the Holocaust.

One of the main influences on the community was Rabbi Lipot Loew,
one of the earliest proponents of the Reform movement in Hungarian Judaism, who served here from 1846 to 1850. (See Szeged.) He lay the
groundwork for a strong Reformed community, which—as in many Hungarian cities—faced bitter opposition by Orthodox Jews during the religious conflicts leading to the Jewish schism of 1869.

From 1837 to 1839, Jewish potter Mor Fischer rented a pottery in Papa
from which at least two very fine, hand-painted earthenware seder plates
remain, both in the collection of the Budapest Jewish Museum. Fischer

went on from Papa to found a full-scale porcelain factory in the nearby village of Herend that became one of the most famous in East-Central Europe.

The synagogue, on Petofi utca, was built in 1845 and reflects Reform practices. It is a big, barnlike building whose simple exterior conceals very striking, if damaged, interior decoration and design incorporating graceful arched galleries and a big rose window over the Aron ha Kodesh. The bimah was situated in front of the Aron ha Kodesh rather than in the middle of the room, as in Orthodox synagogues. Also, space was left in the synagogue for an organ—although one was never installed.

The synagogue looms up over old, low houses and other buildings once part of the old Jewish quarter. It was here that anti-Semitic riots took place at the time of the infamous blood libel case in the eastern Hungarian town of Tiszaeszlar in 1882.

Pecs (Pécs)

Jewish Community: Furdo utca 1. Tel. (72) 315-881

This ancient and important city of 175,000 people lying below forested hills in southern Hungary has numerous museums and the most important relics of the Turkish occupation in Hungary, including two former mosques.

Jews originally settled here during Turkish rule in the early seventeenth century, but in 1692, after the Turks withdrew, they were expelled and the citizens of Pecs ceremoniously swore that no Jews would ever be allowed to live within the walls of the town. This prohibition prevented Jewish settlement for about a century, but by 1841 there were at least thirty Jews living in Pecs. The community prospered and grew quickly after many restrictions on Jewish life were lifted in the mid-nineteenth century, and by 1910 there were more than 4,000 Jews in the town. Nearly 3,500 Jews lived in Pecs before World War II. All were deported to Auschwitz; 700 returned. Today, only about 100, mostly elderly, Jews live in the town.

The synagogue on downtown Kossuth ter, designed by architects Karoly Gerster and Lajos Frey, was built between 1866 and 1869. Still used on holidays by the tiny community, it is a large building featuring tall arched windows and a high, arched central section topped by the tablets of Moses.

Inside, the two tiers of side galleries have beautifully decorated ceilings, and there is a wealth of other intricate decorative elements used throughout.

Satoraljaujhely (Sátoraljaújhely)

Jews settled in this town of 21,000 bordering Slovakia in northeast Hungary in the early eighteenth century. As home to the nineteenth-century tzaddik Moses Teitelbaum, the town was a major Hasidic center. More than 4,000 Jews lived here before World War II. At the end of 1992, there were only seven, all of them elderly.

The town was divided between Hungary and Czechoslovakia after World War I, with most of the urban center remaining in Hungary. There is a former synagogue, built in 1886, at Dozsa Gyorgy utca 13. One old synagogue, however, remained on the Czechoslovak side in what is now the Slovakian town of Slovenske Nove Mesto.

The site of the old Jewish cemetery, near the town center, has been turned into a shrine centered on the elaborate ohel of Reb Teitelbaum (1751–1841), founder of an influential dynasty of Hasidic tzaddikim. (There is also a later Jewish cemetery next to the Christian cemetery on the road leading to the border crossing.) Teitelbaum's followers have built a big domed structure over the entrance to the tomb; in the rest of the cemetery, surrounded by an iron and concrete fence, the extremely weathered old tombstones stand in a barren stone and pebble base.

I wanted to visit the tomb, and a workman from a building site next door helped me find Mrs. Rozsika Roth, who at that time kept the key. Mrs. Roth was an elderly, obviously once beautiful woman and mainstay of the few remaining Jews in town. Every doorpost of her stuffy, rambling, rather run-down apartment had a mezuzah on it: She kissed the one on the outer door repeatedly whenever she left the house.

A Holocaust survivor who lost all her family to the Nazis, she lived within the remnants of a lost Jewish world: Pictures of famous tzaddikim were lined up on her dressing table; candlesticks stood on shelves; her refrigerator was full of kosher meat brought by the ritual slaughterer who made his rounds twice a month.

"Are you married?" was the first thing she asked me, in Yiddish. "Do you maintain *Yiddishkeit?*"

People, several of them Jews looking older than she, streamed into her kitchen for a glass of juice from a pitcher that seemed always full. She instructed one man to clean my muddy boots, then instructed me exactly how much to give him as a tip—in dollars, of course, not forints. In one of her rooms she kept piles and piles of her beautiful hand-embroidered Hungarian folk designs. Won't you buy something, she asked—more of an order than a question. Of course I did, voluntarily falling victim to the moral blackmail of this fervent little pocket of old-world Judaism. Next time I come to town, she said, I must sleep on her sofa.

*Sopron

Jewish Community: Szinhaz utca 4. Tel. (99) 313-558

An extremely beautiful, ancient town of quaint medieval and baroque buildings, Sopron, with 56,000 people, lies amid rolling hills almost on the Austrian border.

Sopron—The medieval synagogue on Uj utca in the heart of the picturesque Old Town of Sopron on the Austrian border. Uj utca once was called Jewish Street. The synagogue dates to around 1300 and today is a museum. Jews lived here in early medieval times but were expelled in 1526.

Jews lived here from early medieval times until they were expelled in 1526. They returned in the eighteenth century, and nearly 2,000 Jews lived in the town on the eve of World War II. All were deported to Nazi death camps; there is a small, elderly community in the town today.

Uj utca (New Street), in the heart of the picturesque, horseshoe-shaped Old Town, was called Jewish Street until the fifteenth century and here, facing each other across the narrow street, are the two oldest synagogues known in Hungary, both discovered within the past forty years. An ancient mikvah also has been uncovered and restored.

At Number 11 is the "New" Synagogue, dating from about 1350. At Number 22 is the Old Synagogue, from the year 1300 or earlier, a splendid Gothic building that is a Jewish Museum. Both ancient synagogues have simple interiors, thick walls, ribbed Gothic vaulted ceilings, and an Aron ha Kodesh formed by a deep niche in the wall reached by a short flight of steps. At Number 22, a carved stone border sets off the Ark.

Other than the ones in Budapest, these are the only two medieval synagogues to have been discovered in Hungary, and some historians believe they were private, family prayer rooms rather than synagogues open to the general public.

In addition to these ancient synagogues—forgotten for centuries— an abandoned, red brick synagogue with a central dome, designed by Janos Schiller and built in the late nineteenth century, stands empty and in dilapidated condition on sycamore-shaded Ifjusag ter.

There is a large cemetery dating to the nineteenth century located on Tomalom utca near Gothic St. Michael's Church. Here there is also a large Holocaust memorial, on which the names of all the local Jews deported and killed in the war are listed.

*Szeged

Jewish Community: Gutenberg utca 20. Tel. (62) 311-402

Kosher Restaurant: Ask at the Community office.

Today a city of 176,000 on the Tisza River a few miles from both the Yugoslav (Serbian) and Romanian borders in the southeast corner of the country, Szeged was devastated by a flood on March 12, 1879 and was rebuilt as a model of late nineteenth-century urban planning. Copying Vienna and Budapest, the city center along the river is encircled by broad ring boulevards.

Jews settled here toward the end of the eighteenth century.

Lipot Loew (1811–1875), pioneer in the Hungarian Jewish Reform movement and one of Hungary's outstanding Jewish figures, served here as rabbi from 1850 until his death and had a tremendous influence on the development of the community. Descended from the famous Rabbi Judah

Szeged—The magnificent Great Synagogue, built at the turn of the century and considered the masterpiece of prolific Hungarian synagogue architect Lipot Baumhorn, has been fully restored and is used both as a synagogue and a concert hall.

Loew ben Bezalel of Prague (see Prague), he was a remarkable personality who served as a chaplain with the anti-Hapsburg revolutionary forces in 1848–1849 and was one of the first Hungarian rabbis to preach sermons in Hungarian. A terracotta portrait bust by Ede Telcs in which he resembles a long-haired, full-bearded biblical patriarch is in the Budapest Jewish Museum.

Szeged's Great Synagogue, one of the most magnificent synagogues in Europe even today, was built between 1900 and 1903 by the architect Lipot Baumhorn, working in close collaboration with the city's then chief rabbi, Immanuel Loew—Lipot Loew's son.

The building is considered Baumhorn's masterpiece—partly thanks to the influence Rabbi Loew had on the decoration. Rabbi Loew, a respected scholar and an enthusiastic amateur botanist, had Baumhorn incorporate intricate floral and plant designs into the sumptuous decoration of the 1,650-seat temple both inside and out and also had him include inscriptions and symbols representing Jewish themes.

The synagogue fell into disrepair after the war, but thanks largely to a former Szeged Jew who now lives in the United States, extensive restoration work was carried out in the late 1980s, and it was rededicated in a lavish ceremony in September 1989. Under an agreement between the Hungarian Jewish community and the Budapest government, the synagogue is to be maintained as a synagogue in perpetuity by state and local authorities, who in turn will be able to use it from time to time for secular concerts and cultural events.

Set in a large garden on Gutenberg utca, it has a forest of pale brick domes and tin-roofed turreted towers. Inside, it shimmers with marble, mosaics, gold fittings, elaborate chandeliers, and brilliant stained glass windows with designs symbolizing the Jewish holidays. An enormous dome, in an intricate design of blue glass and gold stars, soars up above the center of the hall supported above the vaulted ceiling by twenty-four columns. An ornate interior facade frames the Ark with Moorish-style arches and colorful inlay behind which the pipes of a magnificent organ serve as a dramatic backdrop.

Almost next door, on Hajnoczy utca, stands the much smaller and simpler synagogue that the Baumhorn design replaced. This synagogue, built in 1842–1843 by Henryk and Jozsef Lipovszky, is an austere, neoclassical building with a peaked roof and very little outside decoration. At the time of this writing, it had not been in use for years and was closed to the public, awaiting restoration. Plaques set into its outer wall—written in Hebrew and Hungarian—show how high the flood waters came in 1879.

The Great Synagogue is used for services on the High Holy Days and other special occasions. Only a few hundred Jews live in Szeged today, and regular services are held in the fine prayer hall of the nearby Jewish community center at the corner of Gutenberg utca and Josika utca—itself more sumptuously decorated than most other existing Hungarian synagogues. Here there is also a kosher lunchroom.

Before World War II, some 5,000 Jews lived in Szeged. Most of them were deported to Auschwitz under the orders of Adolf Eichmann; about half the deportees perished, and their names are inscribed on the walls of the entry area of the synagogue.

The tombs of Lipot and Immanuel Loew are found in the large, overgrown Jewish cemetery at the edge of town, where there is also a domed ceremonial hall, shaped something like a giant mushroom, designed by Lipot Baumhorn.

Szentendre

An extremely picturesque little town of 18,000 just north of Budapest on the Danube River, Szentendre has long been an artists' colony and major tourist attraction with its quaint architecture and numerous galleries and museums featuring twentieth-century Hungarian art. Two of the museums are of particular Jewish interest.

At Bogdanyi utca 12 is a museum dedicated to the work of Jewish husband and wife artists Imre Amos and Margit Anna. Imre Amos, a noted surrealist whose work also is displayed in the Jewish Museum in Budapest, died during the Holocaust in 1944. He was deported to work in a forced labor brigade and secretly sketched what he saw; many of the works in the museum depict the horrors of those years.

At the corner of Kigyo utca and Hunyadi utca is a museum dedicated to Jewish artist Lajos Vajda, who also died in the Holocaust.

There is an old Jewish cemetery in Szentendre dating back to the eighteenth century; it is in devastated condition, with evidence of vandalism.

Szolnok

Jewish Community: Majus 1 utca 33. Tel. (56) 311-239; 30819

Szolnok is an important industrial center and railway junction of 78,000 people on the Tisza River about sixty miles southeast of Budapest. Jews settled here around 1830, and about 2,500 Jews lived in the city by the outbreak of World War II. They were all deported to Nazi death camps; some 600 survived. A few dozen Jews live here today.

One of the city's most striking architectural landmarks is its former synagogue—a grand, slightly churchlike structure with a soaring central dome—which sits on the riverbank near the heart of town. It was designed by the prolific synagogue architect Lipot Baumhorn in 1898.

The synagogue has been nicely restored as a gallery and exhibition hall, and though the interior has been painted white throughout, it is still possible to see many of the sumptuous architectural and decorative details.

Across the little square in front of the synagogue is the former study house—today, a cinema and video center with a stand inside selling popcorn—which still has the tablets of the Ten Commandments embedded in the outer wall.

Szombathely

Jewish Community: Batthyany ter 9. Tel. (94) 312-500

Szombathely, with a population of about 86,000, is a historic town and industrial center in western Hungary near the Austrian border in the low foothills of the Austrian Alps. It was founded as Savaria by the Roman emperor Claudius in 43 C.E. and was an important trade and cultural center at the northern edge of the Roman Empire. Many Roman ruins still remain.

Jews lived here from the late seventeenth century but were only allowed to settle permanently within the town in 1840.

The former synagogue is one of the town's most imposing structures and one of the most extraordinary-looking synagogues still standing in Hungary. Designed in 1880 by Ludwig Schone, who apparently was influenced by the Dohany utca Synagogue in Budapest, it is a vaguely Moorish-style building, lavishly decorated with fancy brickwork and bulblike cupolas, dominated by two massive cupola-topped towers whose grandeur seems out of proportion to the rest of the building.

The synagogue, which stands opposite the remains of a Roman temple to Isis, is now used as a concert hall (sounds of symphony rehearsals waft out into the parking lot next door) and only the exterior remains as it once was.

About 4,200 Jews lived here before World War II. All were deported to Nazi death camps in 1944; few survived. Prominently situated just next to the synagogue building is a large Holocaust monument in their memory.

Only about 100, mostly elderly, Jews live in Szombathely today. A youth group was started in order to teach the twenty or so young people in the community Jewish traditions and history, but local members of the community say few worshipers attend Shabbat services in the community's pleasant little prayer room.

The Jewish community offices are in the building right next door to the former synagogue. I was greeted with good humor—and a little suspicion—when I knocked on the door. One old man, going over accounts in a ledger, eyed me sharply when I introduced myself and explained that, no, I didn't have any relatives from Szombathely, but I was still interested in the community and its Jewish monuments.

"Here, can you read that?" he suddenly said (we were speaking in German), thrusting an open Hebrew prayer book into my hands.

"Yes," I said—and did. I handed him back the book.

Szombathely—The striking, twin-towered former synagogue, designed in 1880 by Ludwig Schone, was apparently influenced by the Dohany utca Synagogue in Budapest. Only the exterior, with its Moorish elements, remains intact. Inside, the building has been converted into a modern concert hall. To the right of the building is a Holocaust monument.

"Ah." He closed the book, put it away, and didn't say anything more on the subject, but I knew that I had passed a test.

Szombathely has two Jewish cemeteries, one each for the Orthodox and Neolog communities. They are next to each other near new housing developments a mile or so from the synagogue (someone from the community will guide you) and have many memorials to Holocaust victims.

Tarcal

In this tiny wine-producing village in the northeast corner of Hungary near Tokaj is the painfully ruined hulk of a small, eighteenth-century baroque synagogue with the remains of extremely beautiful interior decoration: faded frescoes of lions and a beautifully lettered Hebrew inscription over the place where the Aron ha Kodesh was, plus a very lovely flat blue and russet ceiling incorporating a motif of big colorful stars set in squares of color. There is also a delicate wrought iron railing on the women's gallery, whose ceiling is still a brilliant azure.

Over the door is a weathered Hebrew inscription from Psalm 118: "This is the gate of the Lord, let the righteous enter thereby."

Jews settled in Tarcal in the eighteenth century or earlier and became very active in the wine trade. No more than a few hundred Jews ever lived in the village; all were deported to death camps by the Nazis.

There are two Jewish cemeteries just outside the town, both with beautifully carved stones. One cemetery, right on the road, is unfenced, abandoned, and a desolate, overgrown wreck. The other, next door across a sunken lane, is fenced in and well tended.

*Tokaj

This famous wine-producing town of 6,000 people in the northeast corner of Hungary lies at the confluence of the Bodrog and Tisza rivers in the dreamy low foothills of the Carpathian Mountains. With its winding little streets, baroque architecture, and numerous wine cellars, Tokaj is the "capital" of Hungary's most renowned wine region, where wine production dates back nearly a thousand years.

Jews began settling here in the eighteenth century, and little by little they took over the wine trade, which until then had been in the hands of Greek immigrants.

In 1828, a little more than 100 Jews lived in the town. By 1910, there were more than 1,100. The 800 or so Jews who lived in Tokaj on the eve of World War II were all deported to death camps by the Nazis.

The large synagogue on Achim utca, built in 1890, reflects the prosperity of the Jewish community at the time. It's a large, imposing, bright yellow building with a curved roof. It was undergoing total restoration in the early 1990s, probably for use as an exhibition hall. Next to it is another small Jewish building, a tiny prayer hall that was in regular use until 1981. Several other former Jewish buildings and some characteristic old homes also still stand nearby.

The fascinating, tree-shaded old Jewish cemetery, with about 100 tombstones dating back to as early as 1800, is situated on an island in the Bodrog River—it can be reached by ferry. The new cemetery, with about 500 tombstones dating back to the latter part of the nineteenth century, climbs a slope along the river outside town on the road to Bodrogkeresztur.

There is a small corner devoted to local Jewish history in the town museum.

Lajos Lowy, one of the handful of remaining Jews in Tokaj, has the keys to the small prayer house and the new cemetery. He also has a wealth of documentation, photographs, and other information about the local

Jewish history of Tokaj and surrounding villages. He can be contacted at his shop in central Tokaj, at Rakoczi utca 41.

OTHER PLACES OF JEWISH INTEREST

Abaujszanto (Abaújszántó)—Very interesting old cemetery.

Berettyoujfalu (Berettyóújfalu)—A large nineteenth-century synagogue, now a warehouse, but still with fine interior decoration.

Cegled (Cegléd)—A yellow brick synagogue designed by Lipot Baumhorn; currently used as a sports hall.

Erdobenye (Erdőbenye)—Old cemetery.

Esztergom—Moorish-style synagogue designed by Lipot Baumhorn in 1888 (his first synagogue); now offices.

Gonc (Gönc)—Very old cemetery with some beautifully carved stones, including one of a stag in a forest.

Goncruszka (Göncruszka)—Old cemetery with floral-motif carvings.

Gyongyos (Gyöngyös)—Lipot Baumhorn designed the domed great synagogue, which resembled a Taj Mahal–style oriental palace. Today it has been stripped of decoration and is a department store. Next door is a neoclassical synagogue designed by Karoly Rabl and built between 1816 and 1820. It has been turned into a billiard parlor and video game hall. There's an overgrown cemetery outside town.

Hodmezovasarhely (Hódmezővásárhely)—There is a striking synagogue, built in 1857 and rebuilt in 1906, in a unique, art nouveau–influenced style with an enormous, deep, central arch framing a huge rose window.

Karcag—The synagogue here, dating from 1899, is in fairly good condition and is owned by the Jewish community.

Kiskoros (Kiskorös)—There is an art nouveau–style prayer house, built in 1915, that is now a concert hall. Also, a well-maintained cemetery stands near the railway station.

Kormend (Körmend)—Easily visited nineteenth-century cemetery on main road.

Kovagoors (Kővágóörs)—A village on the northern shore of Lake Balaton with a 200-year-old abandoned synagogue; a rare example of a village synagogue.

Kunszentmarton (Kunszentmárton)—The 1912 synagogue, designed by Jozsef Doborszky, has two distinctively shaped towers and many decorative elements drawn from Hungarian folk art.

Mako (Makó)—Synagogue from 1870 with some interior decoration left.

Mezocsat (Mezőcsát)—Late nineteenth-century synagogue, now a warehouse, retains highly decorated interior; also a large cemetery.

Mezotur (Mezőtúr)—Austere, neoclassic synagogue built in 1840.

Nagykallo (Nagykálló)—In the old cemetery is the ohel of the first Hasidic leader to live permanently in Hungary, Rebbe Isaac Itzkhak Kallo, who died in 1821.

Nyiregyhaza (Nyiregyháza)—The large synagogue, on busy Martirok tere, is used by the local community. It was designed by Lipot Baumhorn in one of his more restrained moments.

Siofok (Siófok)—This Balaton Lake resort has Hungary's newest synagogue, built in 1984–1985, at Szechenyi utca 4.

Szekszard (Szekszárd)—The red-and-yellow-striped synagogue, designed in 1896 by Johann Petschnik, has been turned into a concert and exhibition hall. Outside is a very striking sculptural Holocaust monument.

Varpalota (Várpalota)—Neoclassical synagogue, now a concert and exhibition hall.

Zalaegerszeg—The synagogue, designed in 1903 by Jozsef Stern, has been converted into a concert and exhibition hall. There is also a Jewish cemetery.

Zsujta—Old cemetery.

HOTELS/RESTAURANTS

Hungary is inundated by tourists in the summer months. Hotel rooms may be hard to find in Budapest and main tourist centers, like the Lake Balaton region, if you don't make reservations in advance.

Hotels in Budapest tend to be expensive—expect to pay American rates or only a little less. In the provinces, you can generally find good accommodations for $40 or less a double, though prices are sure to rise as the free-market economy takes hold. Tourist offices provide a free booklet listing almost all hotels and their amenities.

In recent years, there has been a boom in private accommodations and restaurants. Thousands of establishments either offer single rooms (if traveling by car look for signs saying *"Zimmer Frei"*) or have set themselves up as pensions (look for signs reading *"Panzio"*). These are much cheaper and often more comfortable than hotels.

It used to be almost impossible to have a bad meal in Hungary—but small, private restaurants now tend to have better food than bigger, state or cooperatively run establishments.

There has also been an explosion of new tourist and travel agencies. These, in addition to the offices of the state travel agency IBUSZ, can help find private accommodations and are often helpful in provincial towns in helping locate Jewish sites.

BUDAPEST

Hotels

- Forum, Apaczai Csere Janos utca 12-14. Tel. (1) 1178-088. My favorite. It also has very good restaurants.
- Gellert, Szent Gellert ter 1. Tel. (1) 1229-200. Refurbished old hotel with thermal baths attached.
- Hilton, Hess Andras ter 1-3. Tel. (1) 1751-000. Good hotel, beautiful location in Buda.
- Intercontinental, Apaczai Csere Janos utca 4. Tel. (1) 1175-122. Good restaurants, including one serving Hungarian specialties.

Kosher Restaurants

- Salom, Klauzal ter 1/2. Up-market atmosphere.

- Hanna, Dob utca 35. Another entrance is through the courtyard of the Orthodox synagogue. Often crowded, this rather rough-and-ready eatery has good, simple food and a real mixture of clientele.

Restaurants

- Gundel, Allatkerti utca 2. Tel. (1) 1227-024. Elegant setting in the park near Heroes' Square.

BAJA

- Hotel Sugovica, Petofi sziget. Tel. (79) 12-988. Modern, on an island in the river, but within walking distance into town.
- Hotel Duna, Beke ter 6. Tel. (79) 11-765. Old fashioned, on the main square.
- Halaszcsarda (Fisherman's Inn), on Petofi Island across from Sugovica Hotel. It serves fantastic fish soup, the local specialty.

DEBRECEN

- Aranybika Hotel, Voros Hadsereg utca 11-15. Tel. (52) 16-777. Downtown, considered one of the best in eastern Hungary.

SOPRON

- Hotel Sopron, Fovenyverem utca 7. Tel. (99) 14254. Modern, very comfortable, on hill overlooking town center.
- Hotel Palatinus, Uj utca 23. Tel. (99) 11395. Small hotel, perfectly located in Old Town on the street where the medieval synagogues are located.
- Royal Panzio, Sas ter 12. Tel. (99) 12481. Excellent restaurant with a few pleasant and inexpensive rooms to rent.

SZEGED

- Hotel Hungaria, Komocsin Z. ter 2. Tel. (62) 21211. Modern and anonymous.

TOKAJ

- Tokaj Hotel, Rakoczi utca 5. Tel. (41) 52336. Modern, a good center for touring the sites in the northeast corner of Hungary.

ROMANIA

Population: 23 million
Jewish Population before World War II: c. 800,000
Jewish Population in 1994: c. 14,000

A LITTLE HISTORY

Romania, straddling the Carpathian Mountains and stretching to the Black Sea, is a country where two great Jewish worlds come together. Here, Central Europe meets Eastern Europe. The reform-influenced Austro-Hungarian Jewish tradition, as found in Transylvania, meets antiquity: the old-fashioned Jewish shtetl, as found in Moldavia.

Romania as we know it was established after World War I, when Transylvania (which for centuries had been under Hungarian rule) was joined with the Romanian principalities of Walachia and Moldavia, which had combined in the nineteenth century as the independent Romanian Kingdom.

Jews lived in what is now Romania during the ancient Roman era, when Roman legions were stationed there from the second century. They probably were craftsmen and merchants serving the troops.

Little is known about Jewish presence over the next thousand years. From the Middle Ages on, though, Jewish immigrants began settling in Walachia, founded around 1290, and Moldavia, founded fifty or sixty years later. Further settlers arrived after the expulsion from Spain in 1492.

Moldavia and Walachia, which came largely under Ottoman rule in the fifteenth and sixteenth centuries, were on the main trade routes between Poland and Turkey.

In a diary written during a tour of the Ottoman Empire in the mid-sixteenth century, a Christian businessman from Bohemia, Hans Dernschwam, compiled a detailed—if unflattering—description of Jewish merchants who plied these routes.

> . . . The Jews and foreign merchants from Poland, Reussen (White Russia), Wallachia [cq], and Hungary, as is their wont, know how to travel about in Turkey. No limitations are anywhere placed on their importing goods as long as they pay the custom duties to the sultan. . . . They march into a caravansary, wherever they want, run about in their own garb, and some of them have barely twenty or fifty florins worth of goods such as Hungarian knives, caps, Prussian russet-leather, brandy made of beer, linen, etc. Unquestionably all the Jews are spies for both sides (Christians and Turks) and he who has the courage can travel with these fellows anywhere, deep into the interior of Egypt or Asia. They travel in large bands, for the Arabs are desperate robbers. . . .

Polish Jewish merchants set up storehouses and trading posts along their routes and eventually settled permanently in Moldavia and Walachia, both of which were sparsely populated. Local rulers welcomed this input, and Jewish settlement was encouraged: Jews were granted tax exemptions and were guaranteed the possibility of building synagogues and cemeteries. Moldavian rulers even sent special emissaries to Poland to recruit Jewish settlers.

Several towns in northern Moldavia had thriving Jewish communities by the early sixteenth century. Their numbers were swelled by waves of Jewish immigrants fleeing south after the devastation wrought by Bogdan Chmielnicki's Cossack uprising in Poland and the Ukraine in 1648–1649 and the subsequent decades of war and upheavals. (See Poland.)

Polish Jews settled in, carrying out all manner of skilled crafts and commercial endeavors. Polish origins have left their traces in the old cemeteries in northern Romania, where the style and rich carving of gravestones are similar to those in Poland itself. Hasidism, too, spread south from Poland in the eighteenth and nineteenth centuries and gained much influence among Jewish communities.

Episodes of anti-Jewish violence or legislation in Moldavia and Walachia were already occurring in the sixteenth century, largely due to fears of commercial competition. On the whole, however, life for Jews was relatively peaceful until the early nineteenth century.

Under the Turks, Jewish communities in Moldavia and Walachia were organized into guilds, which came under the control of a hereditary supreme Jewish leader called the *Hacham Bashi*. The Hacham Bashi, with his headquarters in Iasi, the Moldavian capital, was in charge of religious, judicial, and secular Jewish affairs, including tax collection. Eventually, there was much opposition to the Hacham Bashi system, particularly from Hasidim and other Polish and Russian Jews who regarded their rabbis as their leaders. As Turkish influence waned, the Hacham Bashi system was abolished in 1834. By this time, the Jewish community had evolved into a prosperous middle class in charge of most of the country's trade—and as such was resented by the vast majority of the population, who were mainly poverty-stricken peasants.

The nineteenth century spelled hardship and persecution for the Jews of Moldavia and Walachia. It was a century that saw the emergence of Romanian nationalism as the Romanians struggled to win independence and unity, first from the Turks and later from the Russians, who occupied the two principalities from 1819 to 1834 and ruled them as a protectorate from 1835 to 1856.

The Russians imposed the type of anti-Semitic restrictions long practiced in Czarist Russia. Jews were denied citizenship and barred from living in villages and carrying out various trades. Jews were accused of ritual murder in a series of blood libel cases, and they were also accused of causing everything from epidemics to natural disasters.

When Moldavia and Walachia united in 1859 as an independent kingdom, the estimated 130,000 Jews made up about three percent of the total population. In 1866, a viciously anti-Semitic regime took power and initiated a large-scale and often violent campaign against the Jews.

Jews were expelled from villages and confronted by a series of restrictions on economic, social, and religious life. The constitution was changed to allow Romanian citizenship only to Christians. The situation was so bad that it triggered repeated protests and condemnation from several Western governments.

At the Congress of Berlin in 1878, which set the seal on the independence of Balkan states following the final Russian defeat of the Turks in the region in 1877, the great powers made independence conditional on the new states guaranteeing full civil rights to their Jewish populations.

The Romanians paid this provision little heed. In the decades leading up to World War I, anti-Semitic persecution was only intensified. Jews were barred from a long list of trades and professions. Anti-Semitic political parties developed; Jewish journalists Elias Schwarzfeld and Moses Gaster were expelled from the country in 1884 for writing articles protesting the persecution; in 1893, Jewish children were barred from state schools. A peasants' revolt in Moldavia in 1907 forced Jews out of many villages after homes and shops were looted and destroyed.

The desperate situation sparked mass Jewish emigration from Romania. Tens of thousands picked up and left, many of them walking thousands of miles by foot to western European ports on their way to America.

After World War I, Romania annexed the former Austro-Hungarian provinces of Transylvania and Bucovina, as well as Russian Bessarabia. This increased the Jewish population from under 240,000 to about 750,000 virtually overnight. But the Jews in these new territories had a different history than those of Old Romania. In Bessarabia, ruled by the Russians, the Jews had been even more persecuted than those in Romania.

In the Austro-Hungarian lands, however, Jews were full citizens who had achieved civil rights and emancipation in the early to mid-nineteenth centuries. Many Jewish communities in Transylvania were heavily influenced by Reform Judaism and had large Neolog, or Reform, congregations. A large number of the Jews from Transylvanian cities such as Arad, Cluj, Tirgu Mures, and Oradea were assimilated into mainstream, upper-middle-class life and followed professions barred to Romanian Jews. Most used the Hungarian language, and some Jewish families in Transylvania had even been raised to the Hungarian nobility.

These diverse Jewish groups never really merged, although the anti-Semitism and "Romanization" that continued to grow throughout the 1920s and 1930s affected them all.

In the late 1920s, right-wing Romanian nationalist student leader Corneliu Zelea Codreanu formed the virulently anti-Semitic paramilitary Iron Guard organization, which gained influence in the Romanian government, particularly after Hitler came to power in Germany in 1933. Discrimination against Jews grew steadily harsher throughout the 1930s.

A census carried out in 1930 showed that there were slightly under 730,000 Jews in Romania, making up four percent of the population. The highest concentrations of Jews were in Bucovina, where they made up nearly eleven percent, in Bessarabia, where they made up over seven percent, and in Moldavia, where they made up six and a half percent.

After the outbreak of World War II, Romania was forced by Germany to cede Bessarabia and part of Bucovina to the Soviet Union, northern Transylvania to Hungary, and part of Dobrudja, near the Black Sea, to Bulgaria.

In Bucharest, General Ion Antonescu came to power on September 6, 1940 as the head of a Nazi-style government allied with the Iron Guard after King Carol abdicated. Romania, as a Nazi ally, introduced a long series of anti-Jewish legislation between January 1938 and May 1942. Jewish property and businesses were confiscated; Jewish citizenship was canceled; Jews were barred from owning radios, and so on. The Iron Guard let loose a reign of terror against Jews, and on January 21, 1941, it revolted against Antonescu in an attempt to gain complete power. This touched off a mini–civil war between the Iron Guard and the Romanian army loyal to Antonescu and also unleashed a horrifying pogrom against Bucharest Jews. (See Bucharest.)

Antonescu clung to power, but only with the support of Hitler, who needed relative calm near the front. Antonescu's policy toward the Jews was somewhat ambivalent. The Germans pressured him to impose harsh measures against the Jews, but he refused to allow the mass deportation of Romanian Jews to Nazi death camps in Poland. He apparently also maintained some contact with Romanian Jewish leaders. Romanian ports, particularly Constanta, were the only European ports open where ships were able to set sail with Jewish refugees bound for Palestine.

Nonetheless, in August 1941, the Romanians began the mass deportations of Jews from Bucovina and Moldavia to a German-occupied part of the Soviet Union known as Transnistria. About 150,000 were deported; only 60,000 survived.

When the Germans invaded Hungary in 1944, they dealt with the Jews of northern Transylvania as they did with all the Jews of provincial Hungary: They herded them into ghettos and then deported them en masse to Auschwitz. About 160,000 Jews from Transylvania suffered this fate.

Romania withdrew from the war in August 1944. Roughly half of the prewar Jewish population of about 800,000 survived the Holocaust. Of these, well over 300,000 emigrated, mostly to Israel, by the late 1960s. Steady emigration continued, and in 1991 only about 17,000 Jews, most of them over sixty, lived in Romania.

Under communist dictator Nicolae Ceausescu, who ruled Romania from 1965 until he was overthrown and executed in December 1989, Romania suffered under what probably was the most oppressive communist government in Eastern Europe. In the late 1960s and 1970s, Ceausescu developed a foreign policy that differed in several significant ways from Moscow's.

One of his "independent" policies was his attitude toward Israel and the Jews. Ceausescu was the only communist leader who did not break diplomatic relations with Israel after the Six-Day War in 1967. He permitted the emigration of Romanian Jews to Israel (although eventually he also extorted large financial payments for each Jew who left the country), and he also allowed foreign Jewish charitable organizations, notably the American Jewish Joint Distribution Committee, to help Romania's remaining Jews. The Federation of Jewish Communities in Romania was able to organize Romanian Jews into active communities that ran Talmud Torah classes, youth choirs, charity services, and kosher restaurants. Cemeteries and many synagogues were maintained (although the overwhelming majority of synagogues were destroyed) and old-age homes were set up.

It is clear that Ceausescu's policy toward Jews and Israel was aimed at winning support—and money—in the West, and indeed, this policy was largely responsible for Romania being granted most-favored-nation trade status by the United States.

Rabbi Moses Rosen, who served as Romania's chief rabbi from 1948 until his death in May 1994, played a highly significant role both in helping Romanian Jews emigrate and in winning concessions and privileges for Romanian Jewish communities at home. Referred to by Romanian Jews as "His Eminence," he was, however, a controversial figure because of his relationship with the Ceausescu regime.

Even before Ceausescu came to power, Rosen walked a delicate political tightrope, trading off public support for the communist regime for religious and community rights for the Jews, including the right to emigrate.

His critics revile him as a lackey of Ceausescu who, both at home and abroad, kept silent about the excesses and corruption of the regime and helped maintain the fiction that Ceausescu was charting an independent course for his people. Rosen, in fact, was a key player in helping Romania get U.S. trade concessions.

On the other hand, his supporters, who include most Romanian Jews, regard Rosen as the savior of his people, the man who got nearly 400,000 Jews out of the country, who prevented synagogues from being torn down, and who enabled the Jews who remained to lead a Jewish life and a life of dignity in the land of their fathers.

Rosen repeatedly maintained that the only way he could help Jews emigrate and obtain better conditions in Romania was by working with Ceausescu.

"My only sin has been to help my people," he told me at Pesach 1991.

Since the violent overthrow and execution of Ceausescu, there has been a marked rise of openly expressed nationalism and anti-Semitism in Romania. Rosen became a target of bitter attacks and repeatedly warned Jews they should consider emigrating if the situation didn't improve.

FOR THE TRAVELER

Where

Romania lies in the northern part of the Balkan peninsula, with the Carpathian Mountains curving through the central, northern, and western parts of the country. It borders Hungary, Yugoslavia (Serbia), Bulgaria, Moldova, and Ukraine and has a coastline along the Black Sea. The mighty Danube River forms much of its southern border.

When

Romania has a temperate climate similar to that of the northeastern United States. Winters can be long and severe, particularly in the mountains, and summers can be blazingly hot, particularly in the southern plains.

How

Romania's Tarom Airlines and other international carriers fly in to Bucharest, and there is international train service from neighboring countries.

There are few four-lane highways, and the two-lane roads throughout most of the country can be in very poor condition. Border crossings can take hours.

The country's tourism infrastructure is inefficient and run-down, and even supposedly first-class hotels may lack heat, hot water, light fixtures, or food.

Visas

Americans need visas for Romania. They are technically available at the border, but it is better to get one in advance from a Romanian consulate.

Languages

Romanian is a Romance language, like Italian or French, based on Latin roots and is spoken all over the country. Hungarian is widely spoken in Transylvania, where there is a large Hungarian minority, and German is also spoken in some areas of Transylvania, where ethnic Germans settled centuries ago.

Personnel at major hotels generally speak English. Many older members of the Jewish community speak Yiddish or German. French is the most widespread second language, although younger people increasingly are learning English.

Helpful Phrases

English	Romanian (Pronunciation)
Synagogue	Sinagogă (Sinagoga)
Jewish cemetery	Cimitir evreiesc (Chimiteer yevrayesk)
Hello/Good day	Bună ziua (Boona zeewa)
Yes	Da (Da)
No	Nu (Noo)
Please	Vă rog (Va rawg)
Thank you	Mulţumesc (Multsumesk)
Good-bye	La revedere (La revedereh)
Where is . . . ?	Unde este . . . ? (Undeh yeste)
How much does it cost?	Cît costă? (Cheet kosta)
Toilet	Toaletă (Twaletta)
Men	Domni, Barbati (Domni, Barbaty)
Women	Doamne, Femei (Dwamne, Femey)
Entrance	Intrare (Intrareh)
Exit	Ieşire (Yesheereh)
One	Unu, Una (Oonoo, Oona)
Two	Doi, Două (Doy, Dowa)
Three	Trei (Tray)
Four	Patru (Pahtroo)
Five	Cinci (Chinch)
Six	Şase (Shaseh)
Seven	Şapte (Shapteh)
Eight	Opt (Opt)
Nine	Nouă (Nowa)
Ten	Zece (Zecheh)

Money

The Romanian currency is the leu (plural, lei). It is impossible to say what its real value is due to frequent devaluations in the official exchange rate since the 1989/1990 revolution, as well as a flourishing black market. Many travel expenses (such as hotels, tours, and airfares) must be paid in Western currency; many other tourist-related charges quoted in lei seem to reflect black market rather than official exchange rates. In addition to money, certain Western commodities (such as Western, preferably Kent, cigarettes) have for years taken on a commercial value of their own: A pack of Kents, for example, may often be accepted in payment for, say, a taxi ride or guarded parking instead of actual money.

Kosher Cuisine

Thanks to the extraordinary organization of the Jewish community in Romania there is a network of kosher restaurants at Jewish community centers throughout the country. Most of them are open only for set-meal lunches, but visitors can probably arrange to get kosher food for dinner, too. As of 1993, there were kosher restaurants in Bucharest, Arad, Bacau, Botosani, Brasov, Cluj-Napoca, Dorohoi, Galati, Iasi, Oradea, and Timisoara. All Jewish communities throughout the country are supplied with matzo and other kosher supplies during Passover.

If You Only Have a Few Days

In addition to Bucharest, there are fascinating Jewish sites and hospitable Jewish communities in every part of Romania, so you can explore Romania's Jewish heritage by contacting local communities wherever you travel. The centuries-old cemeteries and numerous synagogues with unique folk-style-painted interiors in northern Moldavia are perhaps the most interesting and unusual. These historic cemeteries are among the most impressive in all East-Central Europe.

Helpful Addresses

(The direct dialing code for Romania is 40.)

> **Romanian National Tourist Office (ONT)**
> 573 Third Avenue
> New York, NY 10016
> Tel. (212) 697-6971
>
> Main Office
> Bulevardul Magheru 7
> Bucharest
>
> (Most main tourist hotels have an ONT desk)
>
> **U.S. Embassy**
> Str. Tudor Arghezi 7-9
> Bucharest
> Tel. (1) 312-4042

Main Jewish Communities

These will be the most helpful addresses you can have when exploring Jewish heritage. In fact, in most cases it will be essential to meet with community leaders in order to gain access to synagogues and cemeteries. Most Jewish community offices are open in the morning, and Shabbat services are held in all communities listed below. Many have daily services.

Due to inefficiency, food and fuel shortages, and lack of infrastructure, Romania is not an easy (and sometimes not a pleasant) country to travel in—though the marvelous sights and people are well worth the effort. Cemeteries can be very hard to find, and, particularly in Moldavia, it can be difficult to locate synagogues and community offices due to recent extensive urban renewal projects that have totally changed the face of towns and cities.

Therefore, since you are most likely to begin your trip in Bucharest, I strongly suggest that you contact the Federation of Jewish Communities in the capital before setting out into the provinces. (The Federation should also be able to provide up-to-date street addresses; in Romania, as in other former communist countries, many street names are being changed to remove communist associations. Through the Federation I also hired a Jewish student to travel with me as an interpreter.)

There are organized Jewish communities with active synagogues in about sixty Romanian towns and cities. Listed below are those communities that have a kosher restaurant, as well as some of the other larger communities.

Bucharest	Federation of Jewish Communities: Str. Sf. Vineri 9-11. Tel. (1) 613-2538; 143-008.
	Jewish Community of Bucharest: Str. Sf. Vineri 9-11. Tel. 157-441.
	Kosher Restaurant: Str. Popa Soare 18
Arad	Str. Tribunul Dobra 10. Tel. (966) 16097
	Kosher Restaurant: Str. 7 Noiembrie
Bacau	Str. Alexandru cel Bun 11. Tel. (931) 34714
	Kosher Restaurant: Str. Alexandru cel Bun 11
Baia Mare	Str. Somesului 3. Tel. (994) 11231
Botosani	Calea Nationala 220. Tel. (985) 14659
	Kosher Restaurant: Str. 7 Aprilie 69
Brasov	Str. Poarta Schei 27. Tel. (921) 43532
	Kosher Restaurant: Str. Poarta Schei 27
Cluj-Napoca	Str. Tipografiei 25. Tel. (951) 16677
	Kosher Restaurant: Str. Parisu 5-7
Constanta	Str. Sarmisegetuza 3. Tel. (916) 11598
Dorohoi	Str. Dumitru Furtuna 16. Tel. (986) 13424
	Kosher Restaurant: Str. Dumitru Furtuna 16

Galati	Str. Dornei 9-11. Tel. (934) 13662
	Kosher Restaurant: Str. Dornei 7
Iasi (Jassy)	Str. Elena Doamna 15. Tel. (981) 14414
	Kosher Restaurant: Str. Elena Doamna 15
Oradea	Str. Mihai Viteazul 4. Tel. (991) 34843
	Kosher Restaurant: Str. Mihai Viteazul 5
Piatra Neamt	Str. V. I. Lenin 7. Tel. (936) 23815
Ploiesti	Str. Basarabilor 12. Tel. (971) 26017
Roman	Str. Sucedava 131. Tel. (937) 26621
Satu Mare	Str. Decebal 4. Tel. (997) 11728
Sighet	Str. Viseului 10. Tel. (995) 11652
Suceava	Str. Armeneasca 8. Tel. (987) 13084
Timisoara	Str. Gheorghe Lazar 5. Tel. (961) 32813
	Kosher Restaurant: Str. Marasesti 10
Tirgu Mures	Str. Braila 10. Tel. (954) 15001
Tirgu Neamt	Str. Cuza Voda 160. Tel. (936) 62515

Local Jewish Interest Guidebooks

Little is available, but several books in English by Chief Rabbi Moses Rosen are on sale at the Jewish Federation office in Bucharest and at several other community offices around the country. They are collections of Rosen's essays and sermons and make interesting reading, particularly as they show the controversial tightrope he walked in lending support to the repressive communist regime in order to win better conditions for Romanian Jews.

The Federation also sells a few pamphlets and postcards of Jewish sites around the country.

The most interesting book I found in Romania is a book on Romanian Jewish cemeteries, written in Hungarian with an English summary. There are lots of pictures, but the printing quality is terrible. Written by Lajos Erdelyi from Tirgu Mures and called *Regi Zsido Temetok Muveszete*, it was published in 1980 and is probably out of print; you may find it in a secondhand shop, or you may be able to find it at the community offices if you visit Tirgu Mures.

JEWISH HERITAGE IN ROMANIA

Romania is unique in East-Central Europe in that there are scores of well-maintained synagogues and cemeteries in use by Jewish communities scattered all over the country. Thus in Romania, it is possible to see how many of the synagogues left ruined in other countries might look if brought to life again.

In 1994, Romania's 14,000 or more Jews lived in more than 150 cities, towns, and villages. There were organized Jewish communities in more than sixty towns, and more than seventy synagogues were in active use, including more than twenty-five where daily services were held.

Romanian synagogues are of several types. In Transylvania, the architectural styles are similar to those found in Hungary and other parts of the old Austro-Hungarian Empire and include large, impressive, and elaborately decorated synagogues dating from the late nineteenth and early twentieth centuries.

In Moldavia, however, there remain numerous folk-style synagogues, plain on the outside but highly decorated inside, with naive paintings and lavish wood carving. Until recent mass urban renewal schemes, such synagogues in towns like Dorohoi, Botosani, Tirgu Neamt, and Falticeni stood amid crowded streets of one-story wooden houses and shops, perfectly preserving the old atmosphere of traditional shtetls.

In addition, there are known to be nearly 750 Jewish cemeteries in 660 localities, including over 500 localities where Jews no longer live. Each active Jewish community is responsible for the upkeep of Jewish cemeteries in surrounding areas where no Jews live. For example, the community in the town of Baia Mare, in northwest Romania, is responsible for forty-seven cemeteries in nearby villages where there are no longer any Jews. In many cases, non-Jewish peasant families living near or on the cemetery grounds care for the graveyards in return for either payment or the right to use the grass, and so on, to feed their animals and to cultivate empty parts of the cemetery grounds. These people, though not Jewish, take their responsibility very seriously and many provide water and towels so that the rare visitor can wash his hands after visiting the graves.

BUCHAREST

(Romanian: Bucureşti)

Federation of Jewish Communities: Str. Sf. Vineri 9-11. Tel. 613-2538; 143-008.

Jewish Community of Bucharest: Str. Sf. Vineri 9-11. Tel. 157-441.

Kosher Restaurant: Str. Popa Soare 18

The capital of Romania, Bucharest was known between the two world wars as the Little Paris of the East. Today, it is a chaotic, frantic, and rather unpleasant city of more than two million people whose remaining picturesque corners, parks, and gracious nineteenth- and early twentieth-century architecture are overwhelmed by the late dictator Nicolae Ceausescu's grandiose urban renewal schemes, mile after mile of shoddy mass housing, and an overall air of grimy dilapidation.

Founded around the beginning of the fifteenth century, Bucharest early on attracted Jewish merchants and moneylenders from Turkey and elsewhere in the Balkans, including refugees from the Spanish expulsions.

In 1659, the city formally became the capital of Walachia—a semiautonomous Romanian principality that paid tribute to the Turkish sultan—and most of the Jewish population of Walachia was concentrated there. Two centuries later, when Walachia and Moldavia were joined, Bucharest became capital of the united Romanian Kingdom.

Jewish settlers came to Bucharest from Russia and Constantinople in the east, from Balkan regions south of the Danube, and from Germany, Austria, Hungary, and elsewhere in central and western Europe, creating a diverse mixture of varied Jewish life. There are believed to have been about 1,000 Jews in Bucharest in 1800; by 1861, when Moldavia and Walachia joined into the Romanian Kingdom, there were about 6,000, worshiping in more than thirty synagogues.

This fast-growing Jewish community suffered from anti-Semitic legislation, occasional blood libel accusations, and even violence from the latter part of the eighteenth century on, as the relatively tolerant Turkish influence waned and was replaced by Russian dominance in the region during nearly a century of almost constant warfare between the Russians and the Turks. More than 100 Jews, for example, died during anti-Semitic riots in the city in 1801.

Mounting anti-Semitism during the nineteenth century took place against the background of bitter, back-stabbing internal conflicts within the Jewish community itself, mainly within the Ashkenazic community between Orthodox and Reform elements. These culminated in the 1860s in a personal clash between Reform leader Iuliu Barasch and the Orthodox leader, the famous scholar Meir Loeb ben Jehiel Michael, called the MaLBiM, who had become Orthodox rabbi in Bucharest in 1858. In 1864, opponents of the MaLBiM arranged for his expulsion from Romania by informing Romanian authorities that he held foreign citizenship. The MaLBiM was arrested and, in a last humiliating gesture, expelled from the country in a rubbish cart.

The internal Jewish conflicts led the authorities to withdraw the official status of all Jewish communities in the country.

Continuing anti-Semitism throughout the nineteenth century prompted thousands of Jews to leave Bucharest. During this period, one of the most important Jewish personalities in the city was, in fact, an American—Benjamin Franklin Peixotto, who arrived in town as the first American consul in 1870. Peixotto helped found the Bucharest branch of B'nai Brith, but he viewed the situation for Jews in Romania as so bleak that he counseled emigration as the best answer.

On the eve of World War II, Bucharest had a Jewish population of 95,000—more than the entire Jewish population of Yugoslavia.

The fascist Iron Guard carried out vicious anti-Semitic persecutions that culminated in Bucharest with a horrifying pogrom in January 1941. Synagogues, Jewish homes, and Jewish businesses were looted or razed to the ground; Jews were hauled from their homes, arrested, taken out to the snowy forests outside the city, and brutally killed: At least 170 died. The bodies of some of those who were murdered were hung in the local slaughterhouse with signs proclaiming, "Kosher meat."

Photographs at the Jewish Museum in Bucharest show what at the time was regarded as a miracle: a single Torah scroll salvaged from the carnage. The fascists, in their frenzy of destruction, had torn the Torahs from the Aron ha Kodesh in the Great Synagogue and hurled them everywhere: The streets of the Jewish quarter were covered with torn parchment. In the Great Synagogue, though, one Torah was found undamaged, caught in the chandelier under the dome and suspended high in the air. One of the looters apparently had thrown it high, expecting it to smash when it hit the ground; instead, it was saved.

Today, about 8,000 Jews, more than half of Romania's Jewish population, live in Bucharest. Here there is full opportunity for a rich Jewish life: a kosher restaurant, old-age homes, youth organizations and choirs, a newspaper, and extensive social services, including a meals-on-wheels program for the elderly and housebound.

Major Places of Jewish Interest in Bucharest

• Choral Synagogue: Str. Sf. Vineri 9-11

The Choral Temple, designed by architects Enderle and Freiwald, was founded by Reform Jewish leader Iuliu Barasch and built in the 1860s for Bucharest's prosperous Reform community. Its magnificent interior and flat facade, with Moorish turrets and two lower side elements flanking a higher central portion, are reminiscent of several important Central European synagogues and were derived from Ludwig von Forster's design for the Tempelgasse Synagogue in Vienna, like the one in Zagreb destroyed during the war.

The Choral Temple—so called because it incorporated a choir loft and organ—is set back behind iron gates and dominates the courtyard containing the Jewish community and Federation offices.

Once it was a landmark in the old Jewish quarter, Vacaresti—a neighborhood of narrow streets and low wooden houses and shops that over the past decade has been almost completely razed to the ground and replaced by hideous new concrete apartment buildings that hem in the synagogue on all sides. Only a few hundred yards away is the late dictator Nicolae Ceausescu's enormous, megalomaniacal palace looming up from a

Bucharest—The Choral Synagogue. Designed by architects Enderle and Freiwald and built in 1860s for the Reformed congregation, it is today the city's main synagogue. Its facade and ornate interior are reminiscent of several other important Central European synagogues. The offices of the Federation of Jewish Communities and the Bucharest Jewish community are in the building next door.

neighborhood of new apartments and ministry buildings that are supposed to look posh but only look vulgar and already old.

An imposing Holocaust memorial was dedicated in front of the Choral Temple in July 1991.

• The Great Synagogue (Sinagoga Mare): Str. Vasile Adamache 9-11

This gorgeous Sephardic synagogue, built from 1845 to 1847, is even more hemmed in by new apartment-house construction than is the Choral Temple. I had to be guided there by someone from the Federation office who led me through debris-strewn building sites that looked like bombs had hit. To get to the synagogue itself, we had to go through a dank, foul-smelling tunnel under one of the new buildings.

Nonetheless, the synagogue is in use and on the inside is in very good condition: There is lush Moorish-style detail work on the walls and ceiling and an extremely elaborate Aron ha Kodesh decorated with much gilding and carved lions.

• Jewish Museum: Str. Mamoulari 3. Open Sunday mornings and Wednesdays.

The Jewish Museum, opened in 1978, is housed in the former Tailor's Synagogue, originally built around 1850. Curator Bernice Stambler is on hand to explain exhibits to visitors, but—rare in East-Central European museums—much information is also provided in English. There is also a Jewish History Research Center here.

Dominating the museum's main hall in the sanctuary of the old synagogue is a moving memorial to Holocaust victims: a mournful sculpture of a person veiled head to foot in a tallis standing at the end of a carpet. Footprints on the carpet lead to the statue; none come away.

"They lead in one direction; the direction of no return, the way to death," Ms. Stambler explained, adding that the footprints were made by two women who survived Auschwitz.

The museum has a varied and rich display of ritual objects, the works of Jewish artists, and many documents relating to the Holocaust. A special exhibition on the Holocaust is expected to be opened in the near future at the Jewish community center and kosher restaurant on Str. Popa Soare nearby.

• Jewish Cemeteries

Bucharest has two main Jewish cemeteries, both still in use. The large, so-called Philanthropic Cemetery, in the north of town, was founded in the mid-nineteenth century and has some very interesting grave monuments, including many made out of iron plaques erected above fenced-in grave plots. Numerous prosperous or influential Jews are buried here, including a secretary to the queen and the designer of the Romanian crown jewels!

There is a large Sephardic cemetery in the south end of the city, near the major municipal cemeteries.

ELSEWHERE IN ROMANIA

Alba Iulia

Jewish Community: Str. T. Vladimirescu 4. Tel. (968) 27840

An ancient town located at the confluence of the Ampoi and Mures rivers in central Transylvania, Alba Iulia has been a trade, cultural, and defensive center since ancient Roman times. Part of Transylvania, it was ruled by Hungary until 1918. Today, with 65,000 people, it still has numerous important historic monuments in and around its vast, eighteenth-century fortress, but they can seem overwhelmed by modern housing blocks and industry.

בעפר אתה
ואל עפר תשוב

Alba Iulia—Just inside the entrance to the cemetery, an old horse-drawn hearse shelters chickens.

A Jewish community was established here by the sixteenth century, and in 1623 Prince Bethlen Gabor granted liberal residency rights to Jews. After this, Alba Iulia became the main Jewish center in Transylvania. In 1930, about 1,500 Jews out of a total population of 12,300 lived in the town. Between the two world wars, the town was a center of Iron Guard activity, and there were many anti-Semitic incidents, including the Iron Guard bombing of a synagogue in 1938.

Fewer than fifty Jews live in Alba Iulia today. There is a large, white, well-maintained synagogue almost hemmed in by new shops and apartment buildings downtown.

The extensive walled Jewish cemetery on Str. Vasile Alecsandri has numerous gravestones dating to the early nineteenth century or earlier spaced out over grassy slopes. Grand nineteenth- and twentieth-century

Alba Iulia—Desecrated graves at the Jewish cemetery.

mausoleums top the hill near the big ceremonial hall. Near the entrance gate, an old, unused, horse-drawn hearse recalls former times—and serves as shelter for a flock of local chickens. On the residential street outside, children clamor for chewing gum and candy.

Unfortunately, the tranquility of the old graveyard was marred by anti-Semitic vandalism in the months following the 1989/1990 revolution: Unknown persons scrawled huge black crosses across the faces of at least half a dozen gleaming tombstones.

Arad

Jewish Community: Str. Tribunul Dobra 10. Tel. (966) 16097

Kosher Restaurant: Str. 7 Noiembrie 22

A dusty, rather shabby city of about 190,000 people in western Transylvania near the Hungarian border, Arad still preserves some of its former Austro-Hungarian charm in its once-elegant downtown districts.

Jews settled here in the early eighteenth century, and in the first half of the nineteenth century, the town became a leading center of Reform

Judaism under Rabbi Aaron Chorin. Chorin, born in Moravia in 1762, became rabbi in Arad in 1789. He advocated a gradual introduction of changes in the ritual, the use of the German language during services, and even organ music in the synagogue.

About 10,000 Jews lived here before World War II; the community survived the Holocaust, and most of them moved to Israel. At the end of 1990, more than 580 Jews lived in the town and four nearby villages, making the community one of the largest outside Bucharest.

The town has two synagogues, both situated in the extensive and quite picturesque old Jewish quarter of characteristic low houses jammed tightly together amid quiet streets and squares.

The Neolog (Reform) synagogue is part of the Jewish community-center complex, and the large Orthodox synagogue at Str. Cozia 12 has stained glass windows and beautiful bronze doors showing Jewish symbols, including menorahs and hands raised in priestly blessing.

The kosher restaurant is located at the Jewish Home for the Aged.

Bacau (Bacău)

Jewish Community: Str. Alexandru cel Bun 11. Tel. (931) 34714

Kosher Restaurant: Str. Alexandru cel Bun 11

Like most towns in northern Moldavia, Bacau, a city of 180,000 in the foothills of the Carpathians about 275 miles north of Bucharest, is a grim, grimy city, most of whose old neighborhoods were razed to the ground and replaced by anonymous concrete "block houses" as part of Nicolae Ceausescu's sweeping urban renewal programs. The Jewish community courtyard, with its old wooden buildings, is an anachronistic, welcoming island surrounded by dehumanized new construction.

Jews settled in Bacau in the eighteenth century and, as in other towns nearby, flourished as merchants, shopkeepers, and artisans. By the 1930s, the 10,000-strong community made up about thirty percent of the local population. There were thirty functioning synagogues.

Today, fewer than 400 Jews live in Bacau, but there is a rich Jewish life, including Talmud Torah classes, a youth choir, and daily services conducted morning and evening. A ritual slaughterer provides kosher meat both for the community's kosher restaurant and for individuals.

"Just yesterday," said a community official a few days before Pesach 1991, "a ninety-two-year-old man came here all the way from Buhusi—sixteen miles—carrying two chickens to have koshered. He's ninety-two years old, but to keep tradition, he came all the way from there to here!"

Bacau has two synagogues. The main synagogue is typical for Moldavia: fairly nondescript on the outside, but a blaze of folk-style interior decoration, including an ornate carved and painted wooden Aron ha Kodesh, a central bimah surrounded by a wrought iron grille, and bright naive wall and ceiling paintings representing the Tribes of Israel.

The old cemetery, closed long ago, has beautifully carved tombstones.

Baia Mare

Jewish Community: Str. Somesului 3. Tel. (994) 11231

Baia Mare is a mining and industrial city of 140,000 in northwest Romania in the shadow of the Carpathian Mountains near the Ukrainian and Hungarian borders. Its huge factories belch out some of the worst pollution in Romania, but there are still some charming corners in the downtown center.

As part of Transylvania, Baia Mare belonged to Hungary until 1918 and was again annexed to Hungary during World War II. Jews were barred from settling within the city limits until 1848 due to seventeenth-century laws banning Jews from all Hungarian mining towns.

On the eve of World War II, there were about 3,600 Jews out of the total population of 21,000. They were white-collar professionals, merchants, shopkeepers, craftsmen, tailors, and even a few industrialists, particularly in the copper industry.

After the Germans occupied Hungary in 1944, a wartime ghetto was set up in the town. The Hungarian military commander there, Lieutenant Colonel Imre Reviczky, helped save many Jews from certain death by enlisting them into labor brigades that kept them out of the ghettos. Nonetheless, most of Baia Marc's Jews were deported to Auschwitz.

Today, about 150 Jews live in the town. As in most Romanian Jewish communities, most of them are over sixty.

"We have a minyan every evening so we can say kaddish," said Ludwig Kahan, president of the community since 1967. He added that the community even provided bus passes to enable regular minyan attendees to make it to services.

The synagogue, built in 1885, dominates a traditional Jewish courtyard in the old Jewish section of town—a neighborhood that still retains its nineteenth-century charm. In the courtyard are community offices, a meeting hall, and an old kosher butcher shop that still bears a placard advertising kosher meat.

Daily prayers are held informally in a small prayer room in the entry of the synagogue proper, but old habits can die hard: Pensioner Paul Markovits, a "minyan regular" and survivor of the wartime ghetto in Budapest, proudly shows his reserved seat in the large, rather simply decorated main shul, where services are held on special occasions.

*Botosani (Botoşani)

Jewish Community: Calea Nationala 220. Tel. (985) 14659

Kosher Restaurant: Str. 7 Aprilie 69

Historically an important market town in the northeast corner of Romania near the border with Ukraine and Moldova, Botosani today, with over 50,000 people, is one of many Moldavian cities where all but a few old streets have been razed in recent years and replaced by characterless concrete blocks.

Jews probably settled here in the seventeenth century, and in the nineteenth century the community, comprising many merchants and craftsmen, grew to be one of the largest and most lively in Moldavia.

Some 11,000 Jews lived here before World War II. Elderly local Jews recall seventy-two synagogues in the town! Thousands of Jewish refugees poured into Botosani during the war, swelling the Jewish population to as many as 20,000, and at one point civil conditions became so anarchic that Jewish community organizations stepped in to take over many municipal functions from civic authorities.

Most of the 19,000 Jews here at the war's end emigrated to Israel. Today, fewer than 200 Jews live here and only two synagogues remain: the richly decorated, 240-year-old Great Synagogue on Str. Marchian, and a

Botosani—The highly elaborate carved wooden Aron ha Kodesh and part of the eighteenth-century painted ceiling inside the synagogue.

smaller, much simpler shul on the remains of a Jewish street nearby. "We keep that open for use so it won't be destroyed," said an elderly member of the community.

The historic Great Synagogue, one of the oldest in Moldavia but now hemmed in by new apartment buildings, is notable for its intricate chandeliers and original lofty, painted ceiling with exquisite naive representations of scenes of Jerusalem. There are also paintings of zodiac signs and symbols representing the Tribes of Israel. It has a central bimah, enclosed by a trellis, in front of an extremely ornate carved and brightly painted Aron ha Kodesh overhanging into the sanctuary that is topped by a two-headed eagle, the symbol of the Russian Empire.

The old cemetery dates from the seventeenth century and it, too, is surrounded by new construction. Many of its richly carved stones are sunk into the ground. In the newer cemetery, opened in 1871 and still in use, there is a monument to victims of the Holocaust.

Buhusi (Buhuşi)

Jewish Community: Str. Republicii 18, Bloc 18, Sc. B, Apt. 6. Tel. (932) 61859

This old textile center of about 20,000 people fell victim, like most other towns in Moldavia, to Ceausescu's urban renewal frenzy, and much of the old town has been replaced by new concrete housing blocks.

Jews may have first lived here in the late sixteenth or seventeenth centuries. Later, they were invited to settle here in 1823 by the local nobleman. In the mid-to-late nineteenth century, the town became an important Hasidic center as the court of Reb Isaac Friedman (1835–1896) of the famous Ruzhyn dynasty. Pilgrims still come each year to visit the tomb of Reb Friedman in the Buhusi cemetery.

Thousands of Jews lived here before World War II; the community survived the Holocaust, but most emigrated to Israel. Today, only about a score of mostly elderly Jews remain in the town.

Nonetheless, the marvelous synagogue and extraordinary old cemetery are lovingly maintained as witnesses to the past. Built in 1859, the synagogue has a stately, rather ornate exterior and rises up amid the characteristically low, irregular houses of what was once an old Jewish shtetl straight out of a Chagall painting. Today, it is one of the only remaining old neighborhoods in the midst of the anonymous, raw new housing blocks that have taken over the city.

The synagogue was damaged in the mid-1980s, when local youths broke in searching for goods to steal and set fire to one of the rooms, but it has since been painstakingly restored and its frescoes and other painted decoration glow with bright colors.

Lit by the sun streaming through its big, arched windows, the lofty, square sanctuary is decorated with naive wall paintings depicting zodiac symbols representing the months of the year and imaginary landscape scenes, including dreamlike visions of the Holy Land.

The Aron ha Kodesh—again, in a style typical for Moldavia—is a joyously ornate carved fantasy in brightly painted wood, incorporating gilded rococo elements, tromp l'oeil painted curtains, and typically Jewish symbols, such as the Ten Commandments and hands raised in priestly blessing.

The extraordinary cemetery is on a hill at the end of an extremely bad, muddy road (impossible to find without the help of the local community). The massive, richly carved gravestones clearly show Polish Jewish influence in the complex designs incorporating Jewish symbolism: the priestly hands; entwined candelabra on women's graves; mythical beasts; floral fantasies, and the like. Quite a few still show traces of the bright red and blue colors with which they were painted.

The cemetery seems to be at the end of the world. Dusk was falling when we visited; leafless trees cast long shadows. On the edge of the cemetery, as if on the edge of a forest clearing in some long-ago century, a gnarled peasant—the caretaker—lives in a small cottage with his mentally handicapped, grown-up son. Smoke curls from the chimney. The old man, astrakhan hat jammed above his weathered face, followed us closely as we walked among the graves, stone to stone. Under his arm, he carried a whisk broom.

Cluj Napoca

Jewish Community: Str. Tipografiei 25. Tel. (951) 16677

Kosher Restaurant: Str. Parisu 5-7

Once the capital of Transylvania, Cluj, in northwest Romania 277 miles from Bucharest, belonged to Hungary until 1918 and also during World War II. Today, it is a bustling educational and industrial center of more than 300,000 people whose downtown area still has an Austro-Hungarian feel, with its eighteenth- and nineteenth-century buildings and several important earlier monuments, including the fifteenth-century St. Michael's Church.

Jews came here in the eighteenth century, but they were not permitted to settle legally in the town itself until 1848. The development of the Jewish community was similar to that of other Hungarian towns, including the conflict between Orthodox and Reformed Jews resulting in the eventual formal split between Orthodox and Neolog (Reformed) communities in 1869.

The Jews of Cluj also suffered the same fate as the Jews of provincial Hungary. In 1944, a ghetto was set up in the city and soon after, about 16,700 Jews from Cluj and nearby towns and villages were deported to Auschwitz.

"This plaque commemorates my entire family, father, mother, wife, and children," said Iosif Weintraub, president of today's 500-strong Jewish community, pointing to a wall plaque in the entryway of the large but simple synagogue, built in 1922, on Str. Croitorilor. "They were all killed."

Weintraub's congregation is mostly elderly and many have intermarried or are children of mixed marriages. A handful of young people study in the Talmud Torah school and sing in the small choir, but age and—increasingly—poverty are the hallmarks of what still is one of Romania's largest Jewish communities outside Bucharest. Food price increases in the spring of 1991 even put the kosher restaurant out of the range of most local Jews who to date had counted on it for warm meals.

"I lie awake at night worrying about prices," said Andrei Farkas, a pensioner who was manager of the restaurant at the time. With the food price increases, he said, his daily stipend for managing the lunchroom was only enough to buy his wife a meal.

Cluj has three synagogues. Its main synagogue is the so-called Synagogue of the Deportees, built in 1887 by the Reformed community and now dedicated to the memory of those who died in the war. It is a highly decorated, Moorish-style building with four bulbous domes topping its orange facade on Str. Horea, a main street leading from the center of town. Another ornate building once belonging to the Jewish community stands right next door.

In the early 1990s, Cluj's Babes-Bolyai University opened the Dr. Moses Carmilly Institute for Hebrew and Jewish History, which has sponsored seminars, exhibitions, and research as well as academic studies.

Constanta (Constanţa)

Jewish Community: Str. Sarmisegetuza 3. Tel. (916) 11598

Dating back to the sixth century B.C.E.—it was the ancient city of Tomis—Constanta today has a population of 330,000 and is Romania's major port on the Black Sea. Ugly industrial areas surround what in parts is still a pleasant Old Town with important ancient Roman archeological remains. The ancient Roman poet Ovid was exiled here and is believed to have been buried here.

Before World War II, about 2,000 Jews lived in the city. The Nazis destroyed the cemetery, using the tombstones for milestones. The two synagogues were used as warehouses and later as camps for Russian POWs. Today, one hundred or so Jews live in Constanta, and both synagogues have been restored. One is part of the Jewish community complex, the other is on Str. Rosetti.

Constanta was one of the only ports open during World War II for Jewish emigration—much of it illegal. One of the ships that sailed from here in 1942 was the *Struma*, a cattle boat in which 769 Jews desperately tried to reach Palestine. The tragedy of its voyage became a symbol of world indifference to the Jewish fate.

The crowded boat managed to reach Istanbul but was held up there for two months during negotiations between the British and the Turks on whether or not it would be allowed to continue to the Holy Land. The British tried to convince the Turks not to let the boat go forward through the Bosphorus into the Mediterranean, and eventually the Turks forced the boat to turn back into the Black Sea.

On February 24, 1942, it was sunk by a Soviet torpedo.

*Dorohoi

Jewish Community: Str. 6 Martie 16. Tel. (986) 13424

Kosher Restaurant: Str. 6 Martie 16

Until the late 1980s, the small town of Dorohoi, set in fertile rolling hills in the far northeast corner of Romania, was like a step backward in time: a Jewish shtetl whose low wooden houses, jammed tightly together on cobbled squares and narrow streets, perfectly preserved the atmosphere of bygone days when Jews made up the majority of the population.

Today, all is changed. As in most Moldavian towns, most of Dorohoi's old buildings were razed to the ground under the Ceausescu regime and replaced by raw concrete blocks. Granted, these blocks have running water (unlike many old homes in Romanian towns and villages), but they have transformed a town full of wonderful historic character into a concrete replica of every other town in the region. The synagogues, once surrounded by a peaceful, cobbled plaza and old wooden homes and shops, are now isolated and fenced off in the middle of a building site.

Dorohoi was located on major trade routes linking the Baltic Sea and the Black Sea, and Jews from Poland settled here in the seventeenth century.

Hasidism became a major force among the Jewish community, many of whose members were shopkeepers, craftsmen, artisans, and merchants. Ohels of local rabbis stand in the sprawling cemetery on a hill just outside of town on the way to Suceava.

About 5,300 Jews, making up one-third of the town's population, lived in Dorohoi on the eve of World War II. Most of the Jewish population was deported to labor camps in Transnistria on November 11, 1941.

A big monument in the cemetery commemorates the victims of the deportations and other casualties of the Holocaust: Bars of soap said to have been made from Jewish bodies are buried here; and the monument also commemorates the massacre by Romanian soldiers of scores of Jews attending a funeral on July 1, 1940, and the subsequent looting of Jewish property in town. "As they were beginning the pogrom in town, there was a huge rainstorm, a deluge, which stopped them from going further," said Chief Rabbi Moses Rosen. "This saved the Jews."

In 1991, only about 100 Jews lived in Dorohoi. About a dozen lonely souls were cared for in the well-maintained Jewish old-age home, which has since closed.

Elias Isaac Rohrlich, the bluff, red-haired leader of the community, said he could have left for Israel like most of the rest of Dorohoi's Jews, but he felt too much responsibility for the care of the lonely, elderly people who for whatever reasons remained in the town.

"I was raised in the spirit of helping the poor," he said. "Rabbi Rosen's wife once described the community as the handkerchief that dries the tears of the suffering Jew, and over the decades I have tried to make our community such a handkerchief."

Rohrlich's tiny storefront office, warmed by a tiled stove, was in one of the only blocks of old houses in the town. Nearby, Dorohoi's two main synagogues huddled side by side amid the chaotic new concrete construction on Piata Unirii. Both were in good condition, with typical Moldavian naive painting decoration on the inside and distinctive memorial lamps, each bearing the name of the person the lamp commemorates.

Rohrlich finally left for Israel about eighteen months after my visit.

Falticeni (Fălticeni)

Jewish Community: Str. Republicii, Bloc 80. Tel. (989) 41337

A small industrial city founded in the late eighteenth century, Falticeni is another depressingly anonymous Moldavian town whose heart has been cut out and replaced by concrete blocks.

Before World War II, about 4,000 Jews lived in Falticeni, making up one-third of the local population. It was the hometown of Chief Rabbi Rosen, whose own father served here as rabbi. Today, there are only a few dozen Jews in Falticeni and nearby villages.

The big, barnlike nineteenth-century synagogue, with high arched windows and tin peaked roof, appears to be the only old building in the town center. Three separate prayer rooms coexist within the spacious building.

One could scarcely imagine the magnificence of the Great Synagogue, or main sanctuary, by looking at the rather simple exterior of the synagogue building. Under a lofty, blue-painted ceiling sprinkled with gold stars, there is a spectacular and grandiose carved, painted, and gilded wooden Aron ha Kodesh that, supported by two big pillars, curves out into the sanctuary, itself surmounted by a double-headed eagle. It is a splendid and awe-inspiring sight: The brilliant gold, red, blue, and green dazzle the eyes, a true celebration of the Torah. There are tromp l'oeil painted curtains, shiny Stars of David, flags, banners, and even the Romanian coat of arms.

Around the walls are painted banners with symbols representing the Tribes of Israel, as well as painted and gilded pillars and false drapery supporting the women's gallery.

The two other prayer rooms are small and simple. One is a prayer room for everyday use. The other is named after Rabbi Avram Arie Rosen, Chief Rabbi Rosen's father.

Falticeni has a very beautiful, large, old cemetery—already closed in the mid-nineteenth century—with richly carved gravestones. In addition to ritual symbolism, a number of the stones are decorated with unusually fanciful geometric and floral designs framing the Hebrew epitaphs.

Iasi (Iaşi)

Jewish Community: Str. Elena Doamna 15. Tel. (981) 14414

Kosher Restaurant: Str. Elena Doamna 15

The capital of Moldavia from 1565 to 1862, Iasi, also known as Jassy, is a cultural, university, artistic, and commercial center in the far northeast corner of Romania that grew up at the crossroads of important ancient trade routes. Despite much modern construction and a mushrooming population of 315,000, many historic monuments remain, and the city is a lot more human and livable than most other Moldavian towns.

Iasi was one of the great centers of Jewish life and learning in East-Central Europe, famous for its scholarly rabbis and intellectuals, skilled craftsmen, and acute businessmen, as well as for its Jewish schools, hospitals, publications, and other organizations. The world's first professional Yiddish theater opened in Iasi in 1876. It was established by Polish director, composer, and playwright Abraham Goldfaden (1840–1908), an avid exponent of the Haskalah (Jewish enlightenment) and the father of the Yiddish stage.

"About Rome, Italy's capital, one says that no matter in which place you are walking you tread on history," longtime Iasi Jewish community president Simion Caufman once said. "That is quite true. Paraphrasing this expression, we may say that it holds true regarding Iasi as well—no matter where you are walking, you tread on Judaism and Jewish art."

Jewish merchants moving south from Poland settled here in the fifteenth century, and their numbers were swelled by further waves of mainly Polish immigrants over the years. By the outbreak of World War II, the city's 51,000 Jews made up well over half the local population, and some 127 synagogues were in operation.

"This street here was called Synagogue Street," said Caufman, a retired pharmacist, pointing to what is now a nondescript city street. "There were seventeen synagogues on it. We had a cemetery here dating back six hundred years, but it was destroyed by the fascists."

Iasi—The Great Synagogue, built in 1671.

Caufman, a short, sweet-faced man with an underslung lower jaw, lost twenty-seven members of his family in the infamous Iasi pogrom in June 1941, when Romanian soldiers slaughtered at least 10,000 local Jews. He himself was saved by a Christian man, a fellow pharmacist, who hid him.

Addressing about 200 fellow Jews at an Iasi community seder, he reminded them that "What unites Jews is not the blood running in their veins, but the blood that flows from their wounds."

Most of the pogrom victims are buried in four huge concrete bunkers that form a massive Holocaust memorial in the Iasi Jewish cemetery on the eastern edge of the city. Monuments mark the mass graves of other pogrom victims near the towns of Tirgu Frumos and Podul Iloaiei.

Iasi's Great Synagogue, an unusual building with simple lines and a metal-roofed dome, was founded in 1671, or maybe even earlier. Unlike most other synagogues in Moldavia, its inner walls are not decorated with brilliant frescoes.

The synagogue is still in use, but daily services are held in a small prayer room outside the main sanctuary. Upstairs, in what used to be the women's gallery, there is a small but comprehensive museum of local Jewish history. Mr. Caufman rather shyly pointed out his own young face in a mass portrait of Jewish high school students from the 1930s.

*Piatra Neamt (Piatra Neamţ)

Jewish Community: Str. Lenin 7. Tel. (936) 23815

Beautifully situated in the forested foothills of the Carpathians about 220 miles north of Bucharest, Piatra Neamt, with 110,000 people, is another historic Moldavian town whose old sections were razed to the ground and replaced by ugly concrete blocks. Only a few historic buildings remain, like islands in a polluted sea. One of these old sections is the little street, beneath a hill, on which the old Jewish courtyard and two synagogues stand.

One of these synagogues, the so-called Ba'al Shem Tov Synagogue, has been declared a historic landmark and is one of the most fascinating synagogues in Romania—both for its architecture and for the legend that surrounds it.

Jewish merchants from Poland settled in Piatra Neamt centuries ago, probably as early as the fourteenth century. The major wave of settlement came in the seventeenth century after the Chmielnicki uprising forced thousands of Jews to flee Poland and the Ukraine. Over 8,000 Jews lived in Piatra Neamt before World War II, making up one-quarter of the local population. Throughout the 1930s, they suffered serious episodes of anti-Semitic violence and restrictions; Corneliu Codreanu, founder of the Iron Guard, was elected to Parliament from Piatra Neamt in 1931. The community survived the war, but most left for Israel. Today, there are fewer than 250 Jews in the town.

The Ba'al Shem Tov Synagogue, made of wood, dates from the eighteenth century but stands on the spot where an earlier masonry synagogue once stood. The present building is halfway underground, built like this to conform to regulations that forbade synagogues to be higher than surrounding Christian buildings.

The sanctuary is entered down stairs leading from a little outer prayer room where regular services are held. Chandeliers hang from the ribbed wooden dome arching over the dull green walls decorated by stenciled flowers. Carved and gilded lions, griffins, bunches of grapes, and other decorations ornament the elaborate Aron ha Kodesh, which is topped by carved hands raised in priestly blessing.

Along a shelf, silver crowns from centuries-old Torahs are lined up. From the small prayer room outside comes the murmur of ancient prayers.

The Ba'al Shem Tov, legendary and mysterious founder of the Hasidic movement believed to have lived from 1700 to 1760, is said to have worshiped in this shul. Little is known about the Ba'al Shem Tov except for the fact that he existed. One legend says that he lived for a time in a small, lonely village twenty-five miles away in a place known as Jews' Valley, high in the nearby mountains. From time to time, the story goes, he came to Piatra Neamt to pray. (See Poland.)

Next door to the Ba'al Shem Tov Synagogue is the Temple Synagogue, very similar to other folk-style Moldavian shuls. It has a small, raised bimah in the center, with a trellised frame in front of a highly elaborate Aron ha Kodesh with tromp l'oeil curtains. The walls are decorated with frescoes in false frames representing the seven gates of Jerusalem and other Holy Land themes. Frescoes of biblical animals—the stag, the lion, the tiger, and the eagle—are painted on the ceiling.

In early 1991, some 400 people from here and a neighboring town packed into the Temple Synagogue to witness a happy occasion: the first wedding celebrated there in twenty years.

The old Jewish cemetery in Piatra Neamt, dating back to the seventeenth century, is one of the most evocative and extraordinary in Romania. Massive, richly carved tombstones straggle up a steep slope at the foot of a dramatic wooded hill above the town. The Polish-influenced carving is sumptuous, and the silhouettes of the stones across the hillside are reminiscent of the scene in Ingmar Bergman's film *The Seventh Seal* when Death leads a line of people into the hereafter.

Radauti (Rădáuţi)

Jewish Community: Al. Primaverii, Bloc 14, Apt. 1. Tel. (989) 61333

Radauti is a dusty little market town in the far north of Romania a few miles south of the Ukrainian border where Jews have lived from the late eighteenth century. Its claim to fame for most visitors is its position as a base for visiting the beautiful painted Romanian monasteries scattered in the rolling countryside nearby.

For me, Radauti holds another significance—it is the town my paternal grandparents came from. About 5,000 Jews—nearly one-third of the local population—lived here before the war, and the town still has the remnants of a large Jewish quarter. My great-grandmother, Ettel Gruber,

Radauti—A tombstone in the Jewish cemetery with an inscription in Hebrew and in German and a vivid sculptural decoration showing the Tree of Life being broken by a hand, the hand of God or of the angel of death.

Radauti—Three members of the Jewish community sit at table after the Passover seder. At left is community president Simon Leventer. At right is the elderly man who led the seder.

is buried in the Radauti Jewish cemetery. She died in 1947, and I was given my middle name, Ellen, in her honor. Her tombstone, decorated with the traditional candlesticks indicating the grave of a woman, stands tilted over near the right-hand wall in the newer part of the cemetery.

My grandparents left Radauti before World War I; my grandmother was just a child, and my grandfather was the only one of his family to immigrate to America. The others stayed in the village; except for one of his brothers who remained in Romania, those who were not killed in the war all moved to Israel.

I first visited the town in 1978, when I was traveling around Romania with Chief Rabbi Rosen during Hanukkah. In 1991, I returned to celebrate Pesach with the few dozen elderly members of the Radauti Jewish community, attending the second night community seder held in the small prayer room of the big twin-towered synagogue in the middle of town.

It was a curious, moving evening. When I had visited Radauti in 1978, there were still several people who remembered members of my family and could tell stories of some of the more colorful characters. This time, only one old man, the grizzled patriarch who led the seder, recalled much. My great-grandfather, Anschel, he told me, didn't come from Radauti itself but from a little village just outside.

The old man was sick. People said he came out of the hospital just for the seders: On the first night, they said, he got locked into reciting one prayer over and over and over until someone had to stop him.

I, the honored guest, was seated next to him at the head table, facing about two dozen people seated at long tables around the walls of the prayer room. The old man went through the service in a quavering voice. Tall candlesticks guttered. The one child—son of the community president—raced through the Four Questions at top speed and everyone applauded. We ate matzo kugel and hard-boiled eggs, brisket and potatoes; we drank sweet Carmel wine from Israel.

At the end of the seder, after most people had gone home, a few of us sat singing Passover songs. We stalled on *"Had Gadyah"*—the song about buying a baby goat. I knew one tune. The friend from Bucharest with whom I was traveling knew another. And the old man, the leader of the seder? He sat silent for a moment. I could almost feel time dropping away as he reached back across fifty years.

He took a breath, smiled a little, and started singing: It was a tune I'd never heard before; a wavering, almost oriental melody sung in a strange, twanging Yiddish accent—the way my grandparents and their parents before them probably sang it.

Satu Mare

Jewish Community: Str. Decebal 4. Tel. (997) 11728

A Transylvanian city of 130,000 set in rich farmland almost on the border with Hungary in the far northwest corner of Romania, Satu Mare is famous for having been the seat of the great Hasidic Teitelbaum and Gruenwald dynasties.

To this day, pilgrims come to pay their respects at the imposing tombs of the tzaddikim in the Jewish cemetery which, partly on behalf of these pilgrims, was repaired and cleaned during the 1980s. In the cemetery is also a large Holocaust memorial in the form of a chapel with the names of the thousands of local victims.

Satu Mare was part of Hungary until 1918 and was annexed by Hungary during World War II. Most local residents are ethnic Hungarians who call their town by its Hungarian name, Szatmar.

Jews settled here in the early eighteenth century. About 13,000 Jews lived here before World War II; there were eight synagogues and a famous yeshiva. In 1944, the Germans deported the Jewish population to death camps. Today, about 200 Jews live in town and two synagogues remain; only one, the Great Synagogue, is in regular use. It is a flat-fronted building erected in 1920. Some of its interior decoration, including the chandeliers, show an art deco influence, and lying everywhere on tables, desks, and pews are piles of moldering prayer books.

Sighet (Sighetu Marmaţiei)

Jewish Community: Str. Viseului 10. Tel. (995) 11652

A quiet Transylvanian town of 40,000 set amid beautiful mountains and farmland on the Ukrainian border in northwest Romania, Sighet is one of the main towns in Maramures country, an area noted for its folkloric traditions: Beautifully carved wooden gates can be seen in many nearby villages, and at Sighet's lively peasant market, both men and women wear traditional folk costumes.

Jews were living in Sighet by the seventeenth century, and the town eventually became a center both of Hasidism and of the bizarre Frankist sect. (See Poland.) At Sighet was a court of the Hasidic Teitelman dynasty, whose main center was in the Hungarian town of Satoraljaujhely. (See Hungary.) Pilgrims from all over come every year to pay their respects at the tombs of the tzaddikim.

The city is also the birthplace of author and Holocaust survivor Elie Wiesel, born in 1928 and winner of the Nobel Peace Prize, who has written movingly of his childhood there. He has described the warm, familial Jewish life in the town, where his parents were shopkeepers (like so many Jews) and he himself lived for his prayers and studies. He has also written how virtually until their ghettoization and deportation to Auschwitz in 1944, Sighet's Jews were not aware of their impending doom; they could not even conceive of the destruction of their people and way of life, despite occasional reports filtering in from Poland and elsewhere.

The house where Wiesel grew up (someone from the Jewish community will be glad to guide you there) still stands. Until recently, it was inhabited by a Gypsy family who drew water from its well just as the Wiesel family must have done. In late 1991, the Romanian government announced that the house would be turned into a museum honoring Wiesel and the local Jewish community.

Before the war, more than 10,000 Jews lived in Sighet, making up nearly forty percent of the population—the highest proportion of any Hungarian town. Today, there are fewer than 100 Jews. Once there were seven or eight synagogues, today there is only one, a barnlike, simply decorated nineteenth century building situated near the Jewish community offices. Religious life is dwindling: Minyans gather in the synagogue's small prayer room only on Shabbat and holidays.

The Jewish community offices and synagogue are full of pictures of Elie Wiesel, their famous native son, and under the lofty painted ceiling,

Siret—A Romanian Jewish man walks in the dramatic Jewish cemetery, the newer of the two Jewish cemeteries in the town.

there is a small exhibition on the Holocaust. (There is a Holocaust memorial on Gh. Doza Street.)

When I visited, in the spring of 1991, the words "Heil Hitler" were scrawled across the synagogue's doors.

*Siret

This pleasant little town on the Ukrainian border in the Bucovina region of northern Romania was the capital of Moldavia in the fourteenth century and has two of the most spectacular of Romania's Jewish cemeteries. Recognized as historic monuments, they are easily found near the center of town, a few dozen yards from each other. There is something particularly mystical about these two cemeteries, lonely reminders in a town where only a dozen Jews at most still live today.

Siret—A vividly carved gravestone showing hands putting money into a charity box, denoting that the deceased was charitable, and holding a book.

Siret, like other towns in the region a staging point on medieval trade routes, was one of the earliest Jewish settlements in Moldavia: Jews came here as merchants and had already established a community in the early sixteenth century.

The old cemetery, founded in the sixteenth century and thus one of the oldest in the country, has only a few richly carved but weathered tombstones scattered amid brush over a small, but extremely hilly, enclosure surrounded by a wall.

As we entered through the unlocked gate, a peasant woman in the house across the way crossed herself repeatedly. Children followed us, clambering over the wall. It was obvious that this was a sort of playground for them. We chided one boy for hitting one of the old stones with a big stick and got a chilling reply. "Why not?" he said. "It's just a Yid tomb."

The newer cemetery across the way is one of the most impressive I've seen anywhere, a vast expanse of richly carved tombstones set in regular rows on two levels, one high above the other, on and on and on.

*Suceava

Jewish Community: Str. Armeneasca 8. Tel. (987) 13084

An ancient city whose history dates back 2,000 years, Suceava, about 270 miles north of Bucharest, served as capital of Moldavia at one point during the Middle Ages. The town now has a population of about 80,000, and the historic monuments that remain are submerged in the characterless concrete jungle of Ceausescu's urban planning.

The town, like other Moldavian cities a major stop on medieval north-south trade routes, was one of the earliest in Moldavia to be settled by Jews: A community was already established by the beginning of the sixteenth century. Later, in 1761, Moldavian authorities and local landowners invited a further wave of Jewish immigrants from Poland to settle here to repopulate and revitalize the town as a commercial center after it had been ravaged by wars. Soon afterward, Suceava came under Hapsburg rule when its county, Bucovina, was annexed in 1775 by Austria, which ruled it until 1918.

Before World War II, eighteen synagogues and small Hasidic prayer rooms served Suceava's thousands of Jews. Today, the Jewish population is 200 or less, and only one synagogue remains standing. All the others were torn down during the "systematization"—urban renewal—of the town beginning in the 1950s. The last was razed in 1986.

The synagogue that still serves the community was built in 1870 and underwent full restoration that was completed in 1991. Like other Moldavian synagogues, it is unprepossessing on the outside, but its simple, box-like interior is brightly painted with biblical and symbolic scenes and imaginary landscapes.

The lofty ceiling is painted deep sky blue and at its corners are splendid representations of scriptural beasts: the lion, eagle, tiger, and stag. On the walls are zodiac symbols representing the months of the year, as well as symbolic representations of the Tribes of Israel and dreamlike views of Jerusalem. Little windows of pebble glass enclose the women's gallery. There is a central bimah surrounded by a wrought iron fence facing a small but elaborately carved Aron ha Kodesh surmounted by gilded lions.

Suceava's breathtaking ancient Jewish cemetery, which may date to the sixteenth century, is believed to be one of the oldest in Moldavia. Its hundreds of exceptionally fine Polish-style gravestones, many showing traces of polychrome decoration, are crowded into a relatively small, walled enclosure. Chickens from the home of the peasant caretaker at the cemetery's edge wander in clucking flocks amid the stones and their intricate designs of mythical beasts, candlesticks, and Jewish symbols. Some of the stones are pointed, similar to Bohemian gravestones, and the cemetery reminds me, on a much smaller scale, of the Old Jewish Cemetery in Prague.

Timisoara (Timoşoara)

Jewish Community: Str. Gh. Lazar 5. Tel. (961) 32813

Kosher Restaurant: Str. Marasesti 10

Set amid vast fertile plains in western Transylvania near the Yugoslav (Serbian) and Hungarian borders, Timisoara, with 325,000 people, is the city where the 1989 revolution was sparked off during antigovernment riots.

Timisoara was ruled by the Turks from 1552 to 1716 and then became part of Hungary until 1918. Long a center of both Hungarian and German ethnic groups, it is a pretty city with many parks and charming Hungarian art nouveau architecture.

There was a Jewish presence here before the Turkish conquest, but permanent settlement dates from the mid-sixteenth century. The oldest tombstone in the extremely impressive Jewish cemetery is that of a rabbi and surgeon named Azriel Asael, who died in 1636.

In 1716, 155 Jews lived in Timisoara. In 1858, there were 2,200. In 1940, the Jewish population was 11,000, at least ten percent of the local population.

The city was an important center of Zionism, but also a hotbed of anti-Semitic Iron Guard activity in the 1930s. In 1936, the Iron Guard bombed a Jewish theater, killing two and injuring many others.

The majority of Timisoara's Jews survived the war, but most went to Israel. Today, along with Iasi, Timisoara has the largest Jewish community outside Bucharest—about 900 people—and has been the seat of the only other rabbi in the country besides Chief Rabbi Rosen.

With three active synagogues, Talmud Torah classes, a choir, kosher restaurant, and Jewish old-age home, there is ample opportunity for a rich Jewish life.

Prolific Hungarian synagogue architect Lipot Baumhorn built the magnificent Great Synagogue in 1899.

*Tirgu Mures (Tîrgu Mureş)

Jewish Community: Str. Brailei 10. Tel. (954) 15001

A city of 160,000 overlooking the Mures River 200 or so miles northwest of Bucharest, Tirgu Mures preserves a charming downtown district ranged around a parklike main square that is an important complex of Hungarian art nouveau architecture. The fact that it is the center of Romania's natural gas industry may account for the fact that the hotel I stayed in, the Transilvania, was one of the few I encountered with adequate hot water.

As part of northern Transylvania, Tirgu Mures was Hungarian until 1918 and was annexed to Hungary during World War II. Jews settled within the city in the nineteenth century, though Jewish settlements were founded in nearby villages much earlier. Their history paralleled that of Jews in Hungary proper: The Tirgu Mures community split into separate Orthodox and Status Quo communities following the 1869 schism in Hungarian Jewry.

More than 5,500 Jews lived in the city before World War II, making up about thirty percent of the population. All were deported to Nazi death camps in 1944. Today, fewer than 300 Jews live in the town.

The wealth and importance of the prewar Jewish community can be seen by the magnificence of the synagogue: a large, domed, highly ornate building on Str. Scolii designed by architect Jakab Gartner for the Status Quo community to seat more than 550 people and dedicated in 1900. The interior is lavishly decorated with stained glass, frescoes, and carved detail. Rather pompous plaques on the walls honor community leaders who gave contributions for the construction of the synagogue. In front of the Ark is a memorial to Holocaust victims, and there are big Holocaust memorials in the two Jewish cemeteries in town.

In the ceremonial hall of one of these cemeteries is a very moving sculpture by local artist Iszak Martin showing a Jewish family facing deportation.

The oldest Jewish cemeteries in the Tirgu Mures area are in the village of Nazna, about three miles away. There are two small cemeteries here set amid rolling pastureland.

The older one, a very small enclosure with a couple of dozen gravestones in it, dates back to the eighteenth or early nineteenth century. The stones are very weathered, but they display a beautiful, living quality—the carved hands representing the priestly blessing on one stone look almost as if they are alive, and some of the Hebrew calligraphy is fantastically delicate and ornate. Fruit trees planted by the peasant caretaker drop petals from their blossoms among the graves. In the center, in a sort of clearing, stands one stone shaped almost like a human being. Its epitaph tells that here lies a man of integrity; the carved decoration represents a crown and an upside-down heart pierced by an arrow.

*Tirgu Neamt (Tîrgu Neamţ)

Jewish Community: Str. Cuza Voda 160. Tel. (936) 62515

Until 1985, there were nine synagogues still standing in Tirgu Neamt, a small town on the Ozana River in northern Moldavia in the foothills of the eastern Carpathians. Today, there is one. The rest were torn down in the urban renewal that transformed Tirgu Neamt into a carbon copy of almost every other town nearby.

Jews are believed to have settled here in the late fifteenth century. They were expelled in 1579 and didn't return until the seventeenth century. Throughout the history of the Jewish community, there were a number of blood libel accusations and other anti-Semitic incidents encouraged by local monks.

Before World War II, more than 3,000 Jews lived in Tirgu Neamt. Today, there are fewer than fifty. Nonetheless, a group of elderly men still manages to gather for a minyan every evening in the one remaining shul.

The synagogue is a totally nondescript-looking building in one of the isolated remaining old streets of the former shtetl now surrounded by concrete housing blocks. Inside, the small sanctuary is a jewel, with bright naive-style wall paintings of zodiac symbols and a very elaborate carved and painted Aron ha Kodesh surmounted by a two-headed eagle and incorporating primitive carvings of eagles, griffins, and the hands raised in priestly blessing.

Tirgu Neamt has a large and extremely impressive old cemetery. The oldest tombstone found in the city dates to 1677. Well maintained by a peasant family living at the edge of the cemetery grounds, it has hundreds of massive stones with extremely rich carving spread out over a broad, grassy field sheltered by shady trees. Some of the stones, tilted over and sunken into the earth, still exhibit traces of polychrome decoration.

Hotels/Restaurants

Few hotels in Romania come up to Western standards of service and comfort for their categories. Due to inefficiency and economic hardship (particularly in the provinces), even first-class or deluxe hotels may lack heat, hot water, toilet paper—or light bulbs—and hotel staff members may balk at remedying the situation.

Given Romania's food and other shortages, restaurants, too, may have very little selection.

The list below notes hotels in several towns that are considered top-of-the-line.

BUCHAREST

- Intercontinental, B-dul N. Balescu 4-6. Tel. 140400
- Bucuresti, Calea Victoriei 63-81. Tel. 145349
- Continental, Calea Victoriei 56. Tel. 154580
- Restaurant Capsa, Calea Victoriei 36. Founded in 1852, an island of old-world atmosphere. Famous for over a century, and one of the best restaurants in town.

ARAD

- Astoria, B-dul Republicii 79-81. Tel. (966) 16650

BRASOV

- Carpati, B-dul Carpati 9

IASI

- Unirea, Piata Unirii. Tel. (981) 42110

TIMISOARA

- Continental, B-dul 23 August 2. Tel. (961) 34145

TIRGU MURES

- Transilvania, Piata Trandafirilor 43

THE FORMER YUGOSLAVIA

SLOVENIA, CROATIA, YUGOSLAVIA (SERBIA
AND MONTENEGRO), BOSNIA AND
HERZEGOVINA, MACEDONIA

Population: 23 million
Jewish Population before World War II: 80,000
Jewish Population in 1994: 3,000 to 5,000

A LITTLE HISTORY

Lying in the heart of the Balkan peninsula directly on the main overland trade routes between Europe and the Middle East, Yugoslavia (which means Land of the South Slavs) was created after World War I by joining ethnically different territories long ruled by different powers. What became the north and west of the country had been ruled by the Austro-Hungarians; the south and east had been mainly under the Turks. Some places had had brief periods of independence; some had changed hands several times.

Yugoslavia existed until 1991. It was made up of six republics—Slovenia, Croatia, Serbia (with its two provinces, Vojvodina and Kosovo), Bosnia and Herzegovina, Macedonia, and Montenegro—whose people were ethnically diverse, practiced different religions, spoke different languages, and used different alphabets. Their histories were diverse, and they had come under separate cultural influences over the centuries. The gap in economic development between the fairly prosperous north (Slovenia and Croatia) and the underdeveloped south (Macedonia, Kosovo province, and Montenegro) was dramatic. These differences, combined with ethnic nationalism, contributed to the civil war that erupted in 1991 after the declarations of independence by Slovenia, Croatia, and, later, Bosnia and Herzegovina.

A number of important archeological finds testify to Jewish presence in the region in ancient Roman times, but all the subsequent historic variation meant that the history of the Jewish communities also differed.

Ashkenazic Jews from Central Europe predominated in the northern and western parts ruled by the Austro-Hungarian Empire.

Much of the southern, eastern, and coastal parts of the country, particularly the parts under Turkish occupation, were havens for Sephardic Jews fleeing the expulsion from Spain and Portugal in 1492. The entire Ottoman Empire, in fact, was long a refuge for Jews. There were few if any restrictions on residency and trade, and the Muslim rulers did not force Jews to wear special identifying badges, as often happened under Christian rulers. Instead, the Ottoman rulers welcomed Jewish immigration, for it brought in thousands of educated people with specialized skills (doctors, pharmacists, merchants, trained artisans, and craftsmen) and a high cultural level.

During World War II, Yugoslavia was occupied by the Germans and their allies in April 1941, and the country was divided up among various German-allied neighbors.

The Italians occupied much of Slovenia, the Dalmatian coast along the Adriatic Sea, parts of Bosnia and Herzegovina, and Montenegro. Vojvodina went to Hungary. Macedonia went to Bulgaria. Serbia proper was occupied by the Germans, and Croatia became a Nazi-allied puppet state under Ante Pavelic, leader of the Croatian nationalist terrorist organization called the Ustashi.

Jews were persecuted everywhere. They were sent to forced labor camps and local extermination camps as well as deported to Auschwitz and other death camps. By mid-1942, the Nazis boasted that Serbia was *Judenrein*—free from Jews. Altogether, of the nearly 80,000 prewar Jewish population, about 60,000 perished.

As the war against the Nazis raged on, civil war within Yugoslavia also broke out, pitting three separate groups against each other: communist anti-Nazi partisans led by Josip Broz Tito; the Croatian Nazi-allied Ustashi; and the Serbian Chetniks, pro-monarchy guerrilla groups that also eventually collaborated with the Germans and Italians.

A number of Jews joined the communist partisans and after the war were declared national heroes. Foremost among them was Mose Pijade, a bespectacled Marxist intellectual and one of Tito's chief aides. Streets, businesses, and organizations were named for him all over the country.

Yugoslavia under Tito (who ruled from the end of the war until his death in 1980) was communist, but it was not part of the Soviet bloc or allied with Moscow. Nonetheless, Yugoslavia broke relations with Israel after the Six-Day War in 1967.

The civil war that broke out in Yugoslavia in 1991 raged for months in Croatia, then centered on Bosnia and Herzegovina and soon became the bloodiest conflict in Europe since World War II.

Until the outbreak of the civil war, about 6,000 Jews lived in Yugoslavia, most of them in Belgrade, Zagreb, and Sarajevo, with many smaller scattered communities.

JEWISH HERITAGE IN THE FORMER YUGOSLAVIA

Most of the information on Jewish sites included here reflects conditions before the civil war. Besides its tragic human toll, the fighting has damaged or destroyed thousands of historic buildings as well as homes and businesses. As of this writing, Slovenia and Croatia were independent states, although Serbs claimed certain portions of Croatia. Bosnia and Herzegovina was the scene of bloody fighting. Macedonia was nominally independent. Serbia and Montenegro made up a rump Yugoslavia subject to severe international sanctions, including a ban on commercial air traffic. Travel was dangerous or difficult in much of the region. Contact the Jewish communities whose addresses are noted in order to obtain updated information. English-speakers are usually available.

SLOVENIA

Slovenia is a stunningly beautiful lozenge of territory encompassing Alpine mountains, upland valleys, and a small but lovely slice of Adriatic coast. Jews lived here during ancient Roman times, but the more modern settlement came in around the twelfth century with immigrations to the region from Italy and from Central Europe.

Until Yugoslavia was formed after World War I, most of Slovenia was ruled by Austria, and under the Hapsburg monarchy all Jews were expelled from the region between the late fifteenth and early eighteenth centuries. Only a few Jews moved back in the nineteenth and twentieth centuries.

Today, fewer than 100 Jews live in Slovenia, which has not been touched by fighting since the earliest days of the civil war.

Maribor

This ancient city on the Drava River in northeast Slovenia near the Austrian border was the stronghold of Slovenia's medieval Jewish population. A Jewish community was first mentioned here in 1277, and original Jewish settlement may go back even further, as Roman coins were found in the foundations of houses in the old ghetto.

In the fifteenth century, Maribor's Jewish community was fairly prosperous. Jews were in the wine business and carried out trade, and relations with local people were fairly smooth. In the early fifteenth century, historical evidence even shows that several dozen Catholics asked to be converted to Judaism! The rabbi, Israel ben Petahya Isserlein, was a noted scholar and expert in Jewish law and from 1427 to 1435 held the title Chief Rabbi of Styria, Carinthia, and Carniola.

Jews were expelled from Maribor and its surrounding territory in a decree issued by Emperor Maximilian in 1496. Today, only ten or so Jews out of a population of more than 100,000 live in the city.

Nonetheless, traces of the old ghetto remain, including a Gothic synagogue, probably built in 1480, that over the centuries was first transformed into a church (in 1501) and now serves as an art gallery. Nearby, there is the Jewish Tower, a fortified structure built in 1465, that is also now a gallery. One or two medieval Jewish tombstones are in the municipal museum.

Nova Gorica

The town of Gorizia was divided between Italy and Yugoslavia after World War II. Gorizia proper remains the Italian part, while the Yugoslav part—almost entirely new, modern construction built up in a suburb—is called Nova Gorica and is in Slovenia.

Most of the Jewish relics, including the former ghetto area and the small synagogue, remain in the Italian part of the city, but the historic Jewish cemetery, dating back to the eighteenth century, is on the Slovenian side near the main border crossing point and the main highway from Ljubljana.

Piran

This ancient seaside town pokes into the Adriatic on a pointed promontory at the northern end of the Istrian peninsula. Its Old Town maintains its medieval character (with some fine examples of Italian Gothic architecture) almost intact. Once ruled by Venice, Piran still conserves the old medieval ghetto square—Zidovski trg—entered through a low archway and surrounded by evocative, multistory buildings, similar to the ghetto architecture in Venice.

Elsewhere in Slovenia

There are also Jewish cemeteries in the towns of **Murska Sobota** and **Lendava** in the northeast near the border with Croatia. There is a Holocaust memorial at the cemetery in Lendava. In **Ljubljana**, the capital of Slovenia, there is a small Jewish cemetery and a Holocaust monument in a corner of the municipal cemetery. Two narrow streets in the town center—Zidovska ulica (Jewish Street) and Zidovska steza (Jewish Alley)—mark where the medieval ghetto stood.

CROATIA

Modern-day Croatia (which along with Slovenia declared independence in 1991) extends from what was central/western Yugoslavia down along the Dalmatian coast of the Adriatic Sea. Jews lived on the Dalmatian coast in ancient Roman times and are known to have had ancient settlements inland, too. A few Jewish settlements also existed in the Middle Ages.

In 1526, most of inland Croatia came under the rule of the Hapsburgs, who ordered the wholesale expulsion of Jews from the territory. Few if any Jews lived in inland Croatia again until the late eighteenth century, when the Edict of Tolerance issued by Emperor Josef II allowed Jews freedom of movement and other civil rights, although restrictions on occupations still remained in force. Jews could not own houses or land, for example, and could not work in agriculture or in professions protected by guilds. Only in 1873 were Jews in Croatia fully emancipated.

Waves of Ashkenazic Jewish immigrants from Hungary, Bohemia, Moravia, and Austria settled in Croatia in the early to middle nineteenth century and founded most of the Jewish communities in the region. By the late nineteenth/early twentieth centuries, Croatian Jews in these communities were fairly well off and constituted a lively and generally prosperous middle class.

Along the Dalmatian coast, ancient Roman-era settlements persisted for centuries, and major Jewish communities linked to seagoing commerce and trade developed in the Middle Ages. Refugees from Spain, Portugal, and Italy settled on the coast in the sixteenth century, giving the local communities a Sephardic character.

Much of the Dalmatian coast was ruled by Venice; parts were under Turkish influence. Conditions varied in later centuries, depending on which great power was in control.

During World War II, Croatia became the Nazi-allied Independent Croatian State, ruled by the brutal fascist Ustashi under Ante Pavelic. The Ustashi carried out terrible atrocities against the Jews and the Serbs.

Most of Dalmatia, however, was occupied by the Italians, who were much more lenient and refused to carry out mass deportations of Jews to death camps. Most Jews in the area were interned on Rab Island.

Of Croatia's 23,000 prewar Jews, only 5,000 survived the Holocaust, most of them either in the Italian-occupied zone or as soldiers in partisan units.

*Zagreb

Jewish Community: Palmoticeva 16. Tel. (41) 434-619

The capital of Croatia, Zagreb is an attractive town of nearly one million, with a quaint old medieval section on a hilltop above the stately Austro-Hungarian Lower Town spread out around the large, recently restored plaza of Trg Ban Jalacic.

Jews are first believed to have settled in Zagreb in the late Middle Ages. Expelled by the Austrian rulers in the fifteenth and sixteenth centuries, they only returned to the city in the late eighteenth century: twenty Jewish families officially founded the community in 1806.

By 1940, nearly 12,000 Jews, the great majority of them Ashkenazic, lived in Zagreb. The highly assimilated community, along with Belgrade the biggest in the country, was the most prosperous Jewish community in Yugoslavia and included a large number of businessmen, artists, writers, scholars, scientists, doctors, and other intellectuals. Zagreb was the seat of the Zionist Federation of Yugoslavia, and there were numerous Jewish clubs and social organizations.

By 1943, most Zagreb Jews had either been killed outright or deported to nearby Jasenovac concentration camp or Auschwitz.

With close to 2,000 Jews—including many refugees from war-torn regions—the Zagreb community is lively and active, sponsoring a youth group, kindergarten, choir, newspaper, cultural society, and many other activities. There is also a Jewish old-age home.

Many members of the community are young adults—in 1991, all members of the community leadership were under fifty. There are also many children, and education in Jewish life and culture plays a big role. A community Hanukkah party in 1990 was standing-room-only to light dozens of homemade menorahs, hear talks on the meaning of the holiday, and applaud cute kindergarteners costumed as candles and singing Hanukkah songs.

A plaque marks the spot on downtown ul. Praska where the former Great Synagogue stood before it was demolished in 1941. A plaque also marks the building at ul. Palmoticeva 22 that once served as the offices of the Maccabbee sports club.

In the community building at Palmoticeva 16 there is a prayer room used for regular services, a collection of Judaica, and a library with over 22,000 volumes dating from the sixteenth century to the present day that is the largest Jewish library in the Balkans. Zagreb's Arts and Crafts Museum features a Judaica collection.

There is a Jewish section in the city's Mirogoj Cemetery on a hill overlooking the town where an imposing statue of Moses forms a monument to Holocaust victims.

The cemetery is well maintained, and its many impressive tombs— particularly the striking monuments under a big arcade—give an idea of the wealth and importance of the late nineteenth- and early twentieth-century Zagreb community. Some tombs have inscriptions by which you can trace family histories, including intermarriage.

Appearances can be deceptive, however. Despite the appearance of care, the cemetery is devastated. Under local law, graves that are not maintained for a certain period of time (twenty to twenty-five years) may be sold as burial plots to others. Many once-Jewish graves are now occupied by Catholics (or communists). At some of the new gravesites, new monuments have replaced the former tombstones. In many instances, however, the name of the newly buried person (and often a Catholic cross or communist five-pointed star) has simply been added to the inscriptions on the former Jewish memorial.

Terrorist bombs during the civil war in 1991 seriously damaged both the community building and cemetery. After its full restoration, the Jewish community center was reopened with a gala ceremony at Rosh Hashanah 1992.

*Dubrovnik

Jewish Community: Zudioska ulica 3

With its massively walled Old Town thrusting into the sea against a backdrop of mountains plunging into the water, Dubrovnik, known as the Pearl of the Adriatic, is arguably the most beautiful city on the Dalmatian coast. An important maritime and trading center, Dubrovnik for centuries was an independent city-state republic, known as Ragusa, until it fell to the French in 1808.

The first record of Jewish presence here was that of a Jewish doctor mentioned in 1326, but the community really began to flourish with the arrival of refugees following the expulsion from Spain in 1492.

From the mid-sixteenth century on, a cramped Jewish ghetto was set up just off the Placa (Stradun), the beautiful, broad main street of Dubrovnik. This was—and still is—called Zudioska ulica (Jewish Street), a narrow alleyway partly composed of steeply rising steps. Gates, locked at night, were erected at either end, and Jews were forced to pay steep taxes for the "privilege" of living there. As late as the eighteenth century, Jews were barred from being out on the streets at night and from visiting Christian homes.

On Zudioska ulica, on the upper floor of Number 3, stands the oldest preserved synagogue in Croatia, a jewel of a prayer house possibly dating back to the fourteenth century but whose present appearance dates from 1652.

The Jewish community never numbered more than about 260, and on the eve of World War II only 87 Jews lived in the town. Today, fewer than twenty Jews live in Dubrovnik, but the synagogue is still used for services whenever a minyan can be found. It is also maintained as a museum, with ritual objects and textiles on display. In contrast to the simple, almost anonymous Gothic exterior, the interior decoration of the synagogue is baroque, with three interior arches and a small but highly ornate Aron ha Kodesh framed by six spiral columns with Corinthian tops.

The synagogue survived both a major earthquake that devastated Dubrovnik in 1667 as well as World War II. Its Torahs, many ritual objects, and the Aron ha Kodesh itself owe their survival of the Holocaust to the Tolentinos, a local Jewish family who hid them. The building was slightly damaged during shelling in 1991.

Dubrovnik has a fascinating Jewish cemetery at Boninovo, just outside town. Here the tombstones from the old Jewish cemetery dating from the early sixteenth century were moved in 1911. Many are still leaning against the surrounding walls.

There are several distinct types of tombstones. Among them are traditional Spanish-style horizontal Sephardic tombs with ornamental carving and Hebrew inscriptions. Some have a distinct Turkish flavor, as seen in ornamentation including the sun, moon, stars, and plant motifs.

Another type is a horizontal sarcophagus shaped like a peaked or gabled roof, with Hebrew inscriptions on its sides. There are also typical upright Ashkenazic tombstones, including obelisks.

Jasenovac

Near this village just off the Zagreb-Belgrade highway, about sixty miles from Zagreb, was sited the notorious Jasenovac concentration camp, which was set up in 1941. Hundreds of thousands of people, including an estimated 20,000 Jews, were slaughtered in the camp, the main concentration camp established in the Independent Croatian State.

*Split

Jewish Community: Zidovski prolaz 1/1. Tel. (58) 45672

Much of this ancient and beautiful Adriatic coast city is a virtual open-air museum of history and archeology; home to over 235,000 people, it is an important seaport as well as a major seaside resort.

Dominating the center is the sprawling Palace of Diocletian, built by the Roman emperor at the end of the third century, which is so huge that much of the picturesque medieval Old Town was built within the ancient palace walls.

Jews lived here in Roman times: A Jewish tombstone and oil lamps engraved with menorahs dating back to the second and third centuries were found at the site of nearby Salona (now called Solin and a suburb of Split), an important ancient Roman port. The spectacular Roman ruins and excavations at Salona can be visited, and various finds of Jewish interest can be seen in the Archeological Museum (Zrinjsko-Frankopanska 25; open mornings, closed Monday).

After Roman times, Jews are known to have lived in Split in the early Middle Ages. Sephardic Jews expelled from Spain and Portugal began settling here at the end of the fifteenth century.

A number of Jews became prominent over the next centuries, when the city was ruled by Venice. But the Jewish community was forced to live in a ghetto and suffered other restrictions: They were ordered to wear a yellow badge, for example, and in 1553 all Talmudic books were ordered burned.

Only in 1806, when Split came under French rule, were Jews granted full civil rights—rights that were rescinded eight years later when the Austrians took the town. It wasn't until 1867 that Jews in Split were fully emancipated. One of the town's leading citizens in the later nineteenth and early twentieth centuries was a Jew—Vid Morpurgo, a leader in the

Dalmatian nationalist movement who was a banker, an industrialist, and a bookseller, and whose shop was a center for young intellectuals.

Today, remnants of the old ghetto area around Zidovski prolaz (Jewish Passage) still exist. The synagogue, believed to date back to the early sixteenth century but rebuilt and restored many times, stands within the walls of Diocletian's palace, near the entry to the ghetto. It was devastated in 1942, and most of its priceless ritual objects, archives, Torahs, and other artistic and historic objects were burnt publicly in the town's main square. Little was saved, but the synagogue itself was restored to its prewar appearance.

The large cemetery on Mount Marjan, outside Split, dates back to the sixteenth century, too. Many of the oldest graves are typical for the area: horizontal sarcophagi shaped like elongated peaked roofs with Hebrew inscriptions on the sides.

On the eve of World War II, about 280 Jews lived in Split. Some 150 of them survived the Holocaust, and today about 75 Jews live in the town.

Varazdin (Varaždin)

Varazdin's former synagogue, built in 1862, was turned into a cinema, the Park Kino, on the border of the pleasant park near the center of this little town about fifty miles northwest of Zagreb. When I visited (on a bone-chilling winter day), a film called *Hot Lips* was playing.

The building had a slightly unnerving appearance: The blond stone rear portion, with its high, arched windows, still was intact, but the entire front had been replaced by an incongruous and quite hideous red entryway in brutal socialist realism style. At the top, there were a faded five-pointed communist star and crumbling letters reading *Dom Sloboda* (Freedom House).

Jews settled here in 1777, and a Jewish school—the first in Croatia—was founded here in 1826.

The Jewish cemetery, dating to 1810, is just outside town on the road to Koprivnica. It is a walled, secret garden–type cemetery; behind a large, neglected nineteenth-century ceremonial hall, large trees shade the graves, and both trees and tombstones are shrouded in ivy.

Elsewhere in Croatia

Bjelovar—The former synagogue, built in 1917 and seriously damaged during World War II, was restored to its prewar appearance for use as a concert hall. A Jewish cemetery dating to 1876 is incorporated into the municipal cemetery.

Djakovo—The cemetery, dating to 1879, was used as the cemetery for the concentration camp set up here during the war.

Karlovac—The cemetery, dating to 1828, is a national cultural monument with a fine late nineteenth century ceremonial hall. A street called Zidovska varos (Jewish Quarter) marks the site of the old Jewish section.

Koprivnica—The cemetery dating to 1842 is still in use. There is a former synagogue dating to 1875 and monuments to Jewish victims of World War I and World War II.

Krizevci (Križevci)—The synagogue, designed in 1894 by architects Honigsberg and Deutsch, now houses cultural offices. There are two Jewish cemeteries, the older dating to 1840.

Ludbreg—There is a cemetery dating to 1890 and a synagogue dating to 1895, now converted into a dwelling.

Osijek—A synagogue, built in 1903, is now a church. There is a cemetery dating to 1850 and a striking sculptural Holocaust monument situated in front of the Jewish community office at Brace Radice 13. The community building was seriously damaged in the civil strife in 1991.

Sisak—The fine nineteenth-century synagogue is now a music school.

There are also Jewish cemeteries in: **Cakovec** (Čakovec), **Kutina, Lipnik, Daruvar, Cernik, Virovitica, Dolny Miholjac, Nasice** (Našice), **Slavonska Pozena** (Slavonska Požena), **Slavonski Brod, Ilok, Valpovo, Vinkovci, Vukovar, Rijeka**.

YUGOSLAVIA (SERBIA AND MONTENEGRO)

SERBIA

Serbia, with its provinces of Vojvodina and Kosovo, was Yugoslavia's largest republic and today forms the basis of what remains of the Yugoslav state. In medieval times, Serbia was an independent kingdom until it was conquered by the Turks in the late fourteenth and early fifteenth centuries.

Jews lived here in the early Middle Ages, and under most of the nearly five centuries of Turkish occupation, the Jews, centered primarily in Belgrade, became important merchants and traders whose lives were relatively free from violent persecution or tight restrictions.

Most Serbian Jews were Sephardic, due to the waves of refugees who found refuge in the Ottoman Empire after the expulsions from Spain and

Portugal in 1492. They suffered greatly over the centuries during the long series of wars between the Austrians and Turks.

In the early nineteenth century, when Serbia gained a degree of autonomy, Jews flourished under Prince Milos, who had close contacts with the Jewish community and even appointed Jewish violinist Josif Slezinger to be bandmaster of his guards. Milos's successor, Prince Mihajlo, came to power in 1839 and sent the pendulum swinging back again, going so far as to expel Jews from parts of Serbia and, under pressure from non-Jewish merchants, to bar Jews from certain trades, including tailoring and shoe making.

Jews won emancipation only after 1878, when the Congress of Berlin, regulating the Turkish defeat in the Balkans, recognized the independence of Serbia and other Balkan countries only on the condition that Jews be granted full civil rights. In 1889, the Serbian Parliament formally declared all Serbian citizens, regardless of religion or ethnic origin, to be equal.

After the Yugoslav Kingdom was founded following World War I, most Serbian Jews consolidated into a comfortable middle-class life. There was little organized or openly expressed anti-Semitism until the 1930s.

The Germans occupied Belgrade and spread out through Serbia in April 1941, launching immediate violent persecutions against the Jewish population. Shops and homes were ransacked, Jews were forced to wear a yellow star, and thousands were sent to forced labor brigades. Eventually, most of the Serbian Jewish population was massacred in concentration camps near Belgrade or deported to Auschwitz and other death camps in Poland and Germany.

By August 1942, the Germans described Serbia as the only country fully cleared of Jews and Gypsies.

Belgrade (Serbo-Croat: Beograd)

Federation of Jewish Communities: ul. 7 Juli 71A. Tel. (11) 624-359

Jewish Community: ul. 7 Juli 71A. Tel. (11) 624-289

The capital both of Yugoslavia and the Republic of Serbia, Belgrade is situated at the confluence of the Danube and Sava rivers. Thanks in part to this strategic position, Belgrade has had a turbulent history and has been conquered and reconquered countless times. For centuries, it was on the border between the Turkish and Austrian empires, a valuable prize to be fought over again and again. It suffered particularly heavy damage during World War II.

Belgrade means "White City," but except for a newly renovated pedestrian area downtown and the lovely Kalamegdan fortress park overlooking the rivers, it is a drab, grimy town of 1.5 million people, ringed by new high-rise developments.

Belgrade was a thriving Jewish center as far back as the Middle Ages. The earliest medieval Jewish settlers were Ashkenazic refugees from Central Europe; a large Sephardic community grew up after the Turks conquered Belgrade in 1521.

The Jewish quarter of the city was in and around the neighborhood called Dorcol, on the bank of the Danube. The main street was called Jevrejska ulica (Jewish Street) and still exists—though few old Jewish houses remain in the neighborhood.

Before the outbreak of World War II, there were over 12,000 Jews in Belgrade, the overwhelming majority of them Sephardic. The Nazis occupied Belgrade in April 1941, and by May 8, 1942, they boasted that Belgrade was the only large city in Europe cleared of the Jews.

Today, Belgrade has a Jewish community of nearly 2,000, including many refugees from the civil-war fighting. Despite war-related tension and economic problems, there is an active social, religious, and cultural life. Community activities include Hebrew and Jewish culture classes, a choir, and various youth and other groups.

An imposing building at ul. 7 Juli 71A houses the offices of the local community and the Yugoslav Federation of Jewish Communities. Also in the building is the Jewish Historical Museum, open mornings, which has an interesting exhibition touching on the entire sweep of Jewish history in Yugoslavia, from ancient Roman times through the Holocaust. There are artifacts, documents, ritual objects, and—for me the most interesting— many old photographs of vanished people and places that round out the picture of a comfortable, middle-class Jewish life.

Little of Jewish character remains in the old Dorcol neighborhood nearby, but a monument to the memory of Belgrade Jews by Jewish sculptor Nandor Glid was recently erected on the bank of the Danube there.

Erection of another monument was planned on the bank of the Sava River, at the site of the Nazi concentration camp set up at the prewar Belgrade fairground. Here thousands, mainly women and children, were slaughtered in specially made gas chamber trucks.

Before the war, Belgrade had three synagogues; only one remains. An austere but imposing building erected in 1926 at ulica Marsala Birjuzova 19, it was transformed by the Nazis into a military brothel during the war. Today restored, it is used for regular services. On the site of the Beth Israel Synagogue—built in 1908 (King Peter I laid the foundation stone) and destroyed in 1944—now stands the Fresco Museum, at Cara Urosa 20, which has a memorial plaque commemorating the Jewish community.

Two Jewish cemeteries stand right across the street from each other at ulica Mije Kovacevica 1. Here there are imposing monuments both to Holocaust victims and to Jewish victims of the Balkan Wars and World War I.

Jewish wartime communist partisan hero Mose Pijade, one of the closest aides to Marshal Tito, is buried in the Crypt of National Heroes in Kalamegdan Park.

Zemun

Jewish Community: Dubrovacka 21. Tel. (11) 195-626

Zemun today is little more than a suburb of Belgrade on the other side of the Danube River. Historically, however, the town (called Semlin in German) was the last outpost of the Austro-Hungarian Empire facing the Turks, and its center still has an Austro-Hungarian flavor.

The Jewish community was founded here in 1807 by Jews fleeing battles during Serbian wars of independence against the Turks.

Zemun was the home of nineteenth-century Rabbi Jehudah ben Schlomo hai Alkalay, considered one of the earliest exponents of Zionism. Alkalay worked in Zemun for decades, and his ideas may well have been one of the early influences on Zionist pioneer Theodore Herzl. Herzl was born in Budapest, but his family came from Zemun—their graves, in fact, can be seen to this day in the Jewish cemetery, which dates back to the early nineteenth century, and where there is also a Holocaust memorial.

The ruins of the former Sephardic synagogue still stand near the Jewish community office and are marked by a memorial plaque. A plaque also marks the nearby site of the former Jewish school.

Elsewhere in Serbia

In the town of **Nis** (Niš), there is a very impressive Holocaust memorial on Bubanj hill above town. The former synagogue is now an art gallery, and there is an old Jewish cemetery.

VOJVODINA

Vojvodina is a province of Serbia north of Belgrade between the Danube River and the borders of Hungary and Romania. Its history is different from that of Serbia proper, as Vojvodina was a province of the Austro-Hungarian Empire.

Jews were generally banned from living in the region until the eighteenth century, when Ashkenazic Jewish refugees from Austria, Hungary, Bohemia, Moravia, Slovakia, and Poland began settling here in villages.

Most larger settlements were founded in the nineteenth century, and the Jewish population prospered and grew quickly, with many Jews remaining in the villages and small towns, working as merchants, farmers, doctors, and veterinarians.

As the region was under Hungarian administration, the development of the Jewish communities was similar to that in Hungary, including the conflicts between Orthodox and Reform (Neolog) communities in the nineteenth century. (See Hungary.)

Celarevo (Čelarevo)

This is an archeological site about twenty miles west of Novi Sad on the Danube River where some of the most fascinating and puzzling Jewish relics in Yugoslavia have been found.

In excavations at a large graveyard apparently dating to the end of the eighth and beginning of the ninth centuries, when the region was under the domination of the Avar tribe, archeologists have unearthed hundreds of brick fragments inscribed with menorahs and other Jewish symbols, including at least one small six-pointed Star of David. Some brick fragments also were inscribed with Hebrew letters.

Research has shown that the people buried at Celarevo were of the Mongol race, apparently a tribe that had newly migrated into the area from the east. Beyond that, the origin of this Jewish settlement remains a mystery: One hypothesis has suggested that they may have been influenced by the Crimean Khazars, a tribe whose leaders converted to Judaism in the eighth century.

The brick fragments or copies of them can be seen at the Novi Sad municipal museum.

Novi Sad

Jewish Community: Jugosl. nar. armije 35. Tel. 613-882

The capital of Vojvodina province about seventy miles north of Belgrade, Novi Sad was founded in 1694, when the Petrovaradin fortress was built—an Austrian stronghold used to guard a bridge over the Danube from the Turks. Among the first civilian settlers were Serbian refugees fleeing across the river from the havoc of the great Austro-Turkish wars in the last two decades of the seventeenth century. Today, with over 260,000 people, the town has a picturesque center incorporating many eighteenth-century buildings.

The first Jewish presence dates from 1699. They were Jewish merchants who supplied the fortress town. Later, Jewish migrants from Moravia settled here in the early eighteenth century. As elsewhere in the Hapsburg Empire, Jewish life was restricted by numerous laws until the mid-nineteenth century. They were forced into a ghetto on the edge of town, many professions were banned (they could not, for example, be goldsmiths or sell Christian books), and steep taxes were imposed.

Conditions for Jews improved with emancipation following the establishment of the Austro-Hungarian dual monarchy in 1867. From

Novi Sad—The early twentieth-century synagogue, designed by prolific Hungarian synagogue designer Lipot Baumhorn. When the picture was taken, it was under restoration for use as a concert hall.

around 1900 until the outbreak of World War II, Jews in Novi Sad prospered and became a vital and influential community, particularly in business, professional, and cultural circles.

The magnificent domed synagogue, with stained glass inner cupola and two fanciful towers flanking the grandiose entrance, was designed by Lipot Baumhorn, the prolific Hungarian synagogue architect. (See Hungary.) Built in the early years of this century, its grandeur reflects the prosperity and optimism of the community. It still stands on downtown Sloboda trg (Freedom Square), and in 1991 was undergoing restoration for use as a concert hall. The Jewish community office is in the building next door in what was once a traditional Jewish courtyard complex.

In the Municipal Museum in the former artillery building in the Petrovaradin Fortress above the river are exhibits from the Celarevo archeological site, and some items of Judaica are displayed in the regional Vojvodina Museum.

Novi Sad has a large Jewish cemetery whose nineteenth- and twentieth-century gravestones are similar to those in Hungary.

Subotica—The sinuous art nouveau lines of the early twentieth-century synagogue, designed by Kómor and Jakab, incorporating Hungarian folk motifs in the decoration. Today, the synagogue is used as a theater.

On the eve of World War II, 4,100 Jews lived in Novi Sad. Some 1,200 survived. Fewer than 300 Jews live in the town today.

On the bank of the Danube stands an impressive monument to civilian Holocaust victims, including over 1,400 Jews and Serbs who on January 23, 1942, were lined up on the ice of the frozen Danube and shot, their bodies falling into the water through breaks in the ice caused by the shooting.

*Subotica

Jewish Community: Dimitrija Tucovica 13. Tel. 28483

The center of this quiet town near the Hungarian border is a showcase of flamboyant art nouveau buildings, many of them painted in pastel candy colors: pink, mauve, green, teal blue. The 1910 town hall, with an extraordinary tower, dominates the center and is surrounded by a small park. Jewish settlement here dates to 1775.

The former main Neolog synagogue is a five-minute walk from the town hall and is an important component of the art nouveau scheme. It is interesting to compare it to the Szeged Synagogue, a few dozen miles away across the Hungarian border. Built in 1901, its design by architects

Dezso Jakab and Marcell Komor is very similar or identical to the design by Jakab and Komor that was the runner-up to Lipot Baumhorn's winning plan in the design competition for Szeged. (See Hungary.)

In 1940, Subotica had a Jewish population of about 5,000. The synagogue was turned over to the city by the handful of Jews who remained in the town after the war, as they did not have the funds to maintain it. Used for years as a theater, it has undergone some restoration, although the work has slowed (and in 1991 seemed stopped) due to lack of funds.

The synagogue sits in a barren yard surrounded by a wrought iron fence worked in patterns of hearts and Stars of David. It has a tall, central eight-sided dome, patterned in multicolored tiles, rising up from smaller, bulbous domes, sinuous gables, and ornamental buttresses. Each dome is topped by a Star of David. The cream stucco outer walls are edged in red brick or elaborate red ceramic tiles molded into floral or other decorative shapes.

The interior of the central cupola is bright with frescoes based on traditional Hungarian folk-art motifs that recall the colorful floral designs embroidered on Hungarian peasant blouses and textiles. The cream and tan background fades into sky blue toward the central point of the dome, where a stylized sun beams down on stylized garlands of flowers. Designs in the numerous stained glass windows pick up these motifs.

About 150 Jews live in Subotica today. In the Jewish community headquarters there is a tiny and extremely beautiful prayer hall, which is used today for regular services.

The cemetery, similar to Jewish cemeteries in Hungary, with tall nineteenth-century tombstones and obelisks, is in fairly good condition. There is a monument in it to Holocaust victims.

Elsewhere in Vojvodina

There are Jewish cemeteries in **Backa Palanka** (Bačka Palanka), **Mali Idjos** (Mali Idjoš), **Novi Becej** (Novi Bečej), and **Sombor**.

MONTENEGRO

Montenegro means Black Mountain—an apt description. This small, mountainous, and extremely rugged republic bordering Albania and the Adriatic Sea was long independent, ruled by a prince-bishop from the breathtaking old capital at Cetinje, on a high plateau inland from the Adriatic. Except for archeological remains there is little Jewish heritage here.

Podgorica (Titograd)

Today's capital of Montenegro is a sprawling and charmless modern city of 150,000 mostly built after World War II. At archeological excavations at nearby Duklja, an important Roman trade center on the ancient road connecting the Adriatic coast to Macedonia, a Jewish grave dating to the late third or early fourth century was discovered in 1960. The tomb, containing two skeletons, was decorated with striking Jewish symbols. These included a delicate red and blue fresco of a seven-branched menorah, birds, and floral motifs, traces of frescoed vines, a six-pointed star, and the Sukkoth *etrog* fruit.

Ulcinj

An ancient town, now a beach resort, Ulcinj is at the far south end of Montenegro, near the border with Albania. Most of its inhabitants are ethnic Albanians.

It is interesting to Jews as the place where the false Messiah Shabbatai Zevi died in 1676. Zevi, one of most startling and, for better or worse, most influential Jewish figures of his age, was born in Smyrna in 1626 into a family of Spanish Jews.

He became deeply involved in mysticism and the cabala and in 1665 proclaimed that he was the Messiah. In the superstitious, war-ravaged times in which he lived, he obtained a large, enthusiastic following all over Europe and the East. In the end, though, after a confrontation with the sultan at Constantinople, Zevi converted to Islam to save his life. Many of his followers also converted. Zevi, who took the name Mehamed Effendi and became the royal doorkeeper, eventually was banished to Ulcinj, then part of Albania. (See Poland.)

BOSNIA AND HERZEGOVINA

Beginning in early 1992, mountainous, ethnically mixed Bosnia and Herzegovina became the scene of the bloodiest fighting in Europe since World War II. The information here about Jewish sites reflects the situation before the civil war.

The region was ruled by the Ottoman Empire from the mid-fifteenth century until the Austrians took it over in 1878, and today much of the population is still Muslim. Mosque minarets thrust high above village streets; the local cuisine, including flat pitalike bread, has a Middle Eastern flavor; and many women still wear traditional Muslim dress, including head scarves and flowing baggy trousers.

Jews were welcome under the Turkish rulers, and many Sephardic Jews settled in the region after the expulsion from Spain; as in other Sephardic communities, Ladino (based on Spanish) rather than Yiddish (based on German) became the local Jewish language.

Jews in the region wore distinctive clothing, similar to the Turkish style but regulated by law. The men wore the Turkish-style fez, for example, but the Jewish fez could only be black. Only Muslims were permitted to wear the color green, but Jewish women wore beautifully embroidered dresses with a distinct oriental flavor.

Before World War II, some 14,000 Jews lived in Bosnia and Herzegovina—about 12,000 in Sarajevo, and the rest scattered in a score of small communities. Before civil war broke out, about 1,000 Jews lived here.

*Sarajevo

Jewish Community: Dobrovoljacka 83. Tel. (71) 22023

The capital of Bosnia and Herzegovina, Sarajevo, cupped in the middle of mountains, is an extraordinary city where the confrontation between East and West is apparent everywhere you look. Much of the city seems to be transplanted directly from the Middle East: From the sixteenth century onward the Turkish rulers left their mark on the town with magnificent mosques—before the civil war there were seventy-three of them altogether—and other Islamic construction.

The influence of the East is particularly strong in the old market section, Bas Carsija, a Turkish-style bazaar made up of tiny little wooden shops selling golden oriental jewelry, handicrafts, copperwork, and oriental delicacies. A few steps away, however, typical late nineteenth-century Austrian-style buildings look as if they came right out of Vienna.

Embedded in the sidewalk on the corner outside the Young Bosnia Museum at Obala Vojvode Stepe 36 were footprints marking the spot where Gavrilo Princip fired the shots that killed Austrian Archduke Franz Ferdinand and sparked off World War I. (These have been destroyed.)

Sarajevo, with about 500,000 people before the civil war, was one of the most important Jewish cities in the former Yugoslavia, and had some of the country's most fascinating and historic Jewish monuments.

Jews settled here in the sixteenth century, following the expulsion from Spain. In the late sixteenth century, the ruling pasha constructed a special quarter for Jews, including a synagogue, great courtyard, and communal lodgings for poor families. Known as *El Cortio*, it was not considered a ghetto per se, as Jews had freedom of movement in the city and also lived elsewhere. This complex burned down in 1879, but the old synagogue was rebuilt and after World War II became the Jewish Museum.

The Sarajevo Jewish community, maintaining generally good relations with the local Muslim and Christian communities, prospered, though a poor underclass also developed. Many Jews became active as merchants and artisans and particularly in the fields of pharmacy and medicine. At one point in the nineteenth century, all the doctors in town were Jewish. There was a very high degree of intellectual life, and the monumental domed Sephardic synagogue, built between 1927 and 1931, was the largest in the Balkans. It was destroyed during World War II.

After Bosnia and Herzegovina were annexed by Austria in 1878, Ashkenazic Jews from East-Central Europe settled here and founded their own, much smaller community.

Before World War II, there were about 12,000 Jews in Sarajevo. About 8,000 Sarajevo Jews perished in the Holocaust. Before the civil war, nearly 1,000 Jews lived in Sarajevo. All but a few hundred fled the civil war fighting. During the siege of Sarajevo, the local Jewish association La Benevolencija became one of the city's most respected humanitarian aid organizations.

Writing just before World War II in her classic portrait of Yugoslavia, *Black Lamb and Gray Falcon,* Rebecca West described the Jews of Sarajevo as "an amazing community." Here is how she described two Jewish acquaintances, a man named Selim and his wife, called the Bulbul:

> Selim's dignity was magnificent but not pompous, as if it were an inherited garment and its previous wearers had taken the stiffness out of it. He was a very tall man with broad shoulders, broad even for a man of his height. His build suggested the stylized immensity of a god sculpted by a primitive people, and his face also had the quality of sculpture; though his wit and imagination made it mobile, it was at once the tables of the law and the force that shattered them . . .
>
> But the fascination of himself and his wife lay initially in their voices. There is a special music lingering about the tongues of many of these Spanish Jews, but no one else gave it such special performance . . . from his wife's lips that music came in such animal purity that we called her the Bulbul, which is the Persian word for nightingale. Voices like these were the product of an existence built by putting pleasure to pleasure, as houses are built by putting brick to brick. A human being could not speak so unless he or she loved many other sounds—the wind's progress among trees or the subtler passage it makes through grasses; note by note given out by a musical instrument, each note for its own color; the gurgle of wine pouring from a bottle or water trickling through a marble conduit in a garden—all sorts of sounds that many Westerners do not even hear, so corrupted are they by the tyranny of the intellect, which makes them inattentive to any message to the ear which is without an argument. . . .
>
> The Bulbul was not as Western women. In her beauty she resembled the Persian ladies of the miniatures, whose luster I had till then thought an artistic convention but could now recognize

in her great shining eyes, her wet red lips, her black hair with its white reflections, her dazzling skin.

Major Places of Jewish Interest in Sarajevo

• The Jewish Museum: ulica Marsala Tita 98

Sarajevo's Jewish Museum, housed in the reconstructed, massive, stone sixteenth-century synagogue, is a fascinating presentation of local Jewish history. Especially noteworthy are the typical local costumes, which clearly show Ottoman influence. There are documents, ritual objects, and also relics from Spain brought by the early Sephardic immigrants. Just as interesting is the building itself, with its austere design, ceiling vaulting, and wooden central bimah.

• The Synagogue: Dobrovoljacka 83

The synagogue was built in 1902 for use by the Ashkenazic community, but since the war, all local Jews worship here. Its Moorish-style design, with four big towers surmounted by pointed domes, fits right in with the local Muslim architecture prevalent in much of Sarajevo, and the interior is also highly elaborate, with Muslim-style arches and busy arabesques and geometric wall ornamentation.

    It is the only one of eight prewar synagogues in Sarajevo still used as a house of worship. The Jewish community offices are next door.

• Jewish Cemetery: Outside town at Kovacici on Mount Trebevic

Founded in 1630, the Sarajevo Jewish cemetery is one of the most fascinating in the Balkans, with unique tombstones shaped like sawed-off tree trunks. These big, slightly rounded blocks with Hebrew inscriptions on one face, thrust out of the ground on the hillside like miniature pillboxes, making an eerie, unforgettable sight. This type of tombstone in fact resembles the medieval Christian *stecaks*, big, blocky grave markers shaped like sarcophagi and often featuring vigorous relief carvings that are particularly common in Bosnia and Herzegovina. From 1992 the cemetery was on the frontline of fighting in the siege of Sarajevo and was used as a firing position by Bosnian Serbs.

• Holocaust Memorial at Vrace

Vrace Park and Memorial, on a hillside overlooking Sarajevo not far from the Jewish cemetery, commemorates more than 9,000 local people— including 7,500 Jews—killed during World War II. Their names and ages are inscribed on the inner walls of the courtyard of a restored fortress forming the centerpiece to the memorial park.

• The Sarajevo *Haggaddah*

An extremely beautiful example of a medieval illuminated Hebrew manuscript, the Haggaddah—the story of the exodus of the Jews from Egypt, read at the Passover seder dinner—dates from the fourteenth century and was brought to Sarajevo from Spain by Sephardic immigrants. During World War II, it was preserved hidden in a remote mountain village.

Stolac

This picturesque little town on the Bregava River between Mostar and the Adriatic coast has many important Muslim relics and an interesting connection with Judaism.

In 1820, the local pasha in Sarajevo arrested Sarajevo Chief Rabbi Moshe Danon and ten other prominent Jews on the trumped-up charges of having killed the false dervish Ahmet, an Islamicized Jew. He threatened to execute them unless they raised a huge ransom. The Sarajevo Jewish community turned to local Muslims for help. In a move highlighting the good relations between the Jewish and Muslim communities, local Muslims stormed the prison and liberated the hostages, then sent a petition to the sultan demanding that the pasha be dismissed. He was.

The anniversary of the liberation became a feast day for Sarajevo Jews.

Ten years later, Rabbi Danon set off on a journey to Palestine. He fell ill on the way and died in Stolac, where he was buried. Until World War II, his tombstone at Stolac was a revered place of pilgrimage on the anniversary of his death.

Elsewhere in Bosnia and Herzegovina

Before the civil war, former synagogue buildings also stood in **Travnik** (there was also a cemetery), **Visegrad** (Višegrad), **Zvornik**, and **Rogatica**. In **Visoko**, the street where the synagogue once stood is still called Jewish Street (Jevrejska ulica), and a Jewish cemetery exists. In **Mostar**, the synagogue had been turned into a puppet theater, and there was a Jewish cemetery. In **Zenica**, the synagogue had been beautifully restored as the town museum and included a Holocaust memorial plaque and small exhibition of local Jewish history.

MACEDONIA

Macedonia was the poor, mainly mountainous southern republic of the former Yugoslavia that bordered on Albania, Greece, and Bulgaria. It, too, declared independence when Yugoslavia broke up. Historic Macedonia extended over areas of Yugoslavia, Greece, and Bulgaria: It was partitioned among them in 1913 after the Balkan Wars.

Jews lived here in ancient Roman times. There were a few communities active in the centuries before and during the Middle Ages. Refugees from Austria and Hungary settled here in the fourteenth and fifteenth centuries; many more from Spain came in the sixteenth century, welcomed by the Turks who then ruled the region.

Jewish life in Macedonia flourished under Ottoman rule. Rabbis from the sixteenth and seventeenth centuries have left behind them fascinating records of everyday life, chronicling the rise of Jewish commerce, handicrafts, and industry, including mining, textiles, and leatherworks. They also tell of poverty, housing shortages, unsafe roads, and crime— including murder and highway robbery. Such books by Rabbi Josef Ben Lev, born in Bitola in 1502, were published in cities as far away as Amsterdam, Venice, and Constantinople.

A poor Jewish underclass already was beginning to develop in the nineteenth century, particularly in Bitola. The Balkan Wars devastated and further impoverished the region and forced many local people— including many Jews—to emigrate.

On the eve of World War II, there were three main, primarily Sephardic, Jewish communities in Macedonia: Skopje, the capital; Bitola; and Stip (Štip), totaling about 8,000 people in all. On March 11, 1943, nearly all were rounded up and deported to death camps in Poland after Macedonia was annexed to Bulgaria; only a few hundred survived. There are Holocaust memorials in Skopje, Bitola, and Stip.

Only about 100 Jews live in Macedonia today, almost all of them in Skopje, the capital, where the Jewish community headquarters is in a modern building at Borka Talevski 24, Tel. (91) 237-543.

Bitola

No Jews today remain in this town of over 65,000 at the edge of wild mountain country near the Greek border that once was a colorful—if impoverished—Jewish center. Jews lived here in the late Middle Ages, but the community was built up by refugees from Spain in the sixteenth century.

Following the Balkan Wars and World War I, during which much of the town was destroyed, the local Jewish community was generally very poor and lived in three ghettos, or *mahallas*. Little remains of these ghettos—one of them was located around the present ul. Mose Pijade, named for the Jewish wartime partisan leader and close aide to Marshal Tito. There is, however, a historic old cemetery with horizontal, carved gravestones in the Sephardic manner.

About 3,350 Jews lived in the town on the eve of World War II. Fewer than 100 survived. There is a Holocaust memorial here.

Stobi

Archeologists excavating this important ancient Roman commercial center near the confluence of the Vardar and Crna rivers near the present town of Gradsko uncovered some important early Jewish remains. The excavations and exhibition of archeological finds can be visited.

In 1931, a column dating to the third century was found bearing an inscription describing the construction of a synagogue by one Claudius Tiberius Polycharmos. The remains of this synagogue were also uncovered—a well-preserved floor mosaic with Jewish symbolism as well as support elements, unearthed 1.5 meters underneath a fourth-century Christian basilica.

HOTELS/RESTAURANTS

BELGRADE

Hotels

- Intercontinental, Vladimira Popovica 10. Tel. (11) 138708. Deluxe, modern, and efficient, but far from the center.
- Moskva, Balkanska 1. Tel. (11) 327312. Turn-of-the-century hotel, run-down, but a Belgrade landmark in the heart of town.

Restaurants

- Skadarlija—There are several famous cafe-restaurants offering typical music and serving typical local cuisine on this quaint street in downtown Belgrade. They include: Zlatni Bokal, Dva Jelena, Ima Dana, Tre Sesira
- "?"—Questionmark Cafe, ul. 7 Jula 6. An atmospheric old cafe-restaurant on the same street as the Jewish community office and museum.

ZAGREB

Hotels

- Esplanade, Mihanoviceva 1. Tel. (41) 512222. The best in town.
- Intercontinental, Krsnjavoga 1. Tel. (41) 443411. Modern, somewhat out of the center.

Restaurants

- Lovacki Rog, Ilica 14. Tel. (41) 445444. Game specialties.
- Kapelska Klet, Kaptol 5. Tel. (41) 425594. Local dishes.

BULGARIA

Population: 9 million
Jewish Population before World War II: c. 50,000
Jewish Population in 1994: 4,000–6,000

A LITTLE HISTORY

Jews have lived in the Balkan territory now known as Bulgaria since ancient times. Jewish merchants dealing in crafts and farm produce are believed to have arrived with the Phoenicians as early as the first and second centuries B.C.E. Later Jewish settlements are known to have grown up in the second and third centuries C.E., when the region was under Roman domination.

Jewish settlement increased after the founding of the Bulgarian state in 681. Jews seem to have been welcomed in Bulgarian lands in the early Middle Ages and were not harshly persecuted. King Ivan Alexandar (1331–1371) even married a Jewish woman named Sarah, who took the name Theodora when she converted to Christianity and became queen.

Much of the medieval Jewish population in Bulgaria followed the Byzantine or Romaniot rite. In the fourteenth and fifteenth centuries, Ashkenazic Jewish refugees settled there from Hungary, Germany, and France. Among them was Rabbi Sholom of Nitra (Slovakia), who founded a famous yeshiva in the fortress town of Vidin on the Danube River.

Following their expulsion from Spain in 1492, as many as 30,000 or more Sephardic Jewish refugees settled in Bulgaria. By the end of the sixteenth century, all but a small fraction of Bulgaria's Jews followed the Sephardic rite.

Among the Spanish refugees was the great scholar and mystic Joseph Caro, who lived in Nikopol from 1523 to 1536. There he founded a yeshiva and worked on his influential treatise on the Talmud, *The House of Joseph.* Caro eventually moved to Palestine, where he wrote an abbreviated version of his Talmudic commentaries and codification of Jewish law. The *Shulchan Aruch (Prepared Table)* was published in 1567, and it was widely circulated through the then-new art of printing, becoming one of the most influential Jewish books ever published. It was a strict, step-by-step guide to being a Jew.

The Turks conquered Bulgaria in 1396 and ruled there until 1877, when they were defeated by the Russians. As elsewhere in the Ottoman Empire, Jews were welcomed by the Turks. Many Jews were active in international trade and commerce and were even granted special privileges in an effort to encourage trade. Several Jews are known to have held government offices.

Partly because Jews were seen as pro-Turkish, there was considerable anti-Jewish violence in provincial towns after the Turks were defeated by the Russian army in 1877 and withdrew from Bulgaria and neighboring Balkan territories. The Treaty of Berlin in 1878, which paved the way to an independent Bulgaria, Serbia, and Romania, included a clause insisted on by Western powers that guaranteed civil equality for the Jews.

Nonetheless, anti-Semitism grew over the following decades, and Jews were barred from various lines of work, including the civil service. Zionism became a highly influential movement among Bulgarian Jews.

Before World War II, about 50,000 Jews lived in Bulgaria, more than half of them in the capital, Sofia.

During the war, Bulgaria allied itself with the Nazis and enacted tough anti-Semitic legislation: Among other things, Jewish gold and valuables were confiscated, and Jews were forced to wear a yellow badge, they were forbidden to use main roads, and they could not carry out trade or move from one town to another.

The mass deportation of Bulgarian Jews to Nazi death camps began in 1943, but protests by some political and Orthodox church figures, led by parliamentary vice president Dimiter Peshev, forced the government to halt the action. Nonetheless, more than 11,000 Jews from Yugoslav and Greek territories occupied by Bulgaria were deported under extremely cruel conditions, and severe anti-Jewish persecutions and restrictions were maintained on Jews remaining in the country until just before the Russians invaded Bulgaria in September 1944.

Nearly 50,000 Bulgarian Jews survived the war. Between 1944 and 1951, all but a few thousand of them immigrated to Israel.

Under the communists, religious Jewish life practically came to a halt. All but a handful of synagogues were demolished or converted for secular use; most Jewish cemeteries, too, were destroyed. Jews were not actively persecuted, but they were regarded as an ethnic, not a religious, group. The rate of intermarriage was high. Contacts with international Jewish organizations were limited. There were formal, communist-dominated Jewish organizations, but they were culturally, not religiously, oriented, and there was no opportunity for Jewish education.

Since the political changes in 1989, there has been an upsurge in Jewish life. Bulgaria and Israel resumed diplomatic relations broken after the Six-Day War in 1967; contacts with international Jewish organizations blossomed; educational, religious, and social service programs were set up. The former communist-dominated Cultural and Educational Society of Jews in Bulgaria was replaced by the Shalom Organization, founded in March 1990, whose branch offices serve as a coordinating network of Jewish revival throughout the country. At the same time, about 2,000 Bulgarian Jews left for Israel between 1990 and 1994.

FOR THE TRAVELER

Where

Bulgaria, a land of towering mountains and rolling hills, is situated in the eastern part of the Balkan peninsula, on the main overland route between the Middle East and Europe. It borders Yugoslavia (Serbia), Macedonia, Romania, Turkey, and Greece and has a coastline along the Black Sea.

When

Bulgaria has a climate similar to that of the northeast United States, with cold winters and hot summers. Spring and autumn are beautiful. There are several ski resorts popular during the snow season, and there are numerous beach resorts along the Black Sea coast.

How

Bulgaria's Balkanair and other European airlines fly to Sofia; there is international train service from Athens, Belgrade, Bucharest, and Istanbul. Main highways, particularly those leading to the main border crossing points, are very good.

Visas

Americans do not need visas for Bulgaria.

Languages

Bulgarian is a Slavic language, similar to Russian, and many Bulgarians speak Russian. A surprisingly large number of Bulgarian Jews speak Ladino or Spanish. Personnel at major hotels and restaurants in Sofia and other big cities speak English.

Bulgarian, like Russian, uses the Cyrillic alphabet, and outside major tourist centers only occasionally are signs written in Latin characters.

Helpful Phrases

English	Bulgarian (Pronunciation)
Synagogue	Seen'agohga
Jewish cemetery	Evray'sko gro'bishte
Hello/Good day	Dohbur den'
Please	Mohl'ya
Thank you	Blah-goh-dar-ya'
Yes	Da
No	Ne
Good-bye	Doh veezhdaneh

I don't speak Bulgarian	Ne go-vor'-ya bulgarski
Toilet	Klo-zet'
Where is . . . ?	K-deh eh . . . ?
How much does it cost?	Kawl'ko stroo'va
One	Edin
Two	Dva
Three	Tree
Four	Cheteery
Five	Pet
Six	Shest
Seven	Seddem
Eight	Ossem
Nine	Devvet
Ten	Desset

Money

The Bulgarian currency is the lev (plural, leva), divided into 100 stotinki. The exchange rate has fluctuated widely, so check current listings on your arrival.

Kosher Cuisine

Check with the Jewish community in Sofia.

If You Only Have a Few Days

See Sofia and Plovdiv. You can stop in Samokov along the way.

Helpful Addresses

(Direct dialing code to Bulgaria is 359)

Balkantourist State Travel Organization
161 East 86th Street
New York, NY 10028
Tel. (212) 722-1110

Knjaz Donduka 37
Sofia

U.S. Embassy
Blvd. Alexander Stamboliyski 1
Sofia
Tel. (2) 884-801

Jewish Communities

There are regular religious services in Sofia, but thanks to forty-five years of secularization, religious functions in provincial towns are limited. Check with the Shalom Organization offices listed next to find out whether or not religious services are celebrated.

Sofia	Blvd. Alexander Stamboliyski 50. Tel. (92) 870-163
Burgas	Vodenicharov St. 14. Tel. (56) 42117
Haskovo	Tomik St. 55. Tel. (38) 24908
Kjustendil	V. Kolarov St. 60. Tel. (78) 26185
Pleven	Tsvetan Spasov St. 20. Tel. (64) 21242
Plovdiv	Gen. Zaimov St. 20. Tel. (32) 761-376
Ruse	Pentcho Slaveiko St. 4. Tel. (82) 22460
Shumen	Balchik St. 23. Tel. (54) 66120
Sliven	Druzhba St. Block 12. Tel. (44) 81125
Stanke Dimitrov	V. Yakova St. 1. Tel. (701) 24666
Stara Zagora	Gurko St. 28. Tel. (42) 49281
Varna	Musala St. 7. Tel. (52) 224-590
Yampol	Poshtenska Kutaya 147. Tel. (46) 22625

JEWISH HERITAGE IN BULGARIA

Plovdiv

Shalom Organization: Gen. Zaimov St. 20. Tel. (32) 761-376

Bulgaria's second largest city, Plovdiv is a town of 367,000 people about 100 miles southeast of Sofia whose center is a picturesque complex of Turkish and characteristic Balkan architecture: Medieval mosques thrust slim minarets into the air alongside a labyrinth of cobbled streets shaded by charming overhanging buildings. There are also some important Roman remains.

Jews lived in Plovdiv in Roman times. Discovered among the Roman ruins were a mosaic floor and panels depicting menorahs from a synagogue dating to 290.

Since at least Byzantine times, Jews maintained a continuous presence in the town as artisans and merchants based in what long was one of the main trading centers on the overland route between Europe and the Middle East.

More than 5,000 Jews lived in Plovdiv before World War II. About 400 Jews live there today.

"We have a lot of young people, but they don't pray," said David Koen, an elderly Jewish pensioner who lives in a small house next to the synagogue—the only synagogue in Bulgaria other than Sofia still consecrated for religious purposes—and takes care of the building.

Two elderly women nodded agreement; the three spoke among themselves in Ladino. "There is a little prayer room here, but no one comes," they said.

The so-called Zion Synagogue, dating to the nineteenth century, is a hidden treasure. A boxy, outwardly nondescript building, it stands almost surrounded by new housing blocks at Tsar Kaloyan Street 13, in the remnants of a small Jewish courtyard in what was once a large Jewish quarter. Despite the new construction nearby, several picturesque Jewish streets still survive: Some doorways are decorated by Stars of David.

Inside, the synagogue is a glorious, if run-down, burst of color. An exquisite Venetian glass chandelier hangs from the center of the ceiling, which has a richly painted dome. All surfaces are covered in elaborate, very Middle Eastern, geometric designs in once-bright greens and blues. Torahs are still kept in the gilded Aron ha Kodesh.

David Koen locked the door with a big key.

"The young people all want to go to Israel. My own son is there. While we old people are alive, maybe the traditions will be maintained. When we are gone, there will be no one left to take care of the synagogue," he said.

Ruse

Shalom Organization: Pentcho Slaveikov St. 4. Tel. (82) 22460

A pleasant, if polluted, port town of 180,000 people spectacularly located on the Danube River in northern Bulgaria, Ruse is at the Bulgarian end of the only bridge across the river between Bulgaria and Romania—the two-lane "Friendship Bridge" built in the 1950s, where due to inefficient border controls it can take hours and hours to cross from one country to the other.

Thanks to its position as a trading center, Ruse has a rich Jewish tradition dating back centuries, and about 2,000 Jews lived here before World War II. Today the Jewish population is about 250.

Ruse is the hometown of the Nobel Prize–winning author Elias Canetti, who in his autobiography wrote movingly about his childhood in the old Sephardic Jewish quarter, a picturesque neighborhood whose small houses still retain a lot of their traditional character. Canetti's house at 13 Gurko Street still stands and usually can be visited.

Here, the late nineteenth-century Sephardic synagogue, closed in 1952 after most local Jews left for Israel, has been turned into a factory and workshop, its front yard dominated by a huge and very incongruous socialist realist sculpture. The building still shows traces of its distinctive architecture in its small round upper windows and domed ceiling.

Plovdiv—Stars of David on a rotting door in the old Jewish section of town.

Nearby, on a small market square around the corner from the Shalom Organization office, is the former Ashkenazic synagogue, a small, squat building turned into offices for a sports lottery organization.

Izador Ajzner, the president of the local Jewish community, said it was the last synagogue built in Bulgaria: Embedded in its doorstep is the date 1927 in Roman numbers and in Hebrew.

Ajzner, an intense, bearded man who was born just after the end of the war, is typical of many Bulgarian Jews. Being Jewish for him meant an ethnic, not a religious, identity: "No one was brought up to pray," he said. "Judaism was a nationality rather than a religion . . . there were no books, no rabbis, no prayers. Everything we learned came from stories old Jews told us about the past."

Since the political changes this, too, has changed. For the first time in his life, Ajzner took part in a seder at Passover 1991.

He and the Jewish community hope to regain possession of the Ashkenazic synagogue and restore it as a prayer house and little museum.

"You who were brought up without religious education, do you want to pray as a Jew?" I asked Ajzner.

He smiled. "Yes," he said.

Samokov

A small, sleepy town of 13,000 or so in the forested foothills of the Rila Mountains forty miles south of Sofia, Samokov has a pleasant center whose most striking buildings are its centuries-old mosque and its nineteenth-century former synagogue.

The synagogue, built in 1858, is set in a walled yard surrounded by the low houses of the former Jewish quarter. Considered a typical example of Balkan architecture, it is listed as a historic monument and served as a local museum until it was gutted by fire (local people say a fire set by a drunk) in the early 1980s. Today, the outer shell is in good condition, but the interior is filled with scaffolding and debris.

The building has distinctive outer decoration: Rows of tall, arched windows are topped by rows of oval windows enclosed by wrought iron grilles. There are still considerable traces of bright black, red, and blue vinelike frescoes around the outer window frames, and there is a Hebrew inscription in gilded letters over the entryway.

Several hundred Jews lived in Samokov before World War II; today, only two or three Jewish families are still in the town. A Jewish family runs the local cafe on Gen. Velyaminov Street around the corner from the synagogue. They still speak Ladino as well as Bulgarian, and Violeta, the vivacious younger daughter, says she has worn a Star of David around her neck all her life even though she knows little about the actual religious practice of Judaism. She knows something about the holidays, though— and she knows that Jews were always persecuted.

Samokov—The synagogue, built in 1858, is a fine example of Balkan Sephardic style. It was turned into a museum but was gutted by fire and now stands empty, filled only with scaffolding.

Violeta, who's in her 20s, hints broadly that life is dull in the small town, but she is torn as to whether to make aliyah to Israel, even though many relatives live there. Here in Samokov, the family owns a business, they all have work.

Violeta wears tight jeans and paints her face heavily with garish blue eye shadow and big black Cleopatra rings around her eyes. She fingers the Star of David on the gold chain around her neck. There are no nice Jewish boys in Samokov, though. Maybe in Sofia (she smiles); maybe in Israel.

Sofia

Jewish Community: Ekzarkh Josef St. 16 (at the synagogue)

Shalom Organization (Jewish cultural center): Blvd. Alexander Stamboliyski 50. Tel. 870-163

Sofia, the capital of Bulgaria, is an ancient city situated almost in the geo-graphical center of the Balkan peninsula on a high plain ringed by moun-tains. Mount Vitosha, rising at the southwest outskirts of town, provides a dramatic backdrop to a city of more than one million people whose present-day aspect is a mixture of drab communist modernity and turn-of-the-century charm studded with a few ancient churches and remnants of the 500-year Ottoman occupation.

Central Ruski Boulevard and other streets and plazas in the city's heart are paved in yellow brick.

Jews, many of them merchants, lived in Sofia from the Byzantine pe-riod, long before the Turkish conquest in the fourteenth century. In Sofia, as in the rest of Bulgaria, many Jews fell under the spell of the false Mes-siah Shabbatai Zevi in the seventeenth century: Two of Zevi's disciples, Samuel Primo and Nathan of Gaza were particularly active in the city. (See Poland; Ulcinj, Montenegro [Yugoslavia])

As were most of the rest of Bulgaria's Jews, Sofia's Jews were mainly Sephardic. Many older members of the current Jewish population still speak Ladino.

Before World War II, 27,700 Jews—more than half of Bulgaria's Jewish population—lived in Sofia. Most of the country's Jewish population today (over 3,000 people) is still centered in the city.

Since the downfall of the communist regime in 1989, the small prayer room in the synagogue building where regular services are held is often filled to capacity on Friday evenings—with many young people in atten-dance—and on the holidays there is sometimes an overflow. Young people volunteered to clean up the overgrown Sofia Jewish cemetery, and Talmud Torah classes attract scores of children, who also participate in Jewish hol-iday camp programs. A Jewish elementary school and kindergarten opened, and there was even a bar mitzvah for the first time in many years. A young Bulgarian, Maxim Koen, began studying to become the first rabbi in Bulgaria for many years.

At Passover 1991, 1,500 people attended community seders held at a Jewish-owned Sofia restaurant! It was the first community Pesach celebra-tion since 1948, and the turnout was so great that the seders had to be spread out over three nights to allow all the people to attend. More than 2,700 took part in ten community seders in 1992.

Jewish community leaders expected to have a kosher restaurant spe-cializing in traditional Sephardic dishes such as eggplant with veal meat-balls, a meat and pastry dish called *pastel,* and a sweet dessert (special for Pesach) made of sugar, almonds, matzo meal, and lemon called *tishpishti* in operation by 1992.

Sofia's magnificent Great Synagogue, designed by Austrian Friedrich Gruenanger, was built between 1905 and 1910 right in the heart of the capital at the corner of George Washington Street and Ekzarkh Josef Street

Sofia—The magnificent synagogue, built between 1905 and 1910, in the heart of the city was designed by Friedrich Gruenanger in Moorish-Byzantine style. It is one of the largest Sephardic synagogues ever built in Europe.

near the massive sixteenth-century Banya Bashi Mosque. One of the largest Sephardic synagogues ever constructed in Europe, it seats 1,200 and was built in a Byzantine-Moorish style that fits in with many of the other grand buildings in downtown Sofia, such as the gold-domed Alexander Nevsky Cathedral not far away.

The synagogue has a huge, rather flat central dome, with smaller domes and cupola-topped towers around it. Both interior and exterior decoration was highly ornate, with much tracery, arabesques, and other details. The very long, thin windows topped by horseshoe arches are a striking feature as is an enormous chandelier. A new Jewish museum is now open here.

The Jewish cemetery occupies one part of the city cemetery (it's at the last stop of the Number 2 tramway). Overgrown and neglected until recently, it has been cleaned up by youth volunteers. Dating to the late nineteenth century and still in use, the cemetery has many simple grave markers, many including a laminated photograph of the person interred.

Elsewhere in Bulgaria

There are former synagogues, either used for secular purposes or standing empty, in **Vidin** (a large neogothic building on a hill), **Pazardjik**, **Burgas** (an art gallery), and **Varna** (a sports hall).

HOTELS/RESTAURANTS

Fairly good hotels are found in major cities, with prices averaging from $60 to $100 a night for a double. Cheaper accommodation is also available. In Sofia, prices are somewhat higher.

SOFIA

Hotels

- Sheraton Hotel, 5 Lenin Square, 1000 Sofia. Tel. (92) 876-541. An elegant restoration of the old Hotel Balkan in the very center of Sofia offering deluxe accommodations at American prices. The restaurants are said to have the best food in town.
- Grand Hotel Sofia, Narodno Sobranie Square. Tel. (92) 878821. Slightly down-at-the-heels, modern hotel beautifully located across from Alexander Nevsky Cathedral.

Restaurants

- Krim (Russian Club), 2 Dobroudja St. A hangout for the intelligentsia; lots of rich Balkan atmosphere straight out of Eric Ambler, plus a pleasant summer garden.
- Mexana Koprivshtitsa, Vitosha Blvd. 1/3; Bulgarian specialties.

RUSE

- Hotel Riga, 22 Alexander Stamboliyski St. Tel. (82) 2181. Modern hotel, picturesquely situated on the Danube. Good restaurant.
- Leventa Restaurant, at Leventa, three miles south of Ruse. Tel. (82) 28290. Picturesque restaurant serving Balkan specialties, housed in a former Turkish fortress.

GLOSSARY

Aron ha Kodesh (Ark) In Hebrew, Aron ha Kodesh means "Holy Ark" and is the shrinelike place built into or standing against the eastern wall of the synagogue where the Torah scrolls are kept. It represents the Ark of the Covenant, in which the two stone tablets containing the Ten Commandments given by God to Moses were kept. A focal point of the synagogue, it is often highly decorated.

Ashkenazic Derived from the term *Ashkenaz,* a medieval Hebrew term for Germany. Ashkenazic Jews trace their origin and religious rituals to Germany and western Europe, but they later migrated to Central and Eastern Europe.

Baroque An artistic and architectural style of the seventeenth and eighteenth centuries characterized by curving lines, sculpture, niches, and other solid but lush ornamentation and decoration, all of whose diverse elements fit into a whole. The later, lighter, and even more fancifully decorative baroque style is called *rococo.*

Bet ha Midrash Literally "house of study" in Hebrew, the Bet ha Midrash is a small room or building where adult men gather to study the Torah and religious commentaries. It actually is considered a holier place than a synagogue because of the reverence accorded to religious study.

Bet Hayyim Literally "house of the living" in Hebrew; a Jewish cemetery.

Bimah The table, often on a raised platform, from which the Torah is read during religious services in a synagogue. In Ashkenazic synagogues, it is usually placed in the center of the Orthodox synagogues and at the eastern wall in front of the Ark in Reform synagogues. In Sephardic synagogues, it is usually opposite the Ark.

Blood Libel Often used as the pretext for pogroms and other persecutions of Jews, blood libel refers to the accusation that Jews use human blood in the preparation of matzo (unleavened bread) at Passover. Particularly in medieval times, Jews were often accused of kidnapping and murdering children to drain their blood for this purpose. There have been a disquieting number of such accusations even within the past century or so, such as that at Polna, the Czech Republic, in 1899 and in Tiszaeszlar, Hungary, in 1882.

Ceremonial Hall A building often found at Jewish cemeteries where the dead are prepared for burial and funeral services are held.

Cohen A descendant of the priestly house of Aaron, the brother of Moses. The Cohens were the only people authorized to perform religious rites and historically were subject to certain hereditary restrictions and privileges due to their position. The graves of Cohens are often marked with a carving of the priestly gesture of the hands held up with fingers spread in a distinctive way.

Etrog   The fragrant citrus fruit used in rituals on the Sukkoth holiday; and, particularly in ancient times, a distinctly Jewish ornamental motif.

Ghetto   A street or neighborhood where Jews were forced to live as a form of persecution in many European cities from medieval times. It often was locked at night. The word *ghetto* is derived from the Venetian dialect for foundry, dating from when a ghetto was set up near a foundry in Venice in 1515. Ghettos were also set up by the Nazis during World War II in many towns and cities. Often Jews were crowded into these ghettos from other towns and villages as staging points for deportations to death camps.

Golem   In Jewish folklore, a man made from clay without a soul who is brought to life with a magic incantation. Creation of the golem is associated with several famous rabbis, including Rabbi Loew in Prague, who is said to have created the artificial man in order to have him defend the Jews.

Haggaddah   The collection of prayers, blessings, tales, songs, and comments arranged in a set order and recited at the Passover seder. The Haggaddah is usually found in book form and is often highly decorated.

Halachah   Jewish legal or ethical rules of behavior and life.

Hasidism   Hasid literally means fervent or pious, and Hasidism was a Jewish religious revival movement based on mysticism, joy, and love of God, that was founded in the Ukraine in the eighteenth century by the legendary Rebbe Israel Ba'al Shem Tov and rapidly spread through eastern and parts of central Europe. Hasids use much song and dancing in their worship. Eventually, Hasids grouped themselves as followers of individual **tzaddikim** known as **rebbes**.

Haskalah   The Jewish enlightenment; the movement from the mid-eighteenth to late nineteenth centuries that spread modern, western European ideas among Jews who until then followed strict Orthodox traditions.

Judenrein   German term meaning cleared of Jews; territories where the "Jewish problem" had been "resolved."

Kiddush   The blessing recited before drinking wine, and, by extension, the wine and refreshments served after Shabbat services.

Kosher   Ritually clean, generally referring to food prepared according to Jewish dietary laws.

Kvittel   A slip of paper left at the tomb of a great sage or Hasidic tzaddik on which a prayer or request invoking the spirit of the master is written. Often there are special boxes at the tombs to receive **kvittleh**.

Ladino   The language spoken by Sephardic Jews; derived from Spanish (similar to the way in which Yiddish was derived from German).

Maskil   A follower of the Haskalah enlightenment movement.

Mazzevah   Gravestone in the form of an upright, usually rectangular slab. One face is usually decorated with an epitaph and ornamental carving.

Menorah   The seven-branched candelabrum that, along with the six-pointed Star of David, has been the most important, distinctly Jewish symbol. According to the Bible, menorahs were important elements in the temple in Jerusalem and in the tabernacle erected in the wilderness by the children of Israel. Menorahs used during the Hanukkah festival have eight branches and a ninth single candle.

Mezuzah   Literally "doorpost." A small parchment scroll containing two passages from the Book of Deuteronomy affixed to the right-hand door-post of Jewish homes; often contained in a highly decorated wooden, metal, or ceramic case.

Mikvah   The ritual bath using flowing water; used for monthly ritual cleansing by Orthodox Jewish women.

Minyan   The quorum of ten Jewish men required for a religious service.

Moorish   An architectural style often used in nineteenth- and twentieth-century synagogues incorporating vaguely Islamic or Middle Eastern design and decoration (such as horseshoe arches, arabesques, spires resembling minarets, etc.).

Neoclassical   An art and architectural style of the late eighteenth and early nineteenth centuries in which simple lines replaced the frenzied ornamentation of the rococo.

Neolog   Reformed Judaism movement in Hungary that became strong in the nineteenth century.

Ohel   Literally "tent." A small building or protective shelter built around the tomb of a revered rabbi or sage.

Orthodox   Jewish practice strictly adhering to age-old traditions. The *Shulchan Aruch*, the codification of Jewish law published by Joseph Caro in 1567, for centuries was the basis of Orthodox practice.

Rabbi   Today, the ordained religious leader of a Jewish congregation. Traditionally, a rabbi was a teacher or sage, a scholar who had completed studies at a **yeshiva** and was thus well versed in Jewish law and able to play a leading role in the Jewish community.

Rebbe   A Hasidic rabbi, often at the head of a devoted court of followers, who is revered as a holy man often deemed to have special, wonder-working powers enabling him to mediate between man and God. Some revered rebbes founded dynasties, and their position as spiritual leader of their court was passed on to their sons.

Reform Judaism   A movement (associated with the Jewish enlightenment) that emerged in the early nineteenth century and aimed to modernize Jewish practice and modify it to fit the conditions of contemporary life. Among its practices, for example, were using the local language in services, incorporating a choir and organ into the synagogue, and adapting clothing to modern styles.

Sephardic   Derived from *Sepharad,* the Hebrew word for Spain, Sephardic Jews trace their origin to Spain and Portugal or follow the Sephardic religious rite, which is somewhat different from that of Ashkenazic Jews. Sephardic pronunciation of Hebrew also differs slightly from Ashkenazic pronunciation.

Shabbat   The sabbath; the biblically declared weekly day of rest lasting from sunset Friday to sunset Saturday. Jewish law prohibits all work on Shabbat.

Shammas   A salaried individual who serves as caretaker, sexton, or all-around handyman for a synagogue, study hour, or rabbinical court.

Shoah   Literally "catastrophe" in Hebrew; the Holocaust.

Shochet   A ritual slaughterer trained to slaughter animals according to Jewish dietary laws and to determine whether an animal is kosher (ritually clean for eating).

Shtetl   "Little town" in Yiddish. East European small-town Jewish settlement.

Shul   Synagogue.

Shulchan Aruch   The "Prepared Table"; a codification of Jewish law and practice compiled by Rabbi Joseph Caro and published in 1567. It became enshrined as a rigidly Orthodox guide to all facets of Jewish life.

Sukkoth   The Jewish early autumn harvest festival during which observant Jews live and eat out of doors in specially constructed booths.

Synagogue   From the Greek *synagoge;* a Jewish house of prayer.

Tallis   The fringed shawl or cloak, white with blue or black stripes, worn by Jewish men when praying in the synagogue.

Talmud   Two great collections of Hebrew and Aramaic writings including commentaries, debates, and discussions of numerous rabbis, sages, and scholars on the entire range of Jewish life and belief.

Tefillin Phylacteries. These are two leather cases that men attach to their foreheads and left arms during morning prayers.

Torah Literally "law." The first five books of the Old Testament, regarded as the written Jewish law, handwritten on parchment scrolls, and kept in the Aron ha Kodesh. Torah also can mean the entire Bible or Holy Scriptures.

Tzaddik A just man revered for saintly, wise behavior and for doing good deeds who is also believed to have a special relationship with God. Many Hasidic rebbes are considered to be **tzaddikim**.

Yeshiva An advanced Jewish religious school, particularly one dedicated to the study of the Talmud.

Yiddish The language spoken by Ashkenazic Jews; derived originally from German. It is written in Hebrew characters.

Yiddishkeit Jewishness; the world of Jewish traditions.

Zionism The movement developed in the nineteenth century, particularly through the writings of Theodore Herzl, advocating the return of the Jews to the Holy Land.

SELECTED BIBLIOGRAPHY AND FURTHER READING

Following is a brief list of books—fiction and nonfiction—that may be of interest in preparing for a Jewish heritage trip in East-Central Europe.

This selection only skims the surface, but it includes books useful as source and background material in preparing this book, as well as books I have simply enjoyed reading.

Apenszlak, Jacob, ed., *Black Book of Polish Jewry*, The American Federation for Polish Jews, 1943. Contemporary documentation of the Holocaust in Poland.

Baron, Salo W., *A Social and Religious History of the Jews*, Columbia University Press/Jewish Publication Society of America, 1976. An exhaustive multivolume history.

Bartosz, Adam, *Zydowskie Zabytki Wojewodztwa Tarnowskiego* (*Jewish Monuments in Tarnow Wojwodship*), Tarnow, 1989. Good local guide (for Polish speakers).

Benoschofsky, Ilona, and Alexander Scheiber, *The Jewish Museum of Budapest*, Corvina, Budapest, 1987. Well-illustrated, hardback catalog of the museum, available at Budapest bookshops; also has some historical articles.

Berger, Natalia, ed., *Where Cultures Meet: The Story of the Jews of Czechoslovakia*, Beth Hatefutsoth, Tel Aviv, 1990. Hardback illustrated catalog of a major exhibition at the Nahum Goldman Museum of the Diaspora.

Blue, Brian, and Yale Strom, *The Last Jews of Eastern Europe*, Philosophical Library, New York, 1986. Photographs.

Dawidowicz, Lucy S., *The War Against the Jews 1933–45*, Penguin, London, 1975. Classic account of the Holocaust.

Dawidowicz, Lucy S., ed., *The Golden Tradition: Jewish Life and Thought in Eastern Europe*, Schocken Books, New York, 1967. A fascinating sourcebook of writings by Jews on all facets of Jewish life, beliefs, social conditions, and activities, primarily in the region of historic Poland/Lithuania/Ukraine. Many of the selections deal with the deep conflict between traditional Jewish life and the Haskalah, or enlightenment.

De Lange, Nicholas, *Atlas of the Jewish World*, Phaidon, Oxford, 1984. Well-illustrated history with lots of maps.

Dobroszycki, Lucjan, and Barbara Kirshenblatt-Gimblett, *Image Before My Eyes*, Schocken Books, New York, 1977. A fascinating photographic history of Polish Jewish life from 1864 to 1939.

Encyclopaedia Judaica, Keter, Jerusalem, 1972. A seventeen-volume treasurehouse of all aspects of Judaism and Jewish history.

Fener, Tamas, and Alexander Scheiber, . . . *Es Beszeld El Fiadnak,* Corvina, Budapest, 1984. Photographic essay on contemporary Jewish life in Hungary. If you're lucky, you may find a copy in English in a used bookstore.

Fenyvesi, Charles, *When the World Was Whole: Three Centuries of Memories,* Viking, New York, 1990. Evocative description of Jewish life in Hungary.

Fiedler, Jiri, *Jewish Sights of Bohemia and Moravia,* Sefer, Prague, 1991.

Gero, Laszlo, ed., *Magyarorszagi Zsinagogak (Hungarian Synagogues),* Muszaki Konyvkiado, Budapest, 1989. Valuable and beautifully illustrated book, available at Hungarian bookstores. It's worth getting for the pictures even if you don't speak Hungarian.

Gilbert, Martin, *The Holocaust,* William Collins, London, 1986. Anger bursts from the pages of this detailed history of the Shoah.

Gitelman, Zvi, *A Century of Ambivalence; The Jews of Russia and the Soviet Union,* Schocken Books, New York, 1988. Informative text and pictures.

Greenberg, Eliezer, and Irving Howe, eds., *A Treasury of Yiddish Stories,* Schocken Books, New York, 1973. Excellent collection of stories by Sholom Asch, Sholom Aleichem, I. L. Peretz, Mendele Mocher Sforim, I. L. and I. B. Singer, and other great Yiddish writers, plus an introduction that tells much about East European Jewish history and culture.

A Guide to Jewish Cracow, Our Roots, Warsaw, 1990. A must for visitors to Cracow.

A Guide to Jewish Warsaw, Our Roots, Warsaw, 1990. A must for visitors to Warsaw.

Herman, Jan, *Jewish Cemeteries in Bohemia and Moravia,* The Council of Czech Jewish Communities, Prague.

Hoffman, Charles, *Gray Dawn: The Jews of Eastern Europe in the Post-Communist Era,* HarperCollins, New York, 1992.

Jacot, Michael, *The Last Butterfly,* Ballantine, New York, 1974. A novel set in the wartime Terezin Ghetto in Czechoslovakia.

Jews in Yugoslavia, (exhibition catalog), Muzejski Prostor, Zagreb, 1989. Detailed, well-illustrated catalog of a major exhibition.

Kis, Danilo, *Garden, Ashes,* Harcourt Brace Jovanovich, New York, 1975. Autobiographical novel by Yugoslav Jewish author on growing up before World War II.

Krajewska, Monika, *A Tribe of Stones: Jewish Cemeteries in Poland,* Polish Scientific Publishers, Warsaw, 1993. Extremely informative text with striking photographs; an expanded update of Krajewska's earlier book, *Time of Stones.*

Krinsky, Carol Herselle, *Synagogues of Europe,* The Architectural History Foundation and the MIT Press, 1985. Extremely informative, well-illustrated study, with large sections devoted to East-Central Europe. Unfortunately, it's a little too big to carry on an overseas trip. If you know where you will be going, take notes.

Kugelmass, Jack, and Jonathan Boyarin, *From a Ruined Garden: The Memorial Books of Polish Jewry,* Schocken Books, New York, 1983.

Levai, Eugene, *Black Book on the Martyrdom of Hungarian Jewry,* The Central European Times, Zurich, 1948. Postwar documentation of the Holocaust in Hungary.

Levi, Primo, *If This Is a Man/The Truce,* Abacus, London, 1987. Eloquent memoir of his experience at Auschwitz by a brilliant Italian writer who committed suicide in 1987.

Magris, Claudio, *Danube,* Collins Harvill, London, 1989. Historical travel book about the river by an Italian scholar.

Manning, Olivia, *The Balkan Trilogy,* Penguin, London, 1960. An English novel set in and around Bucharest just before World War II.

Marcus, Jacob R., *The Jew in the Medieval World: A Source Book,* 315–1791, Atheneum, New York, 1973. Fascinating original texts.

McCagg Jr., William O., *A History of the Habsburg Jews 1670–98,* Indiana University Press, Bloomington and Indianapolis, 1989.

McCagg Jr., William O., *Jewish Nobles and Geniuses in Modern Hungary,* Columbia University Press, 1972. Esoteric but fascinating account of the nineteenth/twentieth-century Jewish elite in Hungary.

Niezabitowska, Malgorzata, and Tomasz Tomaszewski, *Remnants; The Last Jews of Poland.* The Friendly Press, New York, 1986. Portraits of Polish Jews, in words and pictures.

Pawel, Ernst, *The Nightmare of Reason,* Collins Harvill, London, 1988. This biography of Franz Kafka gives some good insights into late nineteenth/early twentieth-century Jewish life in Prague.

Rosen, Moses, *The Paper Bridge.* Essays and sermons by Romania's chief rabbi; available in Bucharest.

Roth, Cecil, *A History of the Jews,* Schocken Books, New York, 1970. A one-volume Jewish history by a noted Jewish scholar.

Sachar, Abram Leon, *A History of the Jews,* Knopf, New York, 1965. Sometimes idiosyncratic one-volume Jewish history.

Samuel, Maurice, *Prince of the Ghetto,* Meridian Books/Jewish Publication Society, 1959. Wonderful essay on the life and work of I. L. Peretz, the father of Yiddish literature.

Serotta, Edward, *Out of the Shadows*, Birch Lane/Carol, New York, 1991. A brilliant photographic study of contemporary Judaism in East-Central Europe.

Singer, Isaac Bashevis. *In My Father's Court; Satan in Goray; The Family Moskat;* and *Gimpel the Fool.* The works of this Nobel Prize–winning author are easily accessible and include memoirs of growing up in prewar Poland, as well as often mystical fiction. *Reaches of Heaven* retells the story of the Ba'al Shem Tov.

Trzcinski, Andrzej, *The Traces of Monuments of Jewish Culture in the Lublin Region,* Our Roots, Warsaw, 1991. A must for visitors to the Lublin area.

Vishniac, Roman, *A Vanished World.* Classic photographic essay of prewar Jewish life in Eastern Europe.

Wechsberg, Joseph, *The Vienna I Knew: Memories of a European Childhood,* Doubleday, Garden City, NY, 1979. The title is misleading—Wechsberg came from the Moravian town of Ostrava, and his memoir lovingly captures the essence of prewar life among the mainly Reform Jewish community. His book *Homecoming* (Knopf, New York, 1946) tells of going back to the town immediately after the war.

Wiesel, Elie, *Night,* Penguin, London, 1981. The Nobel Prize winner's experiences as a child in the concentration camp—particularly interesting is his description of the lack of awareness of Jews in his hometown shtetl of Sighet, now Romania, about what was about to happen.

Wiesel, Elie, *Souls on Fire* and *Somewhere a Master,* Penguin, London, 1984. Insightful essays incorporating portraits and legends of the great Hasidic masters of the eighteenth and early nineteenth century; a moving and informative book.

Wirth, Peter, *Itt Van Elrejtve,* Europa Konyvkiado, Budapest, 1985. Photographic book on Jewish cemeteries in northeast Hungary.

Zborowski, Mark, and Elizabeth Herzog, *Life Is with People,* Schocken Books, New York, 1952. A classic and fascinating study of life in the shtetl.

Index